A YOUNG ENGLISHMAN IN VICTORIAN HONG KONG

THE DIARIES OF CHALONER
ALABASTER, 1855–1856

A YOUNG ENGLISHMAN IN VICTORIAN HONG KONG

THE DIARIES OF CHALONER ALABASTER, 1855–1856

BENJAMIN PENNY

ANU PRESS

To my friend and teacher, W.J.F. Jenner

ANU PRESS

Published by ANU Press
The Australian National University
Canberra ACT 2600, Australia
Email: anupress@anu.edu.au

Available to download for free at press.anu.edu.au

ISBN (print): 9781760465919
ISBN (online): 9781760465926

WorldCat (print): 1389548678
WorldCat (online): 1389548274

DOI: 10.22459/YEVHK.2023

This title is published under a Creative Commons Attribution-NonCommercial-NoDerivatives 4.0 International (CC BY-NC-ND 4.0) licence.

The full licence terms are available at creativecommons.org/licenses/by-nc-nd/4.0/legalcode

Cover design and layout by ANU Press. Cover photograph: William Pryor Floyd (1834–c. 1900), *Public Garden (from the Albany, Hong Kong)*, 1860s.

This book is published under the aegis of the China in the World editorial board of ANU Press.

This edition © 2023 ANU Press

Contents

List of Plates	ix
Acknowledgements	xi
Introduction	1
Editorial Note	47
The Cast of the Diaries	51
Alabaster Diary, Volume 1	63
Alabaster Diary, Volume 2	93
Alabaster Diary, Volume 3	151
Alabaster Diary, Volume 4	181
Appendix	207
Select Bibliography	211

List of Plates

Plate 1. 'The Late Sir Chaloner Alabaster', *Illustrated London News*, 9 July 1898. — 5

Plate 2. Hong Kong, 'Plan of the Cantonment at Victoria, 1853'. — 8

Plate 3. William Pryor Floyd (1834–c. 1900), Public Garden (*Central View HK*), 1869. — 9

Plate 4. William Pryor Floyd (1834–c. 1900), *Chinese Town, Westpoint*, 1869. — 28

Plate 5. William Pryor Floyd (1834–c. 1900), *Public Garden (from the Albany, Hong Kong)*, 1860s. — 30

Plate 6. 'Fire on Board the Ship "Fort William" at Hong-Kong', *Illustrated London News*, 3 January 1852. — 36

Plate 7. Alabaster's Diary, Volume 2, 14 December 1855, showing two 'sketches'. — 49

Plate 8. Alabaster's Diary, Volume 3, 2 June 1856, showing two 'sketches'. — 50

Plate 9. 'Sing-Song Piejon at Hong-Kong', *Illustrated London News*, 15 August 1857. — 138

Plate 10. The first page of Alabaster's Chinese language notes, at the back of Volume 1. — 208

Acknowledgements

While on a pilgrimage to the Special Collections room at the School of Oriental and African Studies (SOAS) in London in 2015 to consult the archives of the London Missionary Society, I typed 'diary' into the catalogue on the off-chance that one of the missionaries I was interested in had kept a journal and that it had survived. Nothing came of that enquiry, but the heading 'Diaries of Sir Chaloner Alabaster' appeared. I had never heard of Chaloner Alabaster but, curious, I requested them. It did not take long to realise the archival gold they represented.

My first acknowledgment, then, is to the custodians of Alabaster's diaries, the staff of SOAS Special Collections, past and present; in particular, Joanne Ichimura, special collections archivist. I am also deeply grateful to Simon Alabaster, Chaloner's great-grandson, for generously granting me permission to publish his ancestor's diaries. It was through the good offices of the Alabaster Society that I was able to make contact with Simon and I would like also to acknowledge their help, in particular that of John S. Alabaster and Laraine Hake.

My excursions into the world of Hong Kong in the Victorian era have also led me to several other libraries and archives, and I wish to acknowledge the assistance of the many people who have made it possible for me to access their holdings. Those institutions include the UK National Archives, the British Library, the John Rylands Library, the Warwickshire County Record Office, the Hong Kong Public Records Office and, as ever, the National Library of Australia and the library of my own institution, The Australian National University.

I have been fortunate to have the assistance of many people in the writing of this book. They include T.H. Barrett, Cao Xinyu, Sue Shih-wen Chen, Tony Edwards, Paul Farrelly, W.J.F. Jenner, Kam Louie, Caroline Stevenson, Rex Stevenson, Mark Strange, Nathan Woolley, Eloise Wright, Yang Qin and Zhu Yayun. I am deeply grateful to them all. I would also like to thank Rani Kerin for copyediting and Sharon Strange for shepherding this book through ANU Press.

Finally, as in all circumstances and at all times, my deepest thanks go to my partner Gillian Russell and our son Tom Russell-Penny.

Introduction

In August 1855, 16-year-old Chaloner Alabaster left England for Hong Kong to take up a position as a student interpreter in the China Consular Service. He was to stay in China until 1892, rising to the position of consul general of Canton, a post he held from 1886. Retiring at the age of 54, he returned to England and received a knighthood. He died in 1898.[1]

Throughout his adult life, Alabaster kept diaries. In 1987, they were donated to the Library of the School of Oriental and African Studies at the University of London.[2] For much of his career, the diaries list his daily appointments and meetings with only brief notices of personal events; for this he used Letts's brand diaries, one day for each page. However, the first four volumes are different from the others. They are ordinary exercise books and in them Alabaster wrote about his world each night, or more sporadically if he was busy or otherwise distracted. These four, handwritten volumes, in excess of 50,000 words in total, are a unique record of life in Hong Kong from October 1855 to November 1856, representing 14 months of observations, cogitations, anecdotes, outbursts and reports.

Alabaster was a deeply committed servant of the British Empire and was curious about what he saw around him. Unfortunately, for many foreign observers of China (not to mention Chinese authors), what was to be seen on the streets they walked each day rapidly became normalised or trivial or ordinary and not worth recording. For the newly arrived Alabaster, however, everything was new and strange, and in the diaries presented

---

1   I have rendered placenames in this book in the modern standard form, with the exception of those names that have become domesticated in English, for example, Hong Kong, Canton and Peking. Where there may be confusion, for example, with Amoy and Xiamen, I have included the older form in brackets at the first occurrence. Where a placename occurs in the name of a treaty, I have used the original form of the name as it appears in that treaty, for example, the Treaty of Nanking rather than the Treaty of Nanjing.
2   Library of the School of Oriental and African Studies, University of London, Archive and Special Collections, MS 380451.

here he wrote without the jaded knowingness of the long-term expatriate. Thus, he records how the Chinese people around him ironed clothes, dried flour and threshed rice; how they gambled, prepared their food and made bean curd; and what opera, new year festivities and the birthday of Mazu – the Heavenly Empress – were like. Like many a young Victorian, he was also a keen observer of natural history, fascinated by fireflies and ants, corals and sea slugs, and the volcanic origins of the landscape. He was young and enthusiastic, and everyday sights, sounds and smells were still novel for him. The diaries also have the immediacy of a daily journal, preserving Alabaster's first thoughts on a subject, with no awareness of how the events he described would turn out. He could not know if one of the many diseases he – and everybody else – suffered from would lead to death, if a minor skirmish would develop into a battle or if his interest in one of Hong Kong's young British ladies would become serious. There are not many records of Hong Kong in this period – I will cite some below – but Alabaster's is unlike anything else we have, in particular because it was not intended as a public document. Therefore, wonderfully, it lacks the careful editing and judicious hindsight of journalism, of histories or of memoirs, which always have a weather eye to either a current readership or to posterity.

Apart from the surrounding Chinese milieu, and the geography and zoology of Hong Kong, Alabaster's diaries also provide insights into some of the major figures of colonial Hong Kong in this period. Most historical works that deal with his world are based on government archives, published books and, occasionally, contemporary newspapers. All these provide important information, of course, but often suffer from the common faults of official histories: characters tend to be flattened into participants in events, or lifeless carriers of ideas. Alabaster, on the other hand, in the privacy of his diary, lets us see, for example, the giant of nineteenth-century Sinology, Thomas Wade, at 10 in the morning, still 'in his shirt & pitgamas, ½ shaved & looking the rummest monster imaginable'. Alabaster's picture of eminent missionaries is perhaps less surprising. After tea with the Rev. John W. Johnson (1819–1872), an American Baptist, the Rev. George Piercy (1829–1913), the first Wesleyan Methodist missionary in China, arrives and Alabaster writes:

> Mr P. first read a chapter to the Hebrews in a horribly drawling manner & then extemporized ½ an hour's prayer during which I am ashamed to say I was in imminent peril of splitting with laughter as I fancied Adkins [his closest friend] was snoring which it luckily turned out he was not.

We also see His Excellency the governor at dinner: 'We all went to dinner at the Governor's where I had the pleasure of sitting next to H.E. who was fearfully cross because he did not get his onions'. In the diaries, these historical personages come vividly to life, as do the many other, often minor, figures in Hong Kong expatriate life that Alabaster encountered. Simply by virtue of being a British Government official, Alabaster's superior social status in relation to the Chinese people he lived among was granted automatically. However, within government circles, he was on the lowest rung, someone who, at this time in his career, could safely be ignored by his seniors. This relatively lowly position granted him, arguably, a prime position as a chronicler of life as a colonial official, even if such a thought would never have occurred to him.

In his position as student interpreter in the China Consular Service, Alabaster was a junior officer in one of the most far-flung outposts of the British Empire. The China Consular Service was established after Britain had defeated China in the First Opium War and, as a result, gained the right under the Treaty of Nanking of 1843 to establish consulates in the so-called treaty ports. Over the course of the nineteenth century, the number of these ports grew from five to more than 35. All had to be staffed by diplomats and interpreters whose role it was to look after British interests, including those of traders and missionaries, and to liaise with Chinese officials. In Alabaster's time, the Consular Service was run from the Foreign Office in London through Government House in Hong Kong. Coates aptly describes the Consular Service as 'that step-child of the Foreign Office'.[3]

Throughout his professional life, and in these diaries, Alabaster's loyalty to Queen Victoria and to his homeland is profound and ever-present. Sometimes this is evident in his apostrophes – 'Vivat Regina!' – but just as frequently in his dismissal of the citizens of the United States, for whom he seems to have had a particular dislike. Perhaps surprisingly for someone who was living on the doorstep of China, in times when relations between the British and the Chinese empires were difficult and getting worse, his attention appears to have been focused much more strongly on the Crimean

---

3   P.D. Coates, *The China Consuls: British Consular Officers, 1843–1943* (Oxford: Oxford University Press, 1988), vii. This book is the classic reference work on the Consular Service and has proved invaluable for this project.

War, in all its theatres from the Black Sea to arctic Russia, and from the Baltic Sea to the north-western Pacific Ocean, until news of the peace arrived in Hong Kong. The diaries are, therefore, crucial documents for understanding the lived experience of empire at the height of British dominance.[4]

---

4   One of the most important developments in the study of Hong Kong's nineteenth-century history in recent decades – practised by what Christopher Munn calls 'the Hong Kong school' in his *Anglo-China: Chinese People and British Rule in Hong Kong 1841–1880* (Richmond, Surrey: Curzon Press, 2001), 8–9 – has been a specific focus on Hong Kong and the interactions of all of its communities. This Munn contrasts with histories written from the position of the colony's elite ('the colonial school') or those intent on seeing this history through the lens of China's 'hundred years of national humiliation' at the hands of foreigners ('the Beijing school'). One of the defining characteristics of these new histories has been to reinstate Chinese people into the history of Hong Kong. This has entailed researching those places where interactions between the Chinese and foreign communities occurred – law courts, hospitals, businesses, missions, brothels, etc. – and the social, economic, legal and cultural systems and relationships that evolved between the communities. Many works of history from this 'Hong Kong school' are cited in this book. Another feature of this scholarship has been to revisit the nature of Hong Kong's colonial society with an eye to recent studies in the history and nature of colonialism. Some examples of this kind of work are Carl T. Smith, *Chinese Christians: Elites, Middlemen, and the Church in Hong Kong* (Oxford: Oxford University Press, 1985; new edition with introduction by Christopher Munn, Hong Kong: Hong Kong University Press, 2005); Tak-Wing Ngo, ed., *Hong Kong's History: State and Society under Colonial Rule* (London: Routledge, 1999); John M. Carroll, *Edge of Empires: Chinese Elites and British Colonials in Hong Kong* (Cambridge, Mass.: Harvard University Press, 2005); David Faure, *Colonialism and the Hong Kong Mentality* (Hong Kong: Centre of Asian Studies, University of Hong Kong, 2003); Elizabeth Sinn, Wong Siu-lun and Chan Wing-hoi, eds, *Rethinking Hong Kong: New Paradigms, New Perspectives* (Hong Kong: Centre of Asian Studies, University of Hong Kong, 2009); Robert Bickers and Jonathan J. Howlett, eds, *Britain and China, 1840–1970: Empire, Finance and War* (Abingdon: Routledge, 2016), doi.org/10.4324/9781315687735; Elizabeth Sinn and Christopher Munn, *Meeting Place: Encounters across Cultures in Hong Kong, 1841–1984* (Hong Kong: Hong Kong University Press, 2015); Kaori Abe, *Chinese Middlemen in Hong Kong's Colonial Economy, 1830–1890* (Abingdon: Routledge, 2018), doi.org/10.4324/9781315543949; May Holdsworth and Christopher Munn, *Crime, Justice and Punishment in Hong Kong: Central Police Station, Central Magistracy and Victoria Gaol* (Hong Kong: Hong Kong University Press, 2020).

This rethinking has been productive and useful. However, as Munn (*Anglo-China*, 11) notes, 'the chronological centre of gravity of the Hong King school, and the area in which it has produced its most original research, tends to be the late nineteenth century … the period when the Chinese merchant elite came into its own'. *Anglo-China*, significantly, focuses on the early period, which, Munn continues, has 'not been subjected to such intensive study'. Alabaster's diaries fall into the 'early period', so this book will, I hope, add meaningfully to our understanding of the second decade of colonial rule in Hong Kong. That the diaries are not *primarily* concerned with interactions between the Chinese and foreign communities is simply an historical fact. This, however, is itself is illustrative and revealing of the nature of Hong Kong society in Alabaster's time.

INTRODUCTION

Plate 1. 'The Late Sir Chaloner Alabaster', *Illustrated London News*, 9 July 1898.

The observations made so far about the value of the diaries have been focused, broadly, on what we can learn about the history of Hong Kong society and the empire at large in the mid-nineteenth century, but they are also relevant to other enquiries. Alabaster was only 16 and 17 when he wrote the first four volumes; they form, therefore, a kind of inadvertent self-portrait of a young mid-Victorian Englishman. The diaries themselves are, as I discuss below, a manifestation of a cast of mind in which processes of self-examination and self-reproof are regarded as fundamental aspects of character formation. They also describe the activities and aspirations of a young man who lives, works and finds recreation with others like him. In this sense they tell us a great deal about Englishmen of Alabaster's class and status. However, importantly, in the telling, they precisely delineate a specific form of masculine self-representation. It is in this aspect of the diaries, perhaps more than any other, that their private nature sets them apart. Many memoirs and biographies of the nineteenth century and later are clearly based on diaries, letters and journals written years before, whether they present themselves as such or not. This is not the case with Alabaster's diaries. None of his children wrote his biography. He never published a memoir. His diaries have remained in manuscript to this day. In them, we hear his voice.

Who Was Chaloner Alabaster?

Chaloner Alabaster was born in 1838, the youngest of three boys, into a family who had been in the hat- and bonnet-making business in London since the late eighteenth century, at least.[5] While the actual manufacturing work was done in and around Shoreditch in East London, Chaloner's father James (1806–1840) lived in the much more salubrious Brompton, in a then recent development facing the Fulham Road. James's mother, Mary Anne (1786–1838) resided in the premises of the family business on Piccadilly in the West End until her death.[6] Her will indicates the family were well-off

---

5 I am indebted to Adrian Alabaster and John S. Alabaster for their work on Chaloner and his relatives. See Adrian Alabaster, *A Quintet of Alabasters* (Knebworth: Able Publishing, 1997); John S. Alabaster, *Sir Chaloner Alabaster Correspondence (1840–1880)*, Occasional Monograph No. 2 (The Alabaster Society, 2005); John S. Alabaster, *An Alabaster Quest: A Claim to North American Indian Land, 1837*, Occasional Monograph No. 4 (The Alabaster Society, 2011).

6 See 'Charles Alabaster, Bonnet Maker', in London Street Views, 28 February 2017, londonstreetviews.wordpress.com/2017/02/28/charles-alabaster-bonnet-maker/.

and established. As we will see in the careers of Chaloner and his brothers, the Alabasters represent in one family the move from trade to the professions that is characteristic of this period.

When young Chaloner was born, the course his life might have been expected to take was somewhat more comfortable and less exciting than it turned out to be. In 1840, when Chaloner was still only a year old, his mother Harriet (1807–1840) and then his father died of tuberculosis within months of each other. Chaloner, and his elder brothers Charles (1833–1865) and Henry (1836–1884), were taken in by James's sister Mary Ann (1805–1880), who had married Harry Criddle (1807–1857) in 1836. Mary Ann and Harry did not, at that time, have any children of their own, but she later gave birth to Percy (1844–1918), on whom Chaloner appears to have doted.[7]

All three brothers attended King's College School in London, then located in the Strand where the current King's College of the University of London now stands, and each of them was assisted by the provision of a scholarship. King's, remarkably for the mid-nineteenth century, taught Chinese, and when Lord Clarendon, the foreign secretary of the time, sought to recruit young men for the China Consular Service he looked to King's for candidates. Alabaster was selected in June 1855 and departed for Hong Kong in August of that year, still only 16 years of age.

Alabaster's diaries presented in this book begin when he leaves England and end in November 1856, a period of 16 months. During this time, we find him a student interpreter, working in the office of the superintendent of British trade in China, which was located in Hong Kong, and starting his serious study of Chinese.[8] He does not tell us where he lived when he first arrived, only that the accommodation was temporary (and paid for by the governor) before moving into the Albany Building. The Albany had been built in 1844 as a barracks – it is called 'Albany Barracks' in an 1853 map of Hong Kong. From Alabaster's remarks, it was being vacated by a regiment of Indian troops and was being prepared for the student interpreters and other government employees. The Albany was located at the highest point of what are now the Hong Kong Botanical Gardens, where the children's playground now stands, and in Alabaster's time was the building furthest up the slope of the peak. It was demolished in 1935.

---

7   More extensive notes on members of Alabaster's family, as well as his friends and fellow officials, can be found in 'The Cast of the Diaries', after this introduction.
8   On the Superintendency of British Trade, see E.J. Eitel, *Europe in China: The History of Hongkong from the Beginning to the Year 1882* (London: Luzac & Company, 1895).

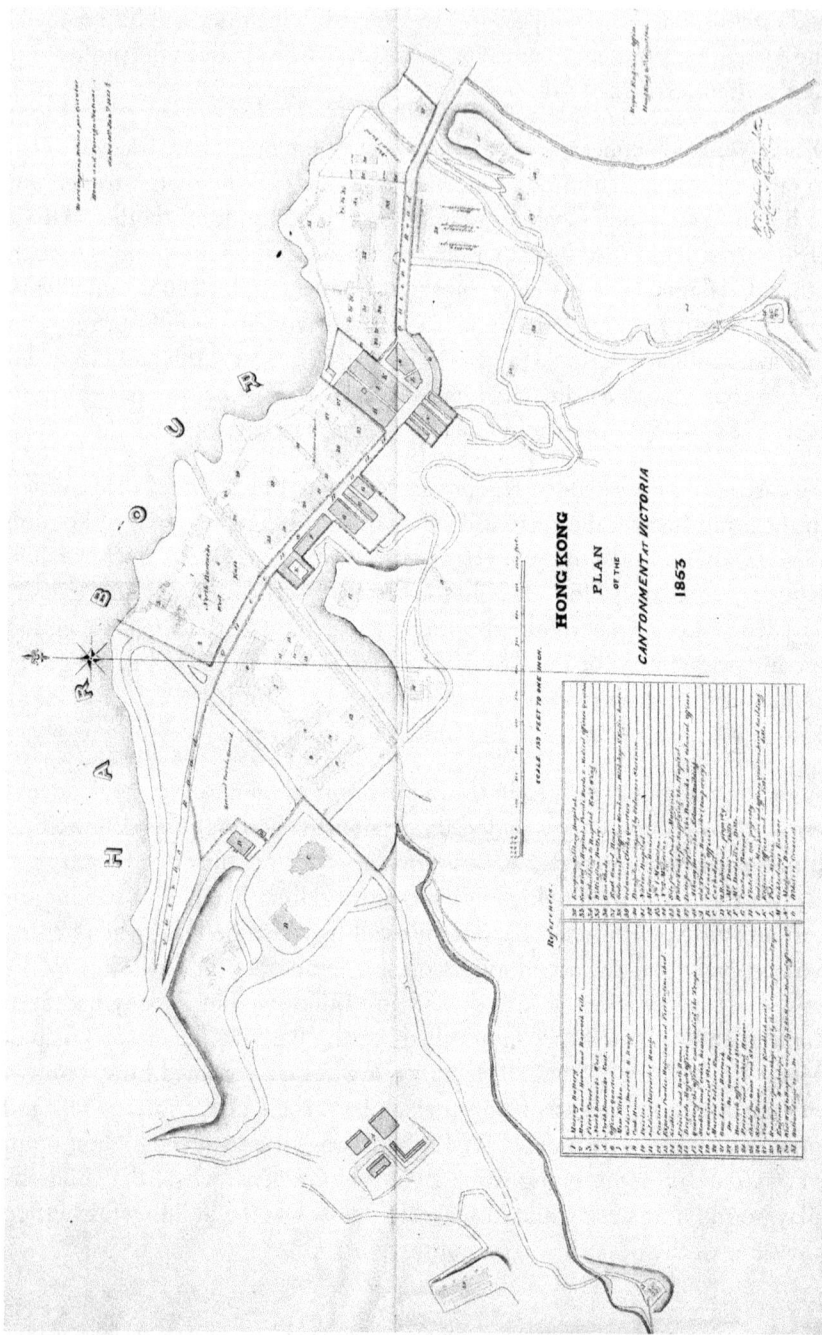

Plate 2. Hong Kong, 'Plan of the Cantonment at Victoria, 1853'.
Permission: The National Archives, WO 55/2962. The Albany Building (here the Albany Barracks) is notated as No. 48 at the lower left of the map.

Plate 3. William Pryor Floyd (1834–c. 1900), Public Garden (*Central View HK*), 1869.
Albumen print. The main building featured is the Albany.
Source: Gift of Mrs W.F. Spinney, 1923, PH17.12. Courtesy of the Peabody Essex Museum.

The British Government position of chief superintendent was established in 1833 when the East India Company monopoly on British trade with China was ended. The office of the Superintendency of British Trade was located in Macao until the British seized the island of Hong Kong in 1841, when it moved to the new colony. At this time, the chief superintendent also became the administrator of Hong Kong, the position that evolved into governor of Hong Kong after the Treaty of Nanking was signed in 1842 and ratified the following year. In the period of Alabaster's first diaries, the governor and chief superintendent was Sir John Bowring (1792–1872).[9] Strictly speaking, the Superintendency was not part of the Hong Kong

---

9   On Bowring's governorship, see Eitel, *Europe in China*, Chapter 17, 'The Administration of Sir J. Bowring', 298–352; G.B. Endacott, *A History of Hong Kong* (London: Oxford University Press, 1958), Chapter 10, 'Sir John Bowring, 1854–59', 87–104; G.B. Endacott, *A Biographical Sketch-Book of Early Hong Kong* (Hong Kong: Hong Kong University Press, 2005), 36–44; Munn's entry on Bowring in May Holdsworth and Christopher Munn, eds, *Dictionary of Hong Kong Biography* (Hong Kong: Hong Kong University Press, 2012), 41–44. See also, Sir John Bowring, *Autobiographical Recollections of Sir John Bowring, with a Brief Memoir of Lewin B. Bowring* (London: Henry S. King, 1877); Philip Bowring, *Free Trade's First Missionary: Sir John Bowring in Europe and Asia* (Hong Kong: Hong Kong University Press, 2014), doi.org/10.5790/hongkong/9789888208722.001.0001.

Government but belonged to the Consular Service, which administered the consulates across China, as well as in other East Asian countries, including Japan and Siam (modern-day Thailand). At the time of these diaries, the acting secretary of the Superintendency, the most senior position under Bowring, was William Caine (1799–1871).[10]

These four diaries end in November 1856. The next diary that survives is from 1859. We do not know whether Alabaster kept diaries for 1857 and 1858 – he may not have as the entries at the end of the fourth volume are less regular and perhaps his enthusiasm for chronicling his affairs had waned. We do know from the *Foreign Office Lists* for this period, however, that from October 1857 until the capture of Canton in early 1858, Alabaster was attached to Admiral Sir Michael Seymour (1802–1887) in what the *Lists* coyly refer to as 'the operations in the Canton River'.[11] These 'operations' are better known now as the Battle of Canton, a pivotal moment in the Second Opium War, otherwise known as the *Arrow* War after the name of the vessel involved in the incident that sparked military action.[12] The *Arrow* was seized on 14 October 1857, but Alabaster makes no mention of this event until 20 October, when he remarks laconically: 'The Canton affair is not settled yet'. Seymour, along with the French commander, was ordered by Lord Elgin to capture the city of Canton, then a walled city, on 21 December. The attack was launched on 28 December and in three days Canton had fallen. British and French troops entered the city itself on 5 January. For his services, Alabaster was awarded the China medal with Canton clasp.

When Canton was captured, the troops also seized the highest ranking Chinese official there, and longstanding bête noire of British governors, Ye Mingchen 葉名琛 (1807–1859). Commissioner Ye, as he was known, held the post of viceroy of the Liang (meaning two) Guang, that is the two provinces of Guangdong and Guangxi, and was brought back to Hong Kong on board the HMS *Inflexible*. He was kept on board as a prisoner in Hong Kong harbour until it was decided that he should be sent to Calcutta.

---

10   On the history of the apparatus of government in Hong Kong, see Ho Pui-yin, *The Administrative History of Hong Kong Government Agencies, 1841–2002* (Hong Kong: Hong Kong University Press, 2004).
11   See, for example, Edward Hertslet, comp., *The Foreign Office List, Forming a Complete British Diplomatic and Consular Handbook, with Maps* (London, Harrison, 1865), 52.
12   On the *Arrow* incident and the Second Opium War more generally, see J.Y. Wong, *Deadly Dreams: Opium and the Arrow War (1856–1860) in China* (Cambridge: Cambridge University Press, 1998), doi.org/10.1017/CBO9780511572807.

The *Inflexible* departed on 20 February and Alabaster was appointed his interpreter. Alabaster stayed with Ye on board, and then in Calcutta, until Ye's death on 9 April 1859.[13]

When he returned to Hong Kong, Alabaster was appointed as interpreter at the consulate in Fuzhou but not long after was attached to Sir Frederick Wright-Bruce (1814–1867, the younger brother of Lord Elgin) on the latter's mission to Peking in May 1859 to exchange the ratified Treaty of Tientsin. This mission went no further than that city, however, as their way was blocked, so they returned south – subsequently, Elgin led the famously punitive mission to Peking that included the destruction of the old summer palace, the Yuanming yuan. From June 1859, Alabaster was interpreter at the Canton Consulate, then over the next 18 months at Xiamen (Amoy), Shantou (Swatow) and Shanghai. The *Lists* note that he 'accompanied various expeditions against the rebels, and was present at the storming and capture of Kah-ding'.[14] The rebels referred to here were those of the Taiping Uprising, and Kah-ding, or Jiading, now in the north-western suburbs of greater Shanghai, was a walled town besieged by British and French troops in 1862. Vice-Admiral Sir James Hope, in a memorandum to Bruce, made special mention of Alabaster's services at this time:

> I avail myself of this opportunity to bring to your notice the name of Mr Chaloner Alabaster, Consular Assistant, whose zeal and ability as interpreter, in which capacity he was invariably attached either to the General or myself during the operations against the rebels, as well as in conducting my communications with the Chinese authorities, have been of the greatest service to me.[15]

For two years, from 1862 to 1864, Alabaster was 'lent to the Chinese Government to assist in the re-organisation of the Sung-kiang force', Sung-kiang, or Songjiang, being a district in the south-west of Shanghai that had been occupied by the Taipings. A strong Chinese Government garrison in Songjiang was considered imperative by the British for the defence of Shanghai, one of the treaty ports with, by then, a substantial

---

13　On Ye Mingchen, see J.Y. Wong, *Yeh Ming-ch'en: Viceroy of Liang-Kuang (1852–8)* (Cambridge: Cambridge University Press, 1976). See also Benjamin Penny, 'The Death of Ye Mingchen' (forthcoming).
14　Hertslet, *The Foreign Office List*, 52.
15　*Further Papers Related to the Rebellion in China* (Enclosure no. 2 in no. 79, Vice-Admiral Sir J. Hope to Mr Bruce) (London: Harrison & Sons, 1862), 111.

foreign community. For this service, Alabaster was awarded a decoration the Chinese Government gave to foreigners, the First Class of the Order of the Star of China.

As he grew older, Alabaster's career in the Consular Service progressed. He was appointed acting vice-consul in Shanghai in 1864, holding that office for periods in Yantai (Chefoo) and Shantou before becoming substantive vice-consul back in Shanghai in 1869. From 1872, he held positions at the acting consul level in Shanghai, Ningbo and Hankou, and then consul in Yantai, Shantou, Shanghai, Ningbo, Xiamen, Yichang and Hankou. His final post was as consul general in Canton from 1886 to 1891. In 1892 he was made KCMG, thus becoming Sir Chaloner Alabaster. He retired in the same year, to Bournemouth, and died in June 1898.

Throughout the diaries, Alabaster often declares his interest (privately, to his diary) in several British women, younger and older, including Bowring's daughter Edith, seven years his senior, and Miss Irwin, the daughter of the colonial chaplain, about whom he wrote: 'Miss Irwin ... is rather a jolly girl but too forward. However, I intend to fall in love with her'.[16] Evidently, he made no progress on this front, or any other potential marriage prospect, until he was 37, when he married Laura Macgowan (1847–1924), the daughter of the remarkable American Baptist medical missionary, scholar and transmitter of scientific knowledge to China, Dr D.J. Macgowan (1815–1893), in 1875 in Shanghai. The Alabasters had six children, the first dying of illness in infancy: Cecil Osborne (1876–1878), Rupert Cecil (1878–1911), Chaloner Grenville (1880–1958), Agnes Dorothea (1882–1976), Evelyn Arblaster (1884–1967) and Eric Osborne (1887–1937).

Alabaster's obituary in the *North-China Herald* summed up his character and career:

> He was one of the cleverest and ablest men in the Consular service; with strong opinions of his own, and absolutely ignorant of fear. He was much too original, too decided, too anti-Chinese, to please Sir Thomas Wade, and he would have got on better if he had been more ready to fall in with his chief's views; but his experience generally, and especially his long and intimate companionship with Yeh, had shown him what the Chinese mandarin is in his heart; and he could not be imposed upon by them as his simpler and more

---

16   In a letter dated 24 August 1857 to his aunt, Alabaster described her in this way: 'a young lady here, Miss Irwin by name, in age 12, but in everything else at least 21'. See John S. Alabaster, *Correspondence*, 17.

soft-hearted chief was ... his friends knew that with all his occasional bitterness he had a heart of pure gold, and would take any amount of trouble to help people who were really in trouble. He had no patience with shams and pretensions; he saw through them directly, and the man had to get up early who proposed to get round 'the Buster,' as he was affectionately termed. It was worth a great deal to spend an evening with 'the Buster,' who would be smoking two cheroots at once, and the Dean [of the Shanghai Cathedral], and hear them discuss men and things, with an incessant flow of wit and humour.[17]

Another portrait of Alabaster – and a rather unkind one – comes from E.T.C. Werner (1864–1954), who served in the Canton Consulate at the beginning of his career and the end of Alabaster's. In his memoir *Autumn Leaves* of 1928, Werner wrote:

'The Buster,' as he was familiarly called, was notoriously a hard taskmaster, difficult to get on with; but we hit it off exceedingly well. His wife, Lady Alabaster, a most charming and kind-hearted lady, who had been a Miss Macgowan, daughter of Dr Macgowan, was said to have had no less than fifty proposals of marriage before she accepted this physically insignificant and crippled dwarf ... Her husband's stature (the result, it is said, of his shoulder having been broken through his nurse dropping him when he was a baby) was so diminutive that the amah once went and tucked him up in bed, mistaking him for one of his children! ... The 'Buster' was not only thus physically deformed, but had a curious growl-like laugh or chuckle, which seemed to come from low down in one side of his throat – the side already lowered by the broken shoulder, and was perhaps conditioned by the physical deformity. On one occasion, at a large dance, when everyone present was sitting round the room between two dances, he (having, it was alleged, indulged somewhat freely during the evening) started walking, or rather hobbling, across the broad polished floor. Having reached the middle, he slipped and fell, and his broken shoulder preventing him from rising up again easily even when in his sober senses, he started twiddling round rapidly like a beetle on a pin, uttering all the while his curious gurgle-like chuckle.[18]

---

17 *North China Herald*, 11 July 1898, 59.
18 E.T.C. Werner, *Autumn Leaves: An Autobiography with a Sheaf of Papers, Sociological & Sinological, Philosophical & Metaphysical* (Shanghai: Kelley & Walsh, 1928), 550–52.

Alabaster was an unusually small man – he writes in the diaries that he was 'asked to ride in the races' that took place annually, so some saw him as a potential jockey – but clearly not one to shrink from the light. His school friend and fellow student interpreter Thomas Adkins wrote to his mother while on board the ship on the way to China that: 'Mr Alabaster bears up well, much better than I expected him to'.[19] He also seems to have been less physically fit than his friends; once, hunting birds, he opted out of following a pheasant they had roused from its hide: 'As I had been walking through cover till thoroughly tired, I let Adkins and Tatham go after him & sat down pro tem'. His physique, however, did not appear to hold him back significantly – as we have seen, he was able to take part in military actions around Shanghai only a few years later. Nevertheless, in his obituary quoted above, the writer concluded that '"The Buster" was not intended by nature to shine in field sports or athletic exercises of any kinds'.[20]

Alabaster was bookish and studious. He often upbraided himself in the diary for his own 'laziness', but this is actually probably an indication of the opposite. He clearly studied his Chinese hard and was frustrated by his lack of progress: after almost a year of study he remarked, 'Chinese studies most unsatisfactory'.

He read what books he could on China assiduously – often written by his forebears in the Consular Service – as well as the novels then in vogue: Le Sage's *Gil Blas,* Henry and Augustus Mayhews' *The Image of his Father* and *The Greatest Plague of Life,* Bulwer-Lytton's *The Caxtons,* and Scott's *Kenilworth* and *The Fortunes of Nigel.* He also read a great deal of Dickens: *David Copperfield, Martin Chuzzlewit, Oliver Twist, Nicholas Nickleby, The Haunted Man* – a Christmas novella from 1848 that Alabaster described as 'nice & pleasant tho' unnatural & mistaken' – and *Little Dorrit,* which 'I think is a most unnatural book like most of Dickens nowadays'. He also subscribed to *The Athenæum* journal, and read the newspaper *Bell's Life in London and Sporting Chronicle.*

Alabaster married the daughter of a missionary, and there is no doubt that he was religious from his diaries. He attended church regularly though this was, of course, de rigeur for respectable Anglican folk. He was not uncritical of the church services, however, sometimes disparaging the sermons and

---

19 Thomas Adkins to Temperance Adkins, 8 August 1855, on board the *Indus*, Warwickshire County Record Office, CR 3554/2.
20 *North China Herald*, 11 July 1898, 59.

the church hierarchy: 'the bishop', he says after having tea with him one afternoon, 'is a great muff & expects to be toadied'. However, in the privacy of his diary, he shows a Christian devotion that appears genuine and sincere. Indeed, the act of keeping a diary in this period was itself associated with religious self-examination, as we will see below. One of the most striking features of the diaries, in this respect, are the raw outbursts of spiritual self-flagellation, such as this plea Alabaster makes only weeks after he arrived in Hong Kong: 'I – lazy, sleepy & stupid – feel all my ambition oozing out and beastly avarice coming in. O Lord! I beseech thee gard me from avarice'. Or this from July 1856, in which he adopts an anachronistic writing style, perhaps because it sounded more 'devout' to him:

> How quick is mine ruin when not upheld by religion. When once he breaks it through, how difficult it is to bind himself again thereby. So I have found it. If I had not in the first place transgressed I should not now be so base as I am. May I regain again my lost position & moral feeling.

In his first month in Hong Kong, Alabaster was instructed to copy a memorial that Lord Shaftesbury had written to Lord Clarendon, and Clarendon's reply. Ashley-Cooper, the seventh Earl of Shaftesbury, was a famous reformer and was firmly opposed to Britain's opium trade. His memorial to Clarendon, the foreign secretary of the time, was on this topic. Alabaster's own ideas about the opium question were very clearly recorded in the diaries:

> The opium trade is truly a gigantic evil and one which will, if not stopped in time, ruin 1st China then India and damage England much. Some damage it has already done. If it be put down suddenly, ruin will attend on many. The first houses [the major trading companies] will break and China like the West Indies go to the dogs, but if it be done gradually, it will not be so much felt and in 10 years the exports from England will be 10 times what they are. If we continue the trade we dishonor ourselves, disobey our God, impoverish and demoralise China & India, which we are doing rapidly. If it be stopped gradually, in 10 years China & Chinese trade will be twice as flourishing as it is now, but we must expect a row for the merchants are powerful & a rash stoppage would raise a commotion not only among the merchants but among the Chinese. To be continued.

This view was not one shared universally in Hong Kong. The large mercantile concerns were founded on the opium trade and even Bowring, an avowed liberal – though still a committed imperialist – let his early commitment to the suppression of the opium trade slide when he reached China. Alabaster's views actually had more in common with those of the missionary community than with most of the officials.

There are strong intimations in both Werner's sketch of Alabaster and in his obituary that he was opinionated and 'difficult to get on with'. If these comments point to an argumentative nature, the diaries provide evidence that they were not a feature of his character acquired late in life. His colleagues Hughes and Payne, in particular, seem to have annoyed him: for example, 'Quarreled with Hughes whom I must consider a mean fool & an impertinent ignoramus', and '[w]e went up to the peak or rather the others did, for I stopped at the first peak after a foolish tiff with Payne'. Alabaster continues, after this last comment, with an observation that indicates that he is, at least, aware of his shortcomings: 'It is strange. I am getting very touchy. It is very foolish'. He also notes at another point, typically upbraiding himself, that he is, 'getting ill-tempered & very snappish which I must correct as this will never do'. To quote the obituary once more:

> Alabaster was a man of intensely strong likes and dislikes; those whom he liked he loved, and those whom he disliked he hated; and as he had a bitter tongue and an ever-ready wit behind it, those whom he disliked called him Thersites.[21]

Learning Chinese

Alabaster's primary task on arrival in Hong Kong was to learn Chinese. Thomas Francis Wade (1818–1895) took charge of this, as he did for all the new student interpreters, in his role at the time of Chinese secretary

---

21   *North China Herald*, 11 July 1898, 59. Thersites is a character in the *Iliad*. Homer describes him (in Samuel Butler's 1898 prose translation) as:
   a man of many words, and those unseemly; a monger of sedition, a railer against all who were in authority, who cared not what he said … He was the ugliest man of all those that came before Troy – bandy-legged, lame of one foot, with his two shoulders rounded and hunched over his chest. His head ran up to a point, but there was little hair on the top of it. (*Iliad*, Book II)

to Governor Bowring.[22] For many years subsequently, Wade remained influential on Alabaster's life and career, to the extent, as we have seen above, of being mentioned in his obituary.

From a military family, Wade's father purchased a commission for him when he was 20. He became lieutenant in 1841 – by then in the 98th Regiment of Foot – and the following year arrived in Hong Kong. A gifted linguist, he began to teach himself Chinese on the ship going out and continued during his military service, acting as interpreter for the garrison. He was later appointed in the same capacity in the Supreme Court of Hong Kong, before becoming vice-consul in Shanghai in 1852. In the period of Alabaster's diaries, Wade was back in Hong Kong working as Chinese secretary. As Alabaster climbed the rungs of his diplomatic career, Wade was often involved in the same missions and negotiations, albeit at a more senior level. The remarks in the obituary point specifically to Alabaster's increasing distance from Wade, his erstwhile mentor, in their attitudes to Chinese officialdom. Alabaster was, according to the obituarist, 'too original, too decided and too anti-Chinese to please Sir Thomas Wade', who is characterised in the same piece as 'soft-hearted'.

Wade served as acting chargé d'affaires in Peking in 1864 and 1865, and again from 1869 for two more years. In 1871 he became envoy extraordinary and minister plenipotentiary and chief superintendent of British trade in China, retiring from the Consular Service in 1883. In 1862, he had been made a Companion of the Bath, and in 1876, Knight Commander in the same order. In 1886, when back in England, he donated more than 650 Chinese books to the Cambridge University Library (where they still reside), and in 1888 was elected that university's first professor of Chinese. The appointment was unpaid and seems to have been an informal quid pro quo for his donation. In his inaugural lecture, Wade commented: 'I assume that my pupils, should I have any, will be intending missionaries or interpreters … My advice to applicants in either category is that they should make their way to China with all speed', which, as T.H. Barrett notes, was likely designed 'to make sure that he might continue to enjoy his books undisturbed'.[23]

---

22   On Wade, see James C. Cooley, *T.F. Wade in China: Pioneer in Global Diplomacy, 1842–1882* (Leiden: Brill, 1981). See also May Holdsworth's entry on Wade in Holdsworth and Munn, *Dictionary of Hong Kong Biography*, 447–48.
23   T.H. Barrett, *Singular Listlessness: A Short History of Chinese Books and British Scholars* (London: Wellsweep Press, 1989), 78.

Wade's name is remembered in Sinology in the system of romanisation of Chinese characters he devised, later revised by Herbert Giles, which goes by the name Wade-Giles. Until the advent of the Hanyu pinyin system in the late 1970s, this was by far the most commonly used system of romanisation in the West.

Alabaster was recruited into the China Consular Service from the Chinese class at King's College. The principal of King's, Robert William Jelf (1798–1871), wrote to Clarendon with his recommendations for supernumerary interpreters on the basis of an examination in Chinese, which, he said, was:

> much more searching and comprehensive than was previously possible; and there seems no reason to doubt, that a much higher degree of proficiency in this difficult language has been attained and evinced on the present occasion than in the past.

The exam results placed Adkins and King in equal first position, followed by Alabaster, Payne, then Glynes. Jelf further noted that 'the characters of all five [are] perfectly satisfactory; the health good; the general intelligence above the usual average'. Alabaster, Adkins and Glynes were also noted to have a 'fair knowledge of French'.[24] Since Jelf was asked to nominate three students for positions, Alabaster, Adkins and King were selected. As it turned out, Payne and Glynes both also ended up in Hong Kong in the Consular Service. The letters of appointment Clarendon wrote to Adkins and Payne survive, listing the conditions of the job in exactly the same wording. Undoubtedly, Alabaster was appointed on the same terms: 'a salary at the rate of 200 pounds per year to commence on the day of your arrival at Hongkong, and a passage to that place will be provided for you at the public expense'.[25]

Clarendon evidently placed great faith in nominations from the principal of King's as the basis for recruitment, but unfortunately, in practice, those (including Alabaster) who had been 'trained' there did not display a great deal of competence in the language when they arrived in Hong Kong. Writing to Clarendon to inform him of the arrival of Alabaster and two other new student interpreters, Bowring expressed his disappointment:

---

24 Jelf to Clarendon, 17 April 1855, FO 228/186, no. 172.
25 Clarendon to Adkins, 14 June 1855, Warwickshire County Record Office, CR 3554/1; Clarendon to Payne, 20 September 1855, FO 228/ 186, no. 175.

> My Lord,
>
> I have to report the arrival of Messrs King, Adkins and Alabaster, Student Interpreters, by the Mail which reached Hong Kong on the 24th ultimo.
>
> We have a great deal of copying in the office from being short of hands, and I propose to detain them at Hong Kong for the present, giving them some training for official duty until after consideration of their aptitudes, and of the best means of giving effect to the objects of their appointment, I can decide as to their future location. They have learned a good many characters, but are wholly ignorant of the true pronunciation of the official language, and seem not to have had their attention directed to any of the classical compositions of the Chinese.[26]

Given that Bowring himself did not know Chinese, it is likely that this was Wade's opinion.[27]

When Alabaster was at King's, the Chinese professor was the Rev. James Summers, who had learned what Chinese he had on the ground, mostly in Shanghai.[28] He had also spent time in Hong Kong, so, to the extent that he was fluent in speech, it was in Cantonese or Shanghainese, not 'the official language' – Mandarin, or the Peking dialect – as noted in Bowring's letter. Alabaster mentions Summers once in his diaries in relation to his Chinese studies in Hong Kong. His comments unwittingly indicate the lackadaisical approach to Chinese language learning at King's in his time there:

> Had a read with the teacher & was confirmed in my idea that working at the tones is rot, for as I found with Summers, if I understand the thing and read as if I were talking not reading a lesson I pronounce the tones sufficiently correctly. At least the teacher says so, yet I could not tell the tone of a single character perhaps & I believe we have the tones just as much in English but are sensible & don't bother about them.

Needless to say, this conclusion would not find many adherents among linguists or teachers of Chinese today.

---

26   Bowring to Clarendon, 6 October 1855, FO 228/183, no. 320.
27   In 1857 Wade submitted a 'Confidential Report on the Ability of Chinese Interpreters' that Bowring had asked him to prepare. Details of its contents can be found in Cooley, *T.F. Wade*, 25–26.
28   On James Summers, see Uganda Sze Pui Kwan, 'Transferring Sinosphere Knowledge to the Public: James Summers (1828–91) as Printer, Editor and Cataloguer', *East Asian Publishing and Society* 8 (2018): 56–84, doi.org/10.1163/22106286-12341317.

On his arrival to Hong Kong, it appears that Alabaster was left to himself in his Chinese studies – his main task, as Bowring noted to Clarendon, was to help out in the office. In early January, however, Wade turned up with Chinese teachers and then 'got us some books but has as yet only given us one. Written by a Manchu of the Canton garrison. Had a read with the teacher'. I have not been able to identify this book, but not many days later, Alabaster was given the *Sacred Edict* or *Shengyu* 聖諭, and the *Thousand Character Classic* or *Qianzi wen* 千字文, both standard texts for students from China for learning to read (and recite). Later, Alabaster read the popular early Qing novel *Yu Jiao Li* 玉嬌梨, known in English as *Two Fair Cousins*,[29] and the *Trimetrical Classic* or *Sanzi jing* 三字經. Reading with a teacher seems to have been the bread and butter of Alabaster's language education, but we should bear in mind that these lessons were conducted in Chinese so they would also have served as conversation classes. He also noted, though, that he 'worked at' 'phrases' and 'the characters', probably his homework.

The conversations with the teachers were not restricted to linguistic matters. They also covered topics such as the 'jolly little dog belonging to the emperor which lights his pipe for him', Chinese mythological lore relating to eclipses and the injunction not to use paper that had writing on it for bathroom purposes: 'The old teacher gave us a long exhortation, which was received with roars of laughter, not to use printed paper for bumfodder & went thro' the motions'. In May 1856, about eight months after his arrival, Wade presented Alabaster (and Adkins, at least) with what he called an 'examination paper'. This appears to have been a comprehensive test of their competence in Chinese and more of an assignment than what we might think of as an exam, as Alabaster worked at it over a number of weeks. From passing remarks in the diaries, it included translations of the *Sacred Edict* into English; English texts into Chinese; 'short colloquial sentences'; an official letter sent by the senior official Xu Guangjin 徐廣縉 to a previous governor, Sir Samuel Bonham, a few years earlier; and essay questions on history and provincial officials.

---

29   Translated into French by Jean-Pierre Abel-Rémusat in 1826, then into English (from this French version rather than the original Chinese) in 1827. See Roland Altenburger, 'Two Cousins: Jean-Pierre Abel-Rémusat's and Stanislas Julien's Translations of *Yu Jiao Li*', in *Crossing Borders: Sinology in Translation Studies*, ed. T. H. Barrett and Lawrence Wang-Chi Wong (Hong Kong: The Chinese University of Hong Kong Press, 2022), 145–80, doi.org/10.2307/j.ctv2pfq2rn.10.

As Alabaster's language improved, Wade got him and Adkins to work on the project that became *The Hsin Ching Lu* or *Book of Experiments*, which was published in three volumes in 1859.[30] The subtitle indicates that this book was intended to be 'the first of a series of contributions to the study of Chinese'. In the Preface, Wade, explaining the origin of the project, wrote:

> The idea of venturing on such a piece of authorship was suggested by the wants of the Student Interpreters in the service of the British Government. A few of these gentlemen were at Hongkong when the writer entered on the duties of Chinese Secretary in 1855. For want of a better text-book he recommended the study of the *Sacred Edict*, a translation of the first chapter of which with a commentary is given in Part II. Subsequently some rough material, more or less in a state of preparation, was worked up as Part I. This chapter, entitled The Category of T'ien, was the foundation-experiment of a projected vocabulary of the Peking language.[31]

These few sentences elucidate a great deal of what we read in the diaries. First, there was no textbook available to use for learning Chinese. Alabaster refers to Joseph Henri Marie de Prémare's (1666–1736) *Notitia Linguae Sinicae*, which had been translated into English in 1847,[32] and to various dictionaries, but Wade chose to use the *Sacred Edict* as an introductory text instead. The *Sacred Edict* was issued by the Kangxi 康熙 Emperor (1654–1722, r. 1661–1722) in 1670 as a concentrated exposition of Confucian principles to be disseminated throughout the empire. Consisting of only 16 behavioural precepts of seven characters each, it was much shorter than the commentary issued by his successor, the Yongzheng 雍正 Emperor (1678–1735, r. 1722–1735) in 1724. Wade reproduced and translated both the original text and the commentary in *The Hsin Ching Lu*. The *Sacred Edict* was already widely known among foreigners in China, and more broadly, as the missionary scholar William Milne had published a translation in 1817.[33] This text is what Alabaster was referring to when he wrote that he had been studying the *Shung yee* or *Shung yü* or *Shangyu* or

---

30 Thomas Francis Wade, *The Hsin Ching Lu* 尋津錄, *or Book of Experiments; Being the First of a Series of Contributions to the Study of Chinese* (Hong Kong: Office of the 'China Mail', 1859).
31 Wade, Preface to *Hsin Ching Lu*, n.p.
32 Joseph Henri Marie de Prémare, *The Notitia Linguae Sinicae of Prémare*, trans. J.G. Bridgman (Canton: Office of the 'Chinese Repository', 1847).
33 William Milne, trans., *The Sacred Edict Containing Sixteen Maxims of the Emperor Kang-Hi, Amplified by His Son, the Emperor Yoong-Ching; Together with a Paraphrase of the Whole by a Mandarin* (London: Black, Kingsbury, Parbury, and Allen, 1817).

Shungyu (his romanisation was unstable). To say that his Chinese teachers would have been thoroughly familiar with the *Shengyu* would be a serious understatement.

Second, Wade used Alabaster and the student interpreters, and their teachers, to work on what became the first part of *The Hsin Ching Lu*. On the title page of this section, Wade used the heading 'T'ien Lei; or The Category of T'ien, Heaven, The Heavens, etc'. This section consists of some 362 sentences on different aspects of the word *tian* 天; that is, 'heaven', and various related terms, such as day, the sun, stars, clouds, etc., translated with short notes. Its format is clearly based on traditional Chinese encyclopedias called *leishu* 類書, the *lei* being the 'category' of Wade's heading. In these books, as Wade remarks, 'the first of the Chinese categories in such encyclopædias is always t'ien, heaven'. What sets this work apart from a traditional Chinese encyclopedia is that 'heaven' is only the first of often many hundreds of different categories.

Towards the end of these diaries, we can observe, perhaps, Wade's huge, unfulfilled ambitions as Alabaster wrote of beginning work on 'man' or *jen* (*ren*) 人, the category that comes second in the sequence: 'I went over t'ien lei & then after tiffin had a satisfactory attack upon jen lei'. Towards the beginning of the diaries, while he was stuck working in the office copying out documents, Alabaster complained that he had not yet been given a teacher but, as noted above, this was rectified when:

> Wade came back today bringing two teachers, Miaou & Siang, both very dirty – especially Miaou – who however to atone for it has a magnificent pronunciation & quite puts Siang, an ex-mandarin, in the shade.

Other student interpreters also had teachers assigned to them. When he wrote home in April 1856 describing their new living quarters in the Albany, Alabaster's friend, Thomas Adkins, recorded that '2 of the downstairs rooms are occupied by the teachers 4 in no'.[34] Thus, at that time, at least four teachers lived in close proximity to the student interpreters, this accommodation being presumably part of their remuneration. The Chinese honorific Alabaster used for the teachers is 'Sinsang', or in modern standard

---

34 Thomas Adkins-Temperance Adkins, 10 April 1856, Warwickshire County Record Office, CR 3554/9.

Chinese, *xiansheng* 先生, a respectful title with connotations of seniority and scholarship, rather than *laoshi* 老師, which is more focused on the professional teaching role.

In all, some seven teachers are mentioned: Miaou (also spelt Meao), Siang (also Seang), Chu, Chang, Seao, Shun and Ying (also 'Old Ying'). While these teachers were clearly a major presence in the lives of Alabaster and his friends and colleagues, it is difficult to identify them. Alabaster provided no characters for their names, but this would not help greatly as we can probably guess which patronyms are represented by his romanisations. More salient is the fact that the teachers typically did not have the appropriate status to find their way into either Chinese- or English-language sources. The only one mentioned above that we do have records of is Ying, because of his long association with Thomas Wade.

Wade notes, in his Preface to the 'Peking Syllabary' of *The Hsin Ching Lu*, that he employed Ying Longtian 應龍田 to be his 'first teacher' in the 'Peking dialect' in 1847, when he was assistant Chinese secretary to Governor John Francis Davis in Hong Kong.[35] In the 1867 Preface to the first edition of his *Yü Yen Tzu Erh Chi*, Wade again described Ying as 'my teacher' (noting that he had died in 1861), then in the Preface to the 1886 second edition as 'a fairly educated Pekingese and an admirable speaker'.[36] Between his appointment as Chinese secretary and his becoming vice-consul in Shanghai in 1853, Wade returned to England suffering from a recurrence of the malaria he had caught a few years earlier. It would appear that he took Ying with him on this trip, as the famous writer and reformer Wang Tao 王韜 (1828–1897) notes in his diary for mid-August 1853 that:

> Ying Yugeng 應雨耕 [Ying Longtian] came. He told me about his trip to England and the many sights he had seen abroad. So I wrote down what he had said and called it 'Yinghai biji' [瀛海筆記 *Notes on the Lands Across the Ocean*].[37]

---

35   Wade, Preface to 'Peking Syllabary' of *Hsin Ching Lu*, n.p.
36   Thomas Francis Wade and Walter Caine Hillier, *Yü Yen Tzu Erh Chi* 語言自邇集: *A Progressive Course Designed to Assist the Student of Colloquial Chinese as Spoken in the Capital and the Metropolitan Department*, 2nd ed. (Shanghai: Statistical Department of the Inspectorate General of Customs, 1886), xvi, xvii, ix.
37   This comes from Wang Tao's manuscript diary covering April 1853 – January 1854, entitled *Yingruan rizhi* 瀛壖日志. See Paul A. Cohen, *Between Tradition and Modernity: Wang T'ao and Reform in Late Ch'ing China* (Cambridge, Mass.: Harvard University Press, 1974), 15 (romanisation converted). *Yinghai biji* 瀛海筆記 (English title: 'Sketch of a Voyage around the Cape and Several Months Residence in Great Britain') was published in the short-lived journal *Xiaer guanzhen* 遐爾貫珍 (English title: *Chinese Serial*), 2, 7 (July 1854), edited by the elder W.H. Medhurst.

Wang also notes that Ying approached Walter Henry Medhurst (1796–1857) of the London Missionary Society in Shanghai in July 1853, seeking instruction in order to convert to Christianity.[38] In 1855, back in Hong Kong as Chinese secretary, Wade was evidently accompanied by Ying. One of Wade's tasks was to oversee the training in Chinese of the student interpreters. Alabaster himself benefited from Ying's teaching and later he was evidently assigned to James Mongan, as he called himself 'teacher to Mr Mongan' when he appeared in court proceedings as a witness in 1858.[39] In these proceedings, Mongan stated that 'three Chinese' were engaged to examine handwritten Chinese documents that were crucial in the case: 'Ying-loong-tim, Shum Cheok Yeen, and Chang-toong Yuen (Mr Wade's teacher)'. Ying-loong-tim, also rendered as Ying-loong-tun and Ying-long-tien, is clearly Ying Longtian. Shum Cheok Yeen, also Sum-cheok-yeen, who said that he was 'a writer and a teacher in the Chinese secretary's office', may be the 'Sun' mentioned in Alabaster's diaries. Chang-toong Yuen, or Yeong, is 'another teacher in Mr Mongan's office'.[40]

'Chinese teachers' were, thus, more than just teachers. They clearly filled the role of language experts, even for those who, like Wade, were already fluent in Chinese. We find, for example, the Rev. George Smith (later Bishop of Hong Kong) describing how missionaries in Shanghai in the 1840s worked collaboratively with the 'teachers' in translating the Bible:

> The three most experienced missionaries were present with their Chinese teachers, one of whom was a literary graduate ... The missionaries, after discussing the passage among themselves, and

---

38 This is recorded in Wang Tao's manuscript record of July–September 1853, *Hucheng wenjian lu* 滬城聞見錄. See Cohen, *Between Tradition and Modernity*, 19.
39 This was in a trial of William Tarrant (c. 1820–1872), editor of the newspaper the *Friend of China*, who had made allegedly libellous comments in relation to the scandal surrounding Daniel Richard Caldwell (1816–1875), the registrar general and protector of Chinese, who was accused of being a criminal associate of the pirate and gangster Wong Ma-Chow. Tarrant was found not guilty. On the legal history of colonial Hong Kong, see Christopher Munn, *Anglo-China*; Gillian Bickley, ed., *A Magistrate's Court in Nineteenth Century Hong Kong: Court in Time* (Hong Kong: Proverse Press, 2005). On Caldwell, see also Christopher Munn's entry on him in Holdsworth and Munn, *Dictionary of Hong Kong Biography*, 60–62.
40 'Papers Relating to Hong Kong', no. 37, 'Copy of a Despatch from Governor Sir Hercules Robinson to His Grace the Duke of Newcastle, &c. &c. &c.' (27 September 1859) concerning the case Regina v. Tarrant in *Parliamentary Papers*, vol. 48 (London: House of Commons, 1860), 302–64, quotations at 307, 309, 310. On the Caldwell Affair and Tarrant, see Christopher Munn, 'Colonialism "in a Chinese Atmosphere": The Caldwell Affair and the Perils of Collaboration in Early Colonial Hong Kong', in *New Frontiers: Imperialism's New Communities in East Asia, 1842–1953*, ed. Robert Bickers and Christian Henriot (Manchester: Manchester University Press, 2000), 12–37.

conveying orally the meaning of the sacred text to the Chinese teachers, proceeded to receive the opinion of the latter on its idiomatic expression in the written language.[41]

Some 20 years later, William Lobscheid, in his *Grammar of the Chinese Language*, bemoans the fact that few foreigners, despite the proficiency of some in Chinese, 'have so far mastered the Chinese pen or brush as to be able to write a document correctly without the aid of a teacher. This is chiefly owing to the facility with which competent Chinese teachers can be engaged'.[42] Learning to converse in Chinese was a difficult enough proposition for the student interpreters, and reading and writing represented another great obstacle to overcome. For even the most accomplished student of Chinese, the intricacies of drafting official documents in Chinese, including using correct phraseology and verbal formulae, not to mention being able to write acceptable characters with a brush and ink, would have required expert assistance.

The reputation of the Chinese teachers was not universally high. George Wingrove Cooke (1816–1865), a London *Times* correspondent who travelled to Hong Kong in 1857, and a particularly jaundiced witness, wrote in 1857 that:

> These 'teachers' are, necessarily, the very scum and refuse of the Chinese literary body – the plucked of the examinations, and the runagates from justice or tyranny. They are hired at a far lower salary than they would obtain in their own country as secretaries to a high official, and if they can write a fair hand, or speak a tolerable idiom, or pronounce with a certain purity of accent (although they may be known to be domestic spies, repeating all they see and hear), they are respected and almost venerated by the English sinologue who maintains them. If one of these learned persons should happen also to be the son of some small mandarin, he becomes to his pupil a great authority on Chinese politics and a Petronius of Chinese ceremonial. Papers are indited and English policy is shaped according to the response of the oracle. The sinologue who derives his inspirations from this source is again taken as an absolute authority by the poor

---

41 George Smith, *A Narrative of an Exploratory Visit to Each of the Consular Cities of China and to the Islands of Hong Kong and Chusan, on behalf of the Church Missionary Society in the Years 1844, 1845, 1846* (London: Seeley, Burnside & Seeley, 1847), 471–72.
42 William Lobscheid, *Grammar of the Chinese Language* (Hong Kong: Office of the 'Daily Press', 1864), 17.

> helpless general, or admiral, or ambassador, who thinks it his duty to adopt what he is told are Chinese customs and to ape the Chinese ceremonial.[43]

Thomas Wade took issue with Cooke's assessment, though we might note that Wade – one of the foreigners most adept in Chinese language and culture of his era – would certainly not have selected 'the very scum and refuse of the Chinese literary body' to teach the student interpreters. In the Preface to *The Hsin Chin Lu*, he wrote:

> It is his [the interpreter's] foremost duty to learn the spoken language; for all our respect for the labours of Morrison, Gonçalves, and others, will not prevent our turning with despair from their dictionaries to our patient living lexicons, our ill-paid Chinese teachers, so recklessly disparaged by Mr Wingrove Cooke. From these men, some of whom, though poor and mean-looking, are perfect mines of literary wealth, to extract such a portion of their store as we require, we must talk, and talk well.[44]

Wade stands out among Westerners in Hong Kong at this time in his desire to immerse himself in the culture of educated Chinese people, evidently regarding his Chinese teachers as far more than 'native speakers' useful in language learning. He sees beyond their appearance – 'poor and mean-looking' – and grants them the respect due to learned scholars and inheritors of a profound literary heritage.

Hong Kong in 1855 and 1856

When Alabaster arrived in Hong Kong in October 1855, the colony had been in British hands for only 14 years.[45] It had been ceded by China in the Treaty of Nanking, and the chief superintendent of British trade in China

---

43 George Wingrove Cooke, *China: Being 'The Times' Special Correspondence from China in the years 1857–58* (London: G. Routledge & Co., 1858), 394.
44 Wade, Preface to *The Hsin Ching Lu*, n.p.
45 On Hong Kong in this period, see Eitel, *Europe in China*; Endacott, *A History of Hong Kong*; Endacott, *A Biographical Sketch-Book*; G.R. Sayer, *Hong Kong 1841–1862: Birth, Adolescence and Coming of Age* (Oxford: Oxford University Press, 1937); Steve Tsang, *A Modern History of Hong Kong, 1841–1997* (London: I.B. Taurus, 1997); Munn, *Anglo-China*. In this context, mention should also be made of a manuscript diary by John Fortescue Evelyn Wright (1827–1891) in the form of a 'letter-book' held in the Alexander Turnbull Collections of the National Library of New Zealand (photocopy held in the Public Record Office of Hong Kong). Wright worked in the Post Office in Hong Kong, and later in Shanghai, before briefly working in business there. In 1854 he migrated permanently to Wellington, New Zealand, and became a sheep farmer. Wright's Hill in Karori in Wellington's western suburbs is likely named for him.

– a position established in 1833 – had shifted his residence from Macau in 1841. From then on, a town gradually grew on the northern side of the island, clinging to the small amount of flat and rising land between the harbour and the steep slopes of Victoria Peak and Mount Gough.

At this stage, the British colony only consisted of Hong Kong Island, ceded 'in perpetuity' in the Treaty of Nanking, signed in August 1842. Kowloon Peninsula across the harbour would become part of the colony with the Convention of Peking of 1860 on the same terms, and the New Territories in 1898, on a 99-year lease. Originally, the harbour was more than twice as wide as it is now, the narrowing due to extensive land reclamations on both sides. The first reclamation project took place as early as 1851, when a disastrous fire in Sheung Wan that affected some 1.75 hectares of built-up land left huge piles of rubble. This rubble was used as fill to reclaim 15 metres of harbour, creating what became Bonham Strand. Before the many reclamations had been undertaken in the central part of the town of Victoria, as the settlement on Hong Kong Island was called, the shoreline was located about halfway between today's Queen's Road and Des Voeux Road.

In the 1855 census, the population of Hong Kong was 72,607, made up of 70,651 Chinese and 1,956 non-Chinese, exclusive of army and navy personnel.[46] Chinese settlement on Hong Kong Island was sparse before its cession to Great Britain – about 3,500 people in 20 or so small villages – and almost all the Chinese people living there in Alabaster's time had migrated from the mainland. Indeed, the Chinese population had doubled in the previous three years with large numbers of people displaced by the ravages of the Taiping Uprising seeking refuge in the colony. The Chinese and Europeans lived in quite separate parts of the town. The Chinese part was a densely populated area known as Taiping shan (after the Chinese name for Victoria Peak, rather than the uprising) in current Sheung Wan in the general vicinity of the Man Mo temple. The European area was strung out from there eastwards, approximately to the current Victoria Park in Causeway Bay. The lack of interaction between the two communities was such that, in September 1858, Bowring noted that 'the separation of the native population from the European is nearly absolute; social intercourse between the races wholly unknown'.[47]

---

46 *Historical and Statistical Abstract of the Colony of Hong Kong, 1841–1920* (Hong Kong: Noronha & Company, Government Printers, 1922). On the Chinese population of Hong Kong in its early years, see Munn, *Anglo-China*, 67–73.
47 Endacott, *A History of Hong Kong*, 122.

Plate 4. William Pryor Floyd (1834–c. 1900), *Chinese Town, Westpoint*, 1869.
Albumen print. This photograph depicts Taiping shan.
Source: Gift of Mrs W.F. Spinney, 1923, PH17.37. Courtesy of the Peabody Essex Museum.

The harbour that lies between Hong Kong Island and the mainland was a primary reason for the British demanding Hong Kong in the treaty negotiations.[48] For them, it represented a safe haven both for their naval forces and for trading vessels. Hong Kong was then, as it continued to be, a hub of maritime activity. In 1855, no fewer than 1,736 ships entered the harbour, and this rose to over 2,000 in 1856. Cooke described the view from his balcony in this way:

> In the harbour, besides the Chinese boats so comfortably fitted with their neat bamboo work – besides, also, several large junks, with their great sightless eyes painted in the bows, their lofty sterns, and their mat sails, there is a fleet of sixty-four European merchant-vessels, whereof ten are steamers. The Yankee and the Dutch flags flaunt about with the Union Jack, for it is Sunday; and every floating thing, from the Yankee *Challenge*, 2,030 tons, to the little British *Squirrel* steamer of 50 tons, rejoices in its display of nationality …

---

48 On Hong Kong as a maritime hub, see Henry Sze Hang Choi, *The Remarkable Hybrid Maritime World of Hong Kong and the West River Region in the Late Qing Period* (Leiden: Brill, 2017).

INTRODUCTION

> But above and more important than these vehicles of opium and rice, ride the vessels of war. From the verandah of this bungalow we can count thirteen pennants. There lies the *Calcutta*, with her three tiers of guns and her admiral's flag; and, dwindled into specks by comparison with her greatness, those saucy little gunboats with their two long guns each – the *Bustard*, the *Forester*, the *Haughty*, the *Opossum*, and the *Staunch* – seem ready for any mischief. There is a French steamer also, and a French brig-of-war, flying their tri-colour; and the Yankee steamer *San Jacinto*, with her fifteen long guns, adds the stars and stripes to this display of warlike force.[49]

Besides these, Cooke reported that another 12 naval vessels were, at the time, on active duty up river towards Canton. The junks in the harbour, he noted, were all 'armed with at least two heavy guns – some have twelve'. 'Probably one quarter of these,' he continued, 'are pirates, who live principally by piracy, and adopt the coasting trade only as a cover to their real profession.'[50]

The British Army residents in Hong Kong were from the 59th (2nd Nottinghamshire) Regiment of Foot, who were stationed in Hong Kong from 1850 until 1858, having been previously based in Ireland. These men were housed in barracks near the harbour. James Bodell, one of the soldiers of the regiment, later wrote a memoir, documenting important information on his time in Hong Kong in the early 1850s, including that, when they arrived at the end of January 1850, there were about 1,200 troops in total there.[51] He also described the ravages that malaria took on the soldiers:

> During July Augt & September, we buried about 300 men. I never seen or heard anything like the Epidemic that got amongst the men and every one, native and European has this Sickness. A man would appear in excellent Health today and in a few hours become raving mad with as the Doctors call it, Remittent Fever and in his grave the next day.[52]

---

49 Cooke, *China*, 12.
50 Cooke, *China*, 69.
51 James Bodell, *A Soldier's View of Empire: The Reminiscences of James Bodell, 1831–92*, ed. Keith Sinclair (London: Bodley Head, 1982), 65. For a general history of the military in Hong Kong, see Kwong Chi Man and Tsoi Yiu Lun, *Eastern Fortress: A Military History of Hong Kong, 1840–1970* (Hong Kong: Hong Kong University Press, 2014), doi.org/10.5790/hongkong/9789888208708.001.0001.
52 Bodell, *A Soldier's View*, 58.

Plate 5. William Pryor Floyd (1834–c. 1900), *Public Garden (from the Albany, Hong Kong)*, 1860s.
Albumen print. Museum purchase made possible by the Frederick Townsend Ward Memorial Fund, PH18.2. Courtesy of the Peabody Essex Museum.

Bodell also observed that the malaria and dysentery affected the regiment so badly that they were unable to do all the guard duties they were required to perform.[53] The numbers who died were appalling but the strength of the garrison was further depleted by desertions: with so many trading vessels coming into Hong Kong harbour, including those from America, opportunities for absconding were numerous. In 1851, he wrote, there was a 'General Parade':

> and of the 650 men that left Cork Barracks in 1849 only 62 remained. They had either died deserted or been invalided out and your humble servant was one of the 62 left and excepting several attacks of the Intermittent Fever (Shakes and Ague) and the prickly heat and one time hundreds of small boils broke out all over my body, I enjoyed good health.[54]

---

53   Bodell, *A Soldier's View*, 59.
54   Bodell, *A Soldier's View*, 61.

By 1852, however, Bodell, reported that 'our Regt was enjoying good health'.[55]

In the period of Alabaster's diaries, there were also other troops present, whom he called 'sepoys', a generic term for soldiers from the Indian subcontinent. Exactly who these troops were is a matter of some uncertainty. Certainly, Indian troops were stationed in Hong Kong throughout this period. However, officially, the three companies of the Ceylon Rifles had left in 1854 and their replacements, the 12th Regiment of the Madras Native Light Infantry, did not arrive until 1857.[56] Thus, in the 16 months of the diaries, no troops from the subcontinent should have been in Hong Kong; but the context of one of his comments – 'The sepoys are having a house built for them & then we shall have possession' – is that when Alabaster arrived, they were living in the Albany Building, into which he would move. Given that he refers, elsewhere, to these troops as 'gun sepoys', it may be that they were stragglers from the Ceylon Rifles. Whoever they were, Alabaster noted that they had left by Easter 1856, 'so now we have lots of outhouses which is a great comfort tho' this is counterbalanced by the loss of their protection'.

Apart from the government and military personnel, most other non-Chinese were engaged in business. Most of the great business houses of colonial Hong Kong had their origins earlier than the establishment of the colony, being engaged in trade with offices and warehouses in Canton and Macau. When Hong Kong was ceded to the British, these firms gradually moved to the new colony and were among the first to buy land there. The great Hongs in Alabaster's time, as these businesses were known, were Jardine, Matheson & Co., and Dent & Co., which were both British. Alabaster's good friend Leonard worked for Dent's, while Tatham, with whom he had a more on-again off-again relationship, was a clerk at J. Burd & Co. in this period, moving to Fletcher & Co. a little later.

---

55 Bodell, *A Soldier's View*, 63. On the general medical situation in Hong Kong, see Moira M.W. Chan-Yeung, *A Medical History of Hong Kong, 1842–1941* (Hong Kong: Chinese University of Hong Kong Press, 2018), doi.org/10.2307/j.ctvbtzp1t; Ka-che Yip, Yuen-sang Leung and Man-kong Wong, *Health Policy and Disease in Colonial and Post-Colonial Hong Kong, 1841–2003* (Abingdon: Routledge, 2016), doi.org/10.4324/9781315672373.
56 Bodell, *A Soldier's View*, 69.

These firms were trading houses and, as G.B. Endacott put it, 'they were primarily agents for manufacturers or wholesalers in Britain, Europe, and India, and sold cargoes or consignments on a commission basis'. This explains, as Endacott noted, the obsession in the historical archive with 'godowns' or warehouses, which were 'indispensable because of goods having to be stored while waiting for a favourable turn in the market'.[57] The British houses were fundamental to the triangular trade between Britain, India and China in tea, silk and opium, although these goods did not comprise the whole of the business. In addition to the trade in goods, transported across the world in the famous fleets of clipper ships they provided, the Hongs engaged in insurance and other financial services.[58] Banking in Hong Kong had been done through branches of Indian- or British-based banks until the establishment of the Hong Kong and Shanghai Bank in 1864. The principals of the trading houses became extremely rich and exerted (or tried to exert) strong influence over the colonial governments.

When Alabaster arrived in Hong Kong, the non-Chinese (and non-military) population was about 2,000. This was, by any account, a very small community, but in practice it was actually broken up into even smaller units. The non-Chinese included French, Germans, Dutch, Spanish, Parsees and, of course, Portuguese who had shifted from Macao.[59] In the latter case, some notable Macanese worked in the British colonial bureaucracy; for example, Leonardo d'Almada e Castro and Januario de Carvalho who held senior appointments in the Colonial Secretary's Office and the Colonial Treasurer's Office, respectively. In addition, Delfino Noronha established himself early on in the printing trade in Hong Kong and from 1849 was printing the *Hong Kong Government Gazette*, before branching out into other ventures, including cross-harbour ferries. However, English- and Portuguese-speaking

---

57   G.B. Endacott, *An Eastern Entrepôt: A Collection of Documents Illustrating the History of Hong Kong* (London: Her Majesty's Stationery Office, 1964), xi.
58   On the history of insurance in Hong Kong, see Feng Bangyan and Nyaw Mee Kau, *Enriching Lives: A History of Insurance in Hong Kong, 1841–2010*, trans. Violet Law (Hong Kong: Hong Kong University Press, 2009).
59   See Cindy Yik-yi Chu, ed., *Foreign Communities in Hong Kong, 1840s–1950s* (Basingstoke, Hampshire: Palgrave MacMillan, 2005). For studies of particular communities in Hong Kong, see, for example, Zhou Xun, '"Cosmopolitan from above": A Jewish Experience in Hong Kong', *European Review of History – Revue européenne d'histoire* 23 (2016): 897–911, doi.org/10.1080/13507486.2016.1203879; François Drémeaux, ed., *Hong Kong, French Connections: From the 19th Century to the Present Day* (Hong Kong: Bonham Media, 2012); Stuart Braga, *Making Impressions: A Portuguese Family in Macau and Hong Kong, 1700–1945* (Macau: Instituto Internacional de Macau, July 2015); António M. Pacheco Jorge da Silva, *The Portuguese Community in Hong Kong: A Pictorial History*, vol. 1 (Macau: Conselho das Comunidades Macaenses; Instituto Internacional de Macau, 2007), and vol. 2 (Macau: Conselho das Comunidades Macaenses; Instituto Internacional de Macau, 2010).

people seem not to have mixed socially (and the government appointments did elicit criticism from some British Hong Kong residents on the grounds that those selected were 'aliens'). In 1866, the Portuguese, in fact, established their own club, the Club Lusitano. They were not the first non-English-speaking group to do this: the Club Germania had been formed in 1859. On the other hand, we might imagine, from the distance of more than 150 years, that expatriates from different English-speaking countries would have mixed more easily. However, a glance at Alabaster's diaries shows this not to be the case. His animus towards the 'Yankees' is palpable: when General Keenan, the US consul was arrested for aiding in the escape of an American ship's captain accused of flogging one of his British seamen, Alabaster's response was: 'Great News!' He even saw fights between drunken sailors through this prism: 'There was a fearful row last night between some Yankees and Englishmen but our Jacks licked them.'

Alabaster's anti-Americanism in the local Hong Kong scene was consistent with the broader geo-political situation of the time. On receiving news that the US Government had dismissed the British minister to Washington, John Crampton, and had also recognised the American mercenary adventurer William Walker as president of Nicaragua, he even went so far as to conclude: 'War seems inevitable with America. They have dismissed Crampton and recognize Walker, &c. Confound them, I hope we shall thrash them into nothing.' Socially, Alabaster's world was very limited. His working hours were almost exclusively spent with the small group in the office and in his time off he mostly associated with the same people, and a few young men from the trading houses. The only Chinese people he got to know well were his teachers, and he was clearly not impressed with them as social companions. His encounters with young non-Chinese women were limited to formal engagements at Government House or sightings at church. A dyspeptic account of Hong Kong society in 1856 written by Henry Ellis, a naval officer who had already spent four years there, does nothing to make the place seem welcoming:

> The English residents at Hong Kong, like many other small communities, were divided by exclusive feelings, which rendered society far less agreeable than it might have been had a better understanding existed among them. As each little coterie was headed by its own peculiar lady patroness, it was a difficult matter to find a half-dozen who would meet any other half-dozen, without their evincing mutual marks of contempt or dislike … The most absurd part of this purse-proud stuck-up-ism, was that with the exception

of a few Government *employés*, they were all more or less rowing in the same boat, i.e. striving to amass as many dollars as opportunity would admit of.[60]

Ellis's views were endorsed by Alfred Woodhead, a clerk in the Hong Kong Supreme Court, in a lecture he gave in England called 'Life in Hong Kong: 1856–1859' some years after he had returned. He described 'petty class distinctions' and a community 'split up into numerous petty cliques or sets, the members of which never think of associating with those out of their immediate circle'. Like the provincial town it was in many respects, 'every one knows every body, and the minutest details of your neighbour's daily lives, manners and conversation, are noted with watchful assiduity'.[61]

Ellis's more general remarks on the nature of Hong Kong life were equally damning:

> There was, as it were, a bleakness of life and prisoner-like sensation, in a residence at the latter place, arising, in a great measure, from a local monotony, from the difficulty experienced in moving more than a mile or two on either side of the town of Victoria, partly from want of practicable roads and partly from the unscrupulous treachery and hostility of the Chinese. There had been roads to one or two police and military stations on the other side of the island of Hong Kong, which is in itself about thirty miles in circumference, but the Chinamen had broken the bridges down for the sake of the iron fastenings, and the rains were continually washing away the embankments on which the roads were laid round its rocky hills; so that these circumstances, together with the necessity of being well armed against predatory bands rendered excursioning, at best, but a search for a change of air and scene under difficulties, and was seldom attempted except in large parties, or by water, in boats, nor were the latter by any means exempt from attack by local pirates. So that unless you could get a few days' leave occasionally over to the Portuguese settlement of Macao, distant about thirty miles, it was exceedingly dull, stupid, and monotonous, to say nothing of the baleful influence of the climate on health and spirits.[62]

---

60   Henry T. Ellis, *Hong Kong to Manilla, and the Lakes of Luzon, in the Philippine Isles in the Year 1856* (London: Smith, Elder & Co., 1859), 5–6. This Henry Ellis should not be confused with the more famous Henry Ellis (1788–1855) who accompanied Lord Amherst on his diplomatic mission to China in 1816.
61   Alfred Woodhead, 'Life in Hong Kong, 1856–1859', n.d., Hong Kong Public Records Office, 34–35.
62   Ellis, *Hong Kong to Manilla*, 4–5. The history of policing in Hong Kong has received significant attention in recent years. See, for example, Sheilah E. Hamilton, *Watching over Hong Kong: Private Policing 1841–1941* (Hong Kong: Hong Kong University Press, 2008); Kam C. Wong, *Policing in Hong Kong: History and Reform* (Boca Raton: CRC Press, 2015) doi.org/10.1201/b18199; Patricia O'Sullivan, *Policing Hong Kong: An Irish History* (Hong Kong: Blacksmith Books, 2017).

Alabaster's life in and around Hong Kong does not appear to be quite as constrained as this account, and others of the time, imply. Perhaps being with a group of other young men, sometimes armed with hunting rifles, made him feel safe, and, being only 16 or 17 and single, he had no reason to become involved with cliques and coteries. In the diaries, he writes of the regatta, the cricket, the race meeting and other regular recreations. He frequents the Reading Rooms, goes bowling in the Hong Kong Club where they had a bowling alley, and attends a meeting of the Royal Asiatic Society (RAS) to hear a paper given by the Rev. S. Beal, later in life professor of Chinese at University College, London, and expert on Chinese Buddhism:

> Beal, Chaplain of the *Sibylle*, reading a paper on Japan, &c. Rather good tho' he had to leave out ½ of it … Tasted some sake which seems to be a composition distilled from cockroaches & ketchup. Lot of Japanese books there. Nice neat little things in curious paper covers.

In his lecture, Woodhead gave a contrasting view of the RAS, which, he said, 'exists, or rather languishes', where 'members might play chess, practise music and get up lectures, soirées, and classes if they liked. But they don't'. He explained why not:

> In the first place such proceedings would involve people belonging to different circles meeting each other, which would be highly improper and objectionable, and besides would necessitate some exertion of the bodily and intellectual faculties, a thing to be deprecated in a hot climate.[63]

Woodhead also mentions that 'private theatricals have always been much cultivated'. It is tempting to think that Alabaster may have been involved in these or at least part of the audience as, in later years in Shanghai, he was very involved in the Amateur Dramatic Society. However, in these diaries, it is Adkins rather than Alabaster who attends theatrical performances.

---

63 Woodhead, 'Life in Hong Kong, 1856–1859', 30.

The Empire and the China Consular Service

Hong Kong was one of the furthest parts of the British Empire from London, and communications and transport were slow in the middle of the nineteenth century. When Alabaster left for Hong Kong on 4 August 1855 on the P&O passenger paddle steamer, the *Indus*, he followed what had become the standard route to Asia. Leaving England from Southampton for the Mediterranean, he reached Alexandria in Egypt after 15 days, with stops in Gibraltar and Malta. From there, he crossed overland via Cairo to Suez at the head of the Gulf of Suez. Alabaster's next ship – he does not record its name, though it might well have been the *Norna* – proceeded down the Red Sea to Aden, then a free port under British control, and across the Arabian Sea to Point de Galle in the British colony of Ceylon (i.e. Galle in modern Sri Lanka). Leaving Ceylon, he travelled across the Bay of Bengal to Penang, then down the strait to Malacca and Singapore, all parts of the British-controlled Straits Settlements. He arrived in Hong Kong on 14 October, the journey having taken 10 weeks.

Plate 6. 'Fire on Board the Ship "Fort William" at Hong-Kong', *Illustrated London News*, 3 January 1852.

The mail, of course, took as long and, just as passenger transport might be held up by inclement weather or other delays, the arrival of the mail was not predictable. Travelling, like passengers, on P&O vessels, the mail was announced by a blast from the guns of the *Fort William*, P&O's so-called receiving hulk moored permanently in the harbour. The excitement at the arrival of the mail in Alabaster's diaries is palpable. It not only brought letters from family and friends, informing him of news from his circle – which he duly notes in the diary – but also the newspapers and journals he subscribed to, including the *Illustrated London News*. Many entries in the diaries that follow the arrival of the mail are full of detail about world events, weeks old by the time the news reached Hong Kong. One such entry, for example, reads:

> Great news. The Calcutta mail came in today. The Russians have sallied out at Sebastipol & been repulsed with 4000 killed. Sveabourg has been bombarded and the town and harbour been smashed and perhaps the batteries. Riga has been smashed at. Supplies are cut off from south part of Sebastipol which must now surrender. The Queen has been to Paris. The Empress is *enceinte*. Parliament is prorogued. Sir de Lacy Evans has brought in a bill to take all the regulars from Hong Kong, &c. The sea of Azof and the White sea have been cleared of the Russians and there have been great successes in Asia. Vivat Regina.

The references here to Sevastopol, Sveabourg (an alternative name for Suomenlinna, in Helsinki) and Riga relate to events in the Crimean War. The bombardment of Sveabourg took place on 9–11 August 1855. The defeat of the Russian counterattack is likely a reference to the Battle of Chernaya, which took place on 16 August. The Queen is Victoria; her visit to France was from 17 to 28 August 1855. The empress is Eugénie, wife of Napoleon III who is pregnant (*enceinte*). Sir De Lacy Evans spoke in Parliament on 14 August proposing the withdrawal of British troops from Hong Kong and other places where they were stationed so they could be redeployed on the front lines of the Crimean War. The sea of Azov lies north-east of the Crimean Peninsula and is connected to the Black Sea by the Strait of Kerch. The White Sea is in the extreme north-west of Russia, south of the Kola Peninsula, emptying into the Barents Sea to the north. All of these events took place in August; as this mail arrived in Hong Kong on 17 October, the news in this case took about two months to arrive.

The Crimean War occupied Alabaster's attention at least as much as Britain's relations with China for the first few months he was in Hong Kong, probably because it was more of a focus in London – and his view of the world was still fundamentally formed by the newspapers and magazines that came with the mail. When Alabaster arrived, the war had already been underway almost two years, and Sevastopol had been under siege for 11 months. The Russians actually retreated from Sevastopol on 9 September – when Alabaster was at sea on his way to take up his position – but he did not hear the news until 26 October. Similarly, the Treaty of Paris ending the war was signed on 30 March 1855, but Hong Kong did not get word until 26 May.

One action that caught Alabaster's attention was the Siege of Petropavlovsk.[64] Concluding more than a year before he got to Hong Kong, it was one of Russia's more unlikely, though small, victories in the Crimean War. Pursuing Russian ships in the Pacific, three French and three British naval vessels (including the HMS *Pique*) chased the Russians down to the port of Petropavlovsk on the eastern side of the Kamchatka Peninsula, north of Japan. Outnumbered and outgunned, the Russian forces should have been defeated by the British and French. However, the night before the assault, the British commander, Rear Admiral David Price, died of a gunshot in his cabin, possibly a suicide. This undoubtedly distracted the officers and sailors under his command, and the French who were fighting alongside them. After a successful first attack from the sea, a misconceived land assault was mounted, leading to a retreat back to the ships. Subsequently, the *Pique* found its way to Hong Kong. Months later, Alabaster, with a great talent for taking down eavesdropped conversations, recorded the following at the races:

> Some fellows off the *Pique* holding forth about Petropaulski: 'Why d'y'see, the French admiral was going in, so we goes up into the riggin' – they made us man the riggin' – to give him 3 cheers & do y'see, he turned back & wouldn't go in & we were between 4 batteries. We lost 46 men first shot. 360 in our company. When we came back we were only 300 & the bloody old admiral shot himself, fear the Roosians should do it'.

---

64   On this campaign, see John D. Grainger, *The First Pacific War, Britain and Russia 1854–1856* (Woodbridge: The Boydell Press, 2008).

Alabaster was sent to Hong Kong in the first place because of the concessions Britain had wrung from China after the First Opium War. Apart from ceding Hong Kong, China was forced to give residence and trading rights to British merchants in the five treaty ports – Shanghai, Ningbo, Fuzhou, Xiamen, and Canton; to grant extraterritoriality to British subjects living there; and to allow Britain to open consulates in each one. This meant, of course, a program of recruitment, as we have seen. Competence in the Chinese language was not widespread among British people at this time, so the new officers came from a variety of backgrounds. Some like Charles (or Karl) Gutzlaff (1803–1851), who was born in what was then Pomerania, and George Tradescant Lay (c. 1800–1845) came from the mission fields and had first learnt Chinese to spread the Word. Others had fallen into the study of the language through a combination of opportunity and curiosity. Thomas Taylor Meadows (1815–1868), for example, was in Germany, 'engaged in various studies', when he:

> commenced the study of the Chinese language at the University of Munich … Happening to notice the announcement of a course of lectures on the language of the Chinese by Professor Neumann, the interest I had always taken in the people, induced me to employ an otherwise vacant hour in learning something of their tongue. But I presently began to devote my whole time to it, with the intention of seeking a place under our Government in China.[65]

Thomas Wade, introduced earlier, was also one of the first recruits into the China Consular Service. Other early members were appointed, in Coates's words, 'in recognition of services rendered in China by their relatives':[66] sons, half-brothers and in-laws of past or serving officers often filled positions.

The realisation that the service needed to put recruitment on a more formal foundation came from Edmund Hammond (1802–1890), who was permanent under-secretary of state for foreign affairs. At the beginning of his tenure in this position, in 1854, he served Lord Clarendon, the foreign secretary, to whom he recommended that new entrants to the service should be recruited only from the Chinese class at King's College and from University College, London. Clarendon broadened this pool to include the Queen's Colleges in Ireland, Belfast, Galway and Cork, of which he was chancellor.

---

65 Thomas Taylor Meadows, *The Chinese and Their Rebellions, Viewed in Connexion with the National Philosophy, Ethics, Legislation, and Administration, to Which Is Added an Essay on Civilisation and Its Present State in the East and West* (London: Smith, Elder & Co., 1856), vii.
66 Coates, *The China Consuls*, 74.

From 1854, nominations for the service were sent through from each of these colleges. Later, a more formal process of selecting student interpreters was put in place, but the former was the system by which Alabaster was nominated.[67] The only two of Alabaster's cohort who did not go to King's were Hughes, from Queen's College in Galway, and Mongan, from Queen's College in Cork. Those appointed at this level to the Consular Service were intended to spend their careers there, climbing the rungs, as Alabaster did, from student interpreter to interpreter, vice-consul, consul and consul general. Some did, but others fell victim to disease and alcoholism, or left to join the Chinese Imperial Customs or to go into business. Summaries of the careers of Alabaster's colleagues can be found in 'The Cast of the Diaries' chapter of this book.

The Diaries

Alabaster's manuscript diaries are held in the Archives and Special Collections of the library of the School of Oriental and African Studies (SOAS) at the University of London. The diaries were donated to the library in 1987 by Dr C.A. Curwen, then lecturer in history at SOAS. The library catalogue says that it holds 'nine of Alabaster's diaries (1854–1875)', and while it is true that this is how they are presented, closer examination shows it not to be correct. The four earliest diaries in the collection are written in plain, lined notebooks and cover 4 August – 31 December 1855, 2 January – 30 May 1855, 1 June – 25 July 1855 and 26 July 1855 – 26 November 1856, respectively. In total, in these 16 months Alabaster wrote over 50,000 words. These are the diaries transcribed and annotated in the current book.

The next diary in the collection, and all subsequent ones, are written in a year diary commercially printed by Letts with one day per page, unlined. These Letts diaries began publication in 1812, so Alabaster's decision to move from the plain book to the specially printed one was not made in response to an innovation in the print market. The 1859 diary is officially entitled *Letts's Diary or Bills Due Book and An Almanack, for 1859, and the Twenty-Second of the Reign of Her Present Majesty Queen Victoria (Accession 20th June 1837)*. The Letts diaries Alabaster used were the no. 8 diary, in Octavo size (6' x 9'), which lists the enterprise Bowra & Co. as their agent in Hong Kong. The 1859 diary is intact with the pages still in their places

---

67   Coates, *The China Consuls*, 75–77.

within the binding. However, after that year, pages have been torn from various bound volumes and placed in between the hard covers of other Letts's diaries for years different from that named on the cover. The last entry we have is from 3 April 1890, when Alabaster was consul general in Canton. These pages all have Alabaster's written notes on them; whether he (or whoever ripped the pages from the diaries) included all the pages with notes, or whether some were chosen and some were discarded, is unknown.

As Alabaster got older, and presumably busier, the diaries change in their nature. The earliest four are a kind of daily journal, where he wrote about what he had seen, how he was feeling, what his work was like, how he felt about his friends and acquaintances, how his studies were progressing and, importantly, how he was failing to live up to his own, or others', expectations. In this, his diaries are typical of Victorian records of self-examination, discussed below. As the years go on, the diaries lose this latter quality and comprise much briefer records of Alabaster's activities and his daily appointments. In this sense, they almost exclusively represent his public life. The four diaries in this book are, however, much more private. Indeed, on 22 June 1856, writing about his 'plots for the gain of honour or of fame', he wrote:

> I will not write them here for fear some prying knave should read them. Some inquisitive rascal with more skill than honor open locks & keys & peeping where he has no business, read all my petty schemes & laugh me to scorn as well.

This clearly indicates that Alabaster kept his diaries under lock and key.

The diaries are, as we would expect, written almost completely in English. However, Alabaster occasionally lapses into French, Latin and Chinese. In none of these languages is he flawless, and sometimes the renderings I have given in English in footnotes are provisional. As a mid-nineteenth-century school student, Latin and French would have been standard subjects in the curriculum. Although Alabaster actually studied Chinese in some manner at King's College, he was really a beginner in the language when he arrived in Hong Kong, as his vocabulary notes at the end of Volume 1 of the diaries, reproduced in the Appendix, demonstrate. Nonetheless, he makes a few forays into Chinese in the diaries. In these, he typically does not use characters but writes in a form of romanisation that, if it was something Thomas Wade taught him, was not yet developed into the standardised system Wade developed and through which his name has echoed along the corridors of Sinology ever since. These passages have been the most difficult to decipher in the diaries, as Chinese is notoriously homophonic, with many characters being pronounced in the same way if their tones are ignored, as Alabaster did. In addition, at this stage of his education he was not particularly fluent in the language. On the other hand, if we assume that Alabaster was trying to make sense, the collocation of syllables and the context of the passages allows a good attempt at a probable reading. If the interpretations I have made are correct, it would appear that Alabaster used Chinese as a means of writing about matters that were of the most private nature, as if to keep them away from any 'prying knave' or 'inquisitive rascal' who would succeed in gaining access to the diaries and 'peeping where he has no business'.

Alabaster's handwriting varies in its readability. At the outset, he was obviously being very careful and proper and the script looks like a final draft of a school assignment. However, later on, whether from tiredness, or from writing quickly, or (in one instance at least) likely being drunk, its legibility declines sharply. His spelling is rarely wrong (though readers of the original should note that Alabaster uses the long 's' in his handwriting), but even when it is, his intended meaning is rarely obscure. Unfortunately, however, there is virtually no punctuation throughout. Full stops are uncommon and the use of capital letters (except for names) is rather idiosyncratic. Thus, the major editorial intervention I have made is to add punctuation – not to have done so would have made the diaries very onerous to read. Nonetheless, on a few occasions when clearly writing breathlessly, Alabaster's style became less mannered as ideas and observations escaped explosively onto the page. In a passage about a fire in Taiping shan, it became almost stream of consciousness:

> Only 5 or 6 houses alight yet, but those blazing fearfully. Other houses blazing now. Here is a police engine. Work it! Here come the Spaniards. Fine fellows. First on the field. Here come the soldiers & the engineers & everyone. Everyone here, no one head. Sir John running about everywhere. All the officers not being as yet able to do anything. We look about us. Here's Ricketts, Caine, Repton, Oakley, Pereira, Leslie. Everyone going to pull that house down. 'Put the rope through the window. Hurrah! Pull away!' I haul away. We all haul. It shakes. Hurrah! It bends down. It is a rotten place. 'Throw out the bed, the chairs, everything! Hurrah!' It has broken out up there. The P&O sheep are all loose. The soldiers are working. 'We want hands. Would you send the sailors?' 'Can't you use these Chinamen?' 'No, they won't work.' 'Well, all right.' I lose Adkins & Payne. Go to Oakley. Dodge about. Plundering going on like blazes.

There tumbles a roof in. 'Look at that flaming street. Is it not grand? Have you seen all the Chinamen saving their property?' 'Lotsee! Some Chinamen are working.' Armstrong is directing a hose. 'Oh! Here you are! Did you see that cat jump from one burning house to another?' 'No.' 'Let us help Armstrong.' All the merchants are here. The Fokis begin to work. 'Haul away!' 'Send the water in!' 'Can't get through there.' 'Get a long hook.' Adkins & Payne rush in, haul away, smash down some woodwork, haul away some more. 'I am ducked!' 'So am I.' 'Never mind.' Here the water comes down my back. 'Haul away!' 'There is an opening!' 'Pump! Pump!' 'Smash that glass in the way!' 'Let us go down this street.' 'Hoof up!' 'I can't stand this. It's awful. I shall be stifled.' 'Come back!' We get a drink. They are going to blow up a house. Houses are being pulled down. Bang! There is the explosion. 'Let us come round and see.' We lose Payne. 'Oh! Here is Hussam.' Well, how does it go on.

One notable feature of Alabaster's writing concerns names, which he often rendered incorrectly. I suspect that in Hong Kong at this time business cards and other day-to-day printed documents were less common than they became later and so he *heard* the names rather than saw them written. Added to this may be the fact that English as spoken in Hong Kong at the time would have had a remarkable variety of accents, from regional British and Irish ones, to American, Portuguese, French, Dutch and South Asian, not to mention Chinese. Thus, Bemvindo became Benevindo, Roger was written Rogers, Bourboulon was Bourbuillon, Wonter Kup was rendered Vandercuyp, Reimers and Caldas became Rymers and Calders, and so on.

Peter Gay, in his monumental *The Bourgeois Experience: Victoria to Freud*, regards the nineteenth century as the 'golden age of the diary', where diaries that recorded the writer's cogitations 'became almost obligatory companions to a class endowed with a modicum of leisure'.[68] One of the primary features of the Victorian diary that set it apart from those of earlier periods was the development of the idea of privacy and the importance granted to it. The notion that an individual had an internal existence, that it was appropriate to retreat from the hurly-burly of everyday life each day to think through events, actions and conversations, and that the best means of achieving the discipline of such daily reflection was to keep a diary, was characteristic of the age. As Gay remarks:

---

68 Peter Gay, *The Bourgeois Experience: Victoria to Freud. Vol. 1, Education of the Senses* (New York: Oxford University Press, 1984), 446–48.

The silent conversation that diarists carried on benefited from another modern cultural phenomenon: privacy. They could write as freely as they did because they hoped that their diary, locked in the drawer of a desk or ingeniously concealed, was assured inviolability.[69]

Alabaster is not explicit about the living arrangements in the Albany and how much privacy he actually had. He and his colleagues all had local servants – of whom they often seem to be suspicious – in their quarters and presumably the student interpreters went into each other's rooms from time to time.[70] Perhaps this is why Alabaster kept the diary, in which he recorded his innermost thoughts, locked away.[71] He did not, fortunately, ensure their privacy for all time by ultimately destroying them, as did Thomas Hardy and Charles Dickens.[72]

As noted above, one of the recurring motifs in Alabaster's diaries is his dissatisfaction with his own behaviour. He upbraided himself for getting into arguments with his friends, for not working hard enough, for various self-perceived moral failings and especially for not being assiduous enough in writing in the diary itself. There is obviously the influence of Alabaster's religion in this and his diaries do show him, in Gay's felicitous phrase, 'taking [his] religious temperature'.[73] Isaac Disraeli (1766–1848), the British essayist (and father of prime minister Benjamin Disraeli), wrote: 'Shaftesbury calls a diary, "A fault-book," intended for self-correction', and '[o]ne of our old writers quaintly observes that, "the ancients used to take their stomach-

---

69   Peter Gay, *The Bourgeois Experience: Victoria to Freud. Vol. 4, The Naked Heart* (New York: Oxford University Press, 1996), 331.
70   See Christopher Munn, 'Hong Kong, 1841–1870: All the Servants in Prison and Nobody to Take Care of the House', in *Masters, Servants, and Magistrates in Britain and the Empire, 1562–1955*, ed. Douglas Hay and Paul Craven (Chapel Hill: University of North Carolina Press, 2004), 365–401.
71   There has been a good deal of academic discussion on the question of whether diaries were truly private. There are scenes recorded in literature as well as in diaries themselves of diaries being read aloud to families, or being swapped among friends and, of course, some diaries – consciously intended for later publication – were written by 'the self-confident or self-promoting few who aspired to lasting fame' (Gay, *The Naked Heart*, 331). See, for example, Kathryn Carter, 'The Cultural Work of Diaries in Mid-Century Victorian Britain', *Victorian Review* 23, no. 2 (Winter 1997): 251–67, doi.org/10.1353/vcr.1997.0013; Anne-Marie Millim, *The Victorian Diary: Authorship and Emotional Labour* (Abingdon: Routledge, 2013); Rebecca Steinitz, *Time, Space, and Gender in the Nineteenth-Century British Diary* (Basingstoke: Palgrave MacMillan, 2011), doi.org/10.1057/9780230339606. Alabaster's diary, however, was clearly meant to stay private.
72   Millim, *The Victorian Diary*, 11. One volume of Dickens's diaries (1838–41) survived accidentally.
73   Gay, *The Naked Heart*, 332.

pill of self-examination every night".'[74] This aptly characterises *some* of the entries in Alabaster's diaries; many others describe the life of a man that we should remember was very young, coming to terms with adult life, his first salary and a degree of independence he would never have previously experienced.

Philippe Lejeune, the great theorist of diary writing, noted: 'Like correspondence, the diary is first and foremost an activity. Keeping a diary is a way of living before it is a way of writing.'[75] It is well to keep this in mind when reading Alabaster's diaries. Like many Victorians, he was a great letter writer as well as a diarist, all the more so because he was living on the other side of the world from his family. The distinction between the two activities was that letter writing always had a recipient in mind. However, for Alabaster at least, keeping diaries was a *practice of writing* with no audience in mind. It was for himself, alone. Paradoxically, more than 150 years later, it is precisely this characteristic that makes Alabaster's diaries so illuminating for us to read.

---

74 Isaac Disraeli, *Curiosities of Literature*, 3 vols, ed. Benjamin Disraeli, vol. 2 (London: Routledge, Warne, and Routledge, 1863), 206. I suspect this Earl of Shaftesbury would have been the third, Anthony Ashley Cooper (1671–1713), author of the *Characteristicks of Men, Manners, Opinions, Times*, first published in 1711. I have not been able to find which 'old writer' Disraeli was referring to here. A mid-eighteenth-century guide for schoolteachers offers instructions on what daily practices they should instil in their pupils that is redolent of Alabaster's diaries when he is in a self-critical mood:

[The pupils should] call themselves to a Strict and Impartial Account how they have spent the day past: That they would Examine their Thoughts, Discourses, Actions, Recreations, and Devotions, and see what has been amiss in any of them; that so they may Confess and Bewail, and Ask God's Pardon for it, and Resolve to Amend it for the future: That they would consider more particularly what Idleness or Uncharity, what Lying or Stubbornness they have been guilty of; or whether they have had a Quarrel with any of their Fellows; and if they have, that they would take Care to be Friends with them before they say their Prayers.

See James Talbott, *The Christian School-Master* (London: J.F. and C. Rivinton, 1782, originally published 1707), 87.

75 Philippe Lejeune, *On Diary*, ed. Jeremy D. Popkin and Julie Rak, trans. Katherine Durnin (Honolulu: Hawaii University Press, 2009), 153, doi.org/10.1515/9780824863784.

Editorial Note

The four volumes of Chaloner Alabaster's diaries that comprise this book are found in the Archive and Special Collections of the Library of the School of Oriental and African Studies, University of London, MS 380451. I have preserved the original division into four sections in my transcription.

I have changed as little as possible in the presentation of the diaries. Alabaster, however, rarely used any punctuation and his capitalisations were idiosyncratic and not consistent. Thus, it was necessary to add *some* punctuation for the sake of readability, but I have done the minimum required. I have maintained spelling, with the exception of changing the long form of *s* – sometimes rendered in print as ſ – into the standard modern form. As was reasonably typical, Alabaster used the long form to write the first letter of the double *s*. I maintain Alabaster's spellings, abbreviations and symbols such as ∵ that he sometimes used for 'because'.

People mentioned in the diaries are identified in footnotes with the exception of those he mentions frequently, namely his family, friends and close colleagues. Biographical notes on these people are found in 'The Cast of the Diaries' chapter. In the diaries themselves, the names of those who appear in this section are rendered in **bold type** on their first appearance.

The only sections of the diary that I have left out are the occasional sketches Alabaster drew within the lines of his diaries. This has been done for two reasons. First, they are very small and rather unclear. Second, including them in the appropriate position in the transcribed text has proved to be very problematic. Where these sketches appear, however, I have included '[sketch]' in the text. Examples can be seen on pages of the diaries that are reproduced as plates.

I have used many sources to identify people who appear in the diaries. Some of those I have used more frequently I list here to avoid needless repetition in the footnotes:

- *The Foreign Office List of 1857*, compiled by Francis W.H. Cavendish and Edward Hertslet, published by Harrison, 59 Pall Mall, London; as well as the equivalents from 1863, 1865, 1866, 1877 and 1881, the latter four compiled by Hertslet alone.
- *The Hongkong Directory*, with its list of foreign residents in China, printed at the Armenian Press, Hongkong, 1859.
- *The China Directory for 1862*, as well as that for 1863, published by A. Shortrede & Co., Hongkong.
- *The Chronicle and Directory for China, Japan and the Philippines for 1864*, as well as those for 1865, 1869 and 1870, published by the Daily Press, Hongkong.

The resources compiled in the estimable website 'Gwulo: Old Hong Kong' (Gwulo.com), established and run by David Bellis, have also proved invaluable, in particular its transcriptions of the Hong Kong Jurors Lists.

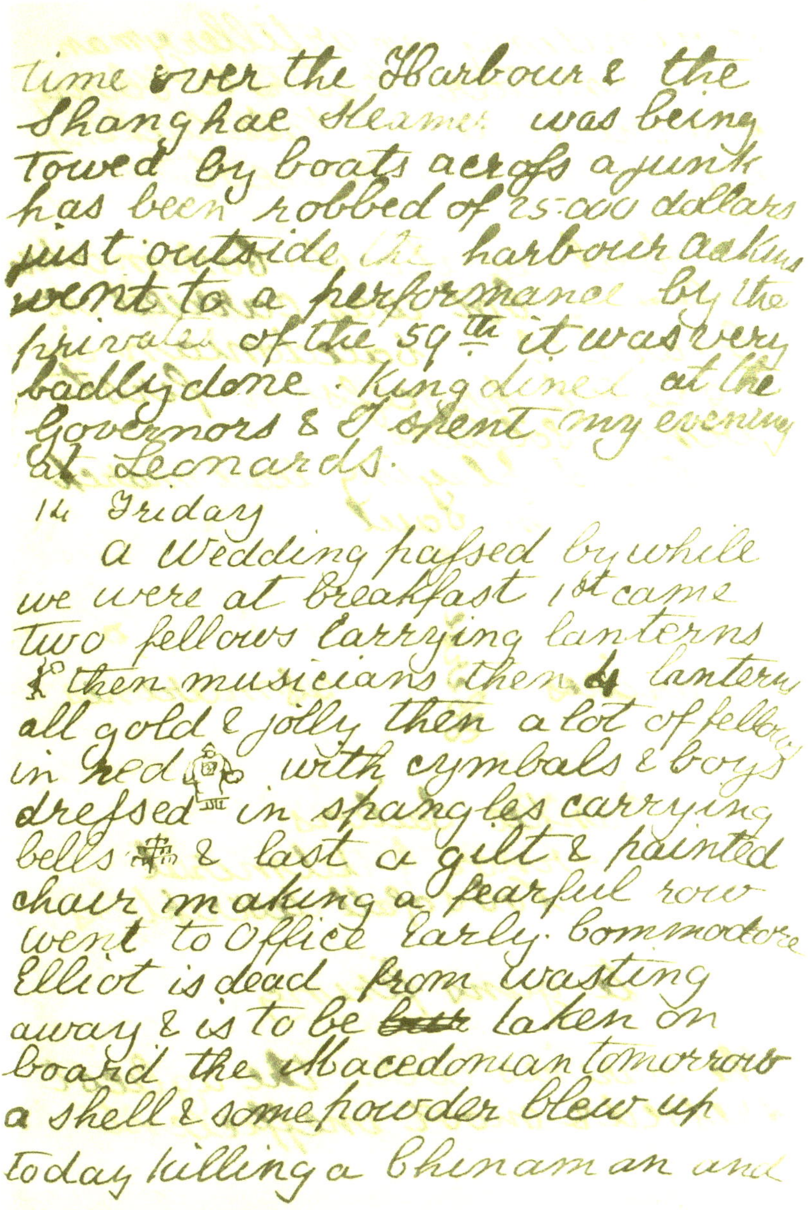

time over the Harbour & the Shanghae Steamer was being Towed by boats across a junk has been robbed of 25,000 dollars just outside the harbour asking went to a performance by the privates of the 59th it was very badly done. King dined at the Governors & I spent my evening at Leonards.

14 Friday
a Wedding passed by while we were at breakfast 1st came two fellows carrying lanterns & then musicians then 4 lanterns all gold & jolly then a lot of fellows in red &c with cymbals & boys dressed in spangles carrying bells &c & last a gilt & painted chair making a fearful row went to Office early. Commodore Elliot is dead from wasting away & is to be but taken on board the Macedonian tomorrow a shell & some powder blew up today killing a Chinaman and

Plate 7. Alabaster's Diary, Volume 2, 14 December 1855, showing two 'sketches'.

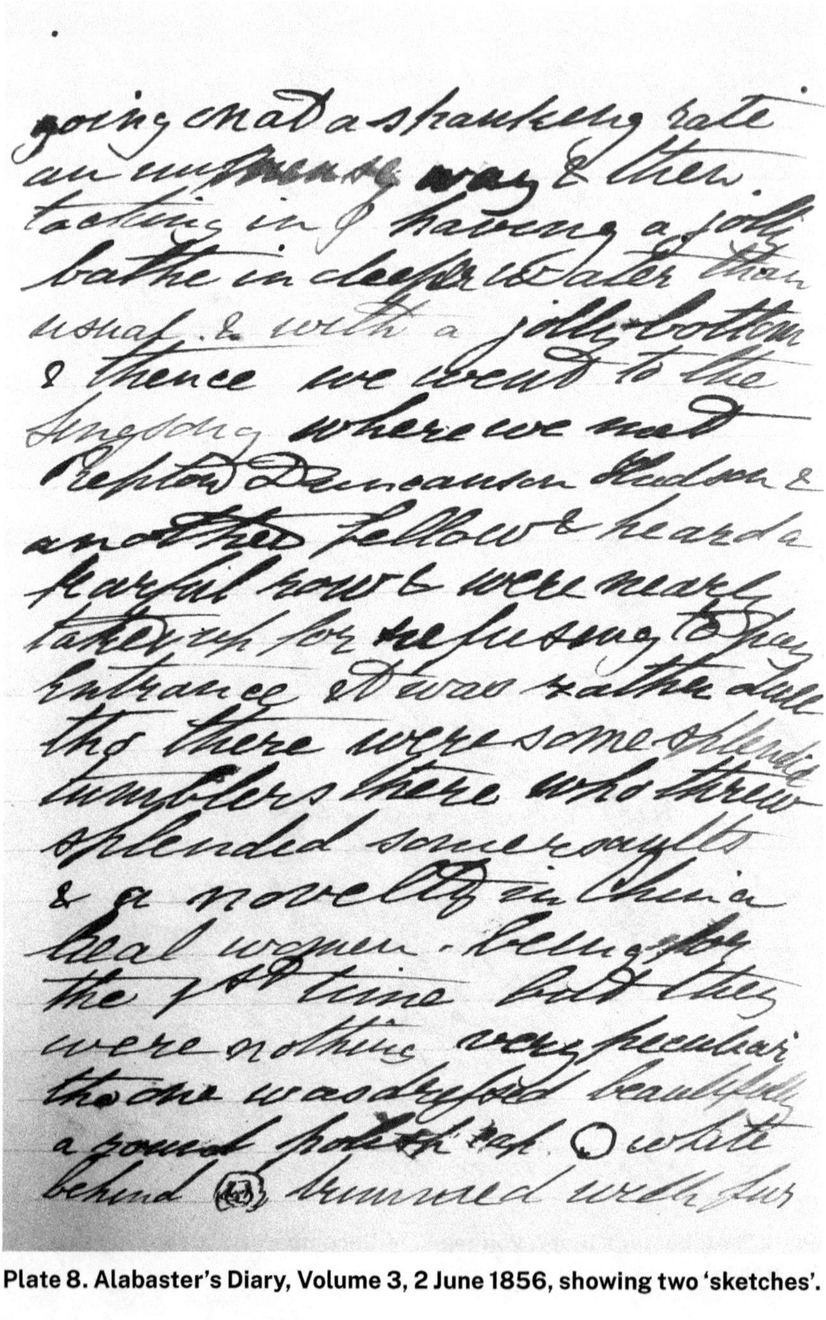

going on at a spanking rate
in an unmeaning way & then
tacking in & having a jolly
bathe in deeper water than
usual & with a jolly bottom
& thence we went to the
Singsong where we met
Repton Duncanson Hudson &
another fellow & heard a
fearful row & were nearly
taken up for refusing to pay
entrance it was rather dull
tho there were some splendid
tumblers there who threw
splendid somersaults
& a novelty in China
real women - being for
the 1st time but they
were nothing very peculiar
tho one was dressed beautifully
a round pork pie hat white
behind trimmed with fur

Plate 8. Alabaster's Diary, Volume 3, 2 June 1856, showing two 'sketches'.

The Cast of the Diaries

The Alabaster Family

Mary Ann Criddle (1805–1880) – **Aunty** in the diaries – was born in Shoreditch in East London.[1] Sent to school in Colchester, she was forced to leave on the death of her father Charles Alabaster in 1820. Charles was a bonnet maker with premises at 58 Piccadilly.[2] After his death, his wife Mary continued the business until her own death in 1838 when her son, and Chaloner's father, James took over the business. Mary Ann's interests were always artistic and in 1824 she finally began taking lessons in drawing and painting with John Hayter (1800–1895), a successful society portraitist; she had been discouraged from following these pursuits earlier as they were thought useless and unsuitable for her. She became a well-known painter herself, exhibiting at the Royal Academy and winning prizes for her work, and was elected a member of the Society of Painters in Water Colours in 1849. In 1834, Mary Ann had married Henry Criddle, adopting James and Sophia's three sons in 1840, and having her own son, Percy, in 1844. Ellen C. Clayton included Mary Ann in her *English Female Painters* of 1876, noting that:

> In 1854 she painted the 'Four Seasons', which were sold to the Baroness Burdett Coutts. They were not admitted for exhibition by the Water Colour Society on account of the borders of flowers around each picture. The vexation caused by this occasioned a severe illness.[3]

---

1 The primary source of biographical information on Mary Ann Criddle is her biography in Ellen C. Clayton, *English Female Painters*, vol. 2 (London: Tinsley Brothers, 1876), 70–74.
2 'Charles Alabaster, Bonnet Maker'.
3 Clayton, *English Female Painters*, 74.

In June 1856, Chaloner referred to either this incident or another refusal to hang the *Four Seasons*, writing that it was the Royal Academy who rejected it. It is unclear if Clayton was mistaken as to the year and the exhibition, or if Mary Ann's work was rejected by both the Water Colour Society and the Royal Academy.

Mary Ann's husband Harry died in 1857. She subsequently moved to Addlestone near Chertsey, some 30 kilometres south-west of London, dying there in 1880.

Uncle was Harry Criddle (1807–1857). Like Mary Ann he came from a family of hatters, which held a royal warrant. His father's business was in New Bond Street. Harry, Mary Ann and their family appear to have lived at 58 Piccadilly until 1850 when they moved to 115 Piccadilly, where Harry is listed as a 'proprietor of houses and superintendent of trade in Leghorn bonnets'.[4] He seems to have been a man of broad interests, in particular archaeology. On 25 May 1852, he was elected an associate of the British Archaeological Association.[5]

Chaloner's eldest brother was **Charles** (1834–1865). Like both his younger brothers, Charles attended King's College in London. In 1852 he was awarded a university distinction in classics and in 1853 was made an associate of King's in general literature and science.[6] He then proceeded to Lincoln College, Oxford, where his bachelor of arts was conferred in April 1857.[7] In 1858 he married Anne O'Connor (1842–1915), a teacher at the parish school of St Ebbe's in central Oxford where he was curate.[8] Charles suffered from tuberculosis and was encouraged to emigrate for his health. In early 1859, Charles and Anne arrived in Lyttleton near Christchurch on the South Island of New Zealand on the *Strathallen*. Soon after he arrived, Charles was elected as a Canterbury diocese delegate to the first General Synod of New Zealand and in April 1859 was appointed assistant curate to Bishop H.J.C. Harper. However, his illness drove him to retirement in 1861. In 1862, he and Anne opened the Lincoln Cottage Preparatory School, with Charles teaching Latin when his health permitted. After his

---

4   'Charles Alabaster, Bonnet Maker'.
5   'Proceedings of the Association', *Journal of the British Archaeological Association* 9 (1853): 195.
6   *Calendar of King's College, London for 1857/8* (London: King's College, 1857), 286–87, doi.org/10.1080/00681288.1853.11887948.
7   *Ecclesiastical Gazette*, 12 May 1857, 257.
8   See Margaret Francis, 'Alabaster, Ann O'Connor', *Dictionary of New Zealand Biography, Te Ara: The Encyclopedia of New Zealand*, first published in 1990, teara.govt.nz/en/biographies/1a5/alabaster-ann-oconnor.

death in January 1865, the school became known as Mrs Alabaster's School. Charles and Anne had two sons, born in 1860 and 1861, whom Anne supported through her work. In the last years of his life, Charles had two pamphlets published in Christchurch: *Do We Do Well to Take Away Our Schools from the Churches?* and *A Few Words about Conversion and Church Truth*.[9] In 1891, aged 49, Anne remarried. Her new husband was Canon Francis Knowles (1830–?) who had arrived in Lyttleton in 1851 and was active in the church in Canterbury, Otago and Southland. His was also a second marriage.

The second brother was **Henry** (1836–1884).[10] Like Chaloner, Henry also attended King's College and studied Chinese. He was recommended to the China Consular Service a year after Chaloner and arrived in Hong Kong in late September or early October 1856. After being very enthusiastic about his brother joining him, Henry's arrival did not turn out as well as expected. Only a couple of days later, Chaloner noted, with characteristic acerbity, 'he wanted to come the elder brother ... whereon I told him that I did not come here to be lectured by him or anyone else'. Henry is best known for the important role he played in Thailand. In 1855, Bowring had gone to Siam, as it was then, and negotiated a treaty with the kingdom in April of that year, now known as the 'Bowring Treaty'. This allowed for the establishment of a consulate in Bangkok. Charles Batten Hillier (c. 1820–1856) was appointed first consul. Hillier died not long after from fever. On 1 May 1857, Sir Robert Schomburgk (1804–1865) arrived as consul. His arrival was, however, preceded by Henry who was appointed student interpreter in Bangkok in January 1857. He served on the consular staff there until 1870, when he returned to England with his wife Palacia – they would ultimately have four children. While working in the British Consulate, Henry also proved invaluable to the Thai King Mongkut, or Rama IV, with his skills in surveying. Back in England he wrote a book on Buddhism from a Thai perspective called *The Wheel of the Law*.[11] He returned to Bangkok in 1873, this time to work directly for the new Thai King Chulalongkorn, Rama V,

---

9   *Do We Do Well to Take Away Our Schools from the Churches?: Five Letters to the Lyttleton Times* (Christchurch: Printed at the Times Office, 1864); *A Few Words about Conversion and Church Truth* (Christchurch: Ward and Reeves, 1865).
10   I have been greatly aided in these biographical notes by Angela Alabaster's chapter on Henry in Adrian Alabaster, *A Quintet of Alabasters*. Unfortunately, I have not been able to consult John S. Alabaster's *Henry Alabaster of Siam: Serving Two Masters*, Occasional Monograph No. 5 (The Alabaster Society, 2012).
11   Henry Alabaster, *The Wheel of the Law: Buddhism Illustrated from Siamese Sources by The Modern Buddhist, A Life of the Buddha, and An Account of the Phrabat* (London: Trübner & Co, 1871).

for whom he oversaw the building of roads and bridges, established both Thailand's first museum and botanical gardens, catalogued the king's library, made maps using modern cartographic methods, dealt with the foreign community in Bangkok and advised on foreign relations more generally. He married a second wife, a Thai woman called Perm, with whom he had two more children. He died in Bangkok. Palacia died 20 years after Henry, in London. Henry and Perm's Thai descendants have the family name Savetsila, meaning 'white rock' (i.e. Alabaster). One of Henry's grandsons, Siddhi Savetsila served as Thailand's foreign minister from 1980 to 1990.

When Mary Ann and Harry's own son **Percy** Criddle (1844–1918) was born, he appears to have become a favourite of his cousins. Letters from Henry and Chaloner to Percy when he was small survive in Alabaster family collections.[12] He attended a private school for four years run by a Mr King not far from Lord's Cricket Ground.[13] Apparently less directed than the Alabaster brothers, Percy went to Heidelberg University to study German, history and music before returning to London in 1863. In August 1864, Chaloner wrote from China, where (at the time) he had duties as a magistrate, expressing his frustrations: 'I wish I had Percy here. I'd commit him a vagrant.'[14] In 1865, we find him listed in a choir in Addlestone with Mary Ann. In 1866 he returned to Heidelberg to visit Elise Harrer (1840–1903), four years his senior. She became pregnant and returned to England with Percy in 1867, but he apparently kept her a secret from his family. In the fullness of time, they had five children together. In 1874, Percy (formally) married Alice Nicol (1849–1918), the cousin of George Nicol with whom Percy had gone to Heidelberg. In the early 1870s, he advertised his services as a 'Professor of Music' and is also listed as being a partner in a wine merchant's business. Percy was likely supported by Mary Ann in these years. Two years after she died, in 1882, he, Elise, her five children, as well as Alice and her four children (by that stage) emigrated to Canada. Alice would bear him three more children in Canada. Apparently, the first time Alice and Elise met was on board ship where Elise and her children travelled in steerage rather than in intermediate class where Percy, Alice and their children were passengers. During the passage, Percy had Elise change her family name from Criddle to Vane. The two families homesteaded in

---

12   Five of Henry's letters have been published in *The Alabaster Chronicle* 13 (1999), see alabaster.byethost18.com/chron13.htm.
13   For much of this information on Percy Criddle, I have relied on Oriole Vane Veldhuis, 'Percy Criddle's Education', *The Alabaster Chronicle* 27 (Spring 2007), alabaster.byethost18.com/chron27b.htm.
14   Veldhuis, 'Percy Criddle's Education'.

Awame, near Brandon in Manitoba where Elise lived on the property as their servant.[15] The farming proved a struggle, but Percy engaged in many gentlemanly pursuits including tennis, golf, astronomy, natural history and, of course, music.

Hong Kong Contemporaries[16]

The young men who people Alabaster's diaries, with whom he seems to have spent most of his time, fall into two groups: junior consular officials like him and those who worked for trading houses.

Almost all of the student interpreters mentioned in the diaries followed the same path as Alabaster, studying at King's College then entering into the Chinese Consular Service. The only exceptions were Patrick Joseph Hughes (1834–1903) and James Mongan (1831–1880), both Irishmen. **Hughes** was born in Newry, County Down, in what is now Northern Ireland,[17] and was appointed to the Consular Service on the recommendation of Queen's College, Galway, while Mongan came from Dundrum in Dublin and was recommended by Queen's College, Cork. Both Hughes and Mongan arrived in 1854, Hughes being sent straight to the Fuzhou Consulate but returning to Hong Kong in 1855 as fourth assistant in the Superintendency and was subsequently promoted to third and second assistant. He later served in Ningbo, Jiujiang and Hankou, ultimately being appointed consul in Hankou in 1872, and consul general in Shanghai in 1880. In 1891, he retired for health reasons and died in Nice, France, on 3 March 1903, aged 69.[18]

---

15 Two books by descendants of Alice and Elise, respectively, that concern Percy and the history of his family present divergent views: Alma Criddle, *Criddle-de-diddle-ensis: A Biographical History of the Criddles of Aweme, Manitoba, Pioneers of the 1880s* (privately printed, 1973); Oriole A. Vane Veldhuis, *For Elise: Unveiling the Forgotten Woman on the Criddle Homestead* (Winnipeg: Heartland Associates, 2012). Many photographs of the families can be found in an online exhibition of the Sipiweske Museum, Wawanesa, Manitoba called 'The Criddle/Vane Legend and Legacy', which can be found on the www.communitystories.ca site. See also, Dorothy Dobbie, 'Early Manitoba Bigamist Leaves Lasting Legacy', *Manitoba Post*, 28 January 2018, www.manitobapost.com/manitoba-news/early-manitoba-bigamist-leaves-lasting-legacy-112762.
16 For Thomas Wade, see Introduction.
17 A photograph survives of Hughes taken in around 1869 in the Edward Bangs Drew collection at Harvard University, www.hpcbristol.net/visual/hv35-49.
18 See 'Notes', www.hpcbristol.net/visual/hv35-49.

When Hughes was sent to Fuzhou, **Mongan** went to Shanghai as a student interpreter and stayed there until he was promoted to assistant in the Chinese Secretary's Office in Hong Kong in June 1856. He acted as head of the office from mid-1857 and was formally assistant secretary from 1858. In 1859 he accompanied Admiral Hope to the north of China and was present at the failed attack on the Dagu (Taku) forts. He was interpreter for Van Straubenzee, the head of the British military in China, in Canton until 1860 when he went north again, this time with Sir Hope Grant, when the Dagu forts were captured and Tianjin was occupied. He was appointed acting consul in Tianjin in 1860 and consul in 1861. Mongan suffered from severe depression in Tianjin and when on home leave beginning in 1877 his wife died. According to Rutherford Alcock (in Coates's words), Mongan 'had become insane but was threatening to return to China with a Belgian mistress'.[19] He retired for health reasons while in England and died not long after.

William Marsh **Cooper** (1833–1896) was also appointed as a student interpreter in 1854, in his case from King's College school when he was 21. He worked at the Xiamen Consulate from 1855, became third assistant in Hong Kong in 1858 and later worked in Canton and Shantou. After acting as interpreter on several naval expeditions up the China coast and to Formosa, he held consular positions in Shantou in 1866, then in Jiujiang, Taiwan and Yantai. In 1877, he was appointed consul in Ningbo. He retired in 1888 for reasons of ill health, dying in Southsea, Portsmouth, in 1896.

F.E.J. **Forrest** (1837–1858) was also appointed to the Consular Service in 1854 from King's. In 1855, he accompanied Bowring to Bangkok when the 'Bowring Treaty' liberalising trade between Britain and Siam was signed. He remained there to learn Thai and was promoted to second assistant when the consulate was established. He died of dysentery shortly after, in February 1858.

Thomas Adkins (1836–1912), Walter Edward King (1837–1917) and William N. Payne (1835–?) were all from King's and were in the same intake to the Consular Service as Alabaster, arriving in Hong Kong in 1855.

---

19   Coates, *The China Consuls*, 282.

Adkins came from Milcote in Warwickshire not far south of Stratford-upon-Avon. A member of the same Chinese class at King's College school as Alabaster, he was appointed to be a student interpreter at the same time and proceeded to Hong Kong on the same ship. In the time of the diaries he appears to have been Alabaster's closest friend. His first appointment was to the Ningbo Consulate in 1857, but in 1858 he was attached to Lord Elgin as his interpreter, a post that took him on Elgin's expedition to Peking in 1860 when the British and French forces destroyed and looted the Old Summer Palace. When Elgin returned south, Adkins remained in Peking as the sole representative of the British Government over the winter of 1860–61. He later served in consular positions in Jiujiang, Shanghai, Taiwan and Xiamen, being promoted to British consul at Niuzhuang in 1869. After returning to England on leave in 1873 and marrying, he returned to China, only to retire for health reasons in 1879. He returned to his native Warwickshire until his death in 1912, filling the role of grandee of the local community, supported by his pension. According to his obituary in the *Evesham and Four Shires Advertiser*, he was known as 'China Tom'.[20] Almost 150 of Adkins's letters home survive and have proved a valuable resource for this project. They are held in the Warwickshire County Record Office in Warwick.

King was 17 when he arrived in Hong Kong and was sent to Fuzhou in January 1856, which disappointed both Alabaster and Adkins. In the second half of 1858, he accompanied Lord Elgin on his famous and destructive trip north. He served as a consular officer in Xiamen, Hankou and Jiujiang. In 1876, he was appointed consul in Taiwan, a post he did not take up for some reason. He did, however, become the first British consul in Yichang that year under hostile and difficult circumstances.[21] He retired for health reasons in 1878.

Payne's career did not progress as successfully as some of his colleagues. After being appointed to positions in Shanghai, Ningbo and Canton, he was forced to resign in 1868. Coates writes that 'Payne was so busy drinking himself to death when sent home in disgrace that it was doubtful he would reach home alive'.[22]

---

20   See 'Thomas "China Tom" Adkins, b. 1836', Adkins Family – Histories, last modified 17 May 2022, www.adkins-family.org.uk/hist-china_thomas_1836_obit.htm.
21   See, Coates, *The China Consuls*, 273.
22   Coates, *The China Consuls*, 358.

James K. **Leonard** (c. 1830–?) arrived in Hong Kong on the same ship as Alabaster and Adkins. Adkins wrote to his father on 13 January 1856:

> I have made but one intimate here. He was a fellow passenger and we all here have got very thick with him. He is in Dent's house now and we are still very friendly. He came out here on speck and soon got a place of 300 a year and board and lodging but then he is between 5 and 6 and twenty and has had a good deal of experience. His name is Leonard and he comes from near Aberdeen.[23]

Leonard was a mercantile assistant at Dent & Co. in 1857. In 1862–63, he was commissioner of the Imperial Maritime Customs in Jinjiang where Adkins was vice-consul. In 1865, he held the same position in Huangpu (Whampoa) and, in 1869, deputy commissioner at the Office of Maritime Customs, Shanghai. In 1879, he was commissioner of customs at Ningbo.

In 1857 and 1858 Thomas **Tatham** (?–?) was a merchant's clerk at J. Burd & Co., then at Fletcher & Co. in 1859. He must have moved to Japan soon after, as he was a commission agent in Yokohama in 1861 and remained there until 1865, by which time he had become a merchant. Thomas Tatham was no longer there in 1868, but a 'C.G. Tatham' (possibly a relative) was in residence.

In 1858, Edward Packenham **Repton** (1832–c. 1865) was a merchant's clerk – the juror's list for that year only gives his address as Hollywood Road without providing a company name. He had left Hong Kong by the next year as he does not appear in the 1859 list. He was married in 1863 to Maria Georgina Stevens in Bombay, with the wedding notice giving his father's name as Edward E.H. Repton of the Bengal Civil Service who died aged 34 in 1843.[24] Repton had died by 1865 as he is listed as 'deceased' in a notice for the dissolution of a partnership in the company of Arbuthnot, Ewart & Co. of Manchester and Bombay.[25]

Sir John **Bowring** (1792–1872) was the governor of Hong Kong at the time of the diaries.[26] However, this period represented only one portion of a notable nineteenth-century life. Bowring came from Exeter in Devon. His father was a wool merchant and a Unitarian, a faith that Bowring inherited

---

23 Thomas Adkins to J.C. Adkins, 13 January 1856, Warwickshire County Record Office, CR 3554/7.
24 *The Gentleman's Magazine* 214 (March 1863): 369.
25 *The Liverpool Commercial List 1871–72* (London: Estell & Co., 1871), Appendix, 10.
26 I have relied largely on Gerald Stone's essay on Bowring in the *Oxford Dictionary of National Biography* for these notes on Bowring. See also Introduction, footnote 9.

and maintained throughout his life. Unitarians, as dissenters from the Church of England, were not permitted to attend Oxford or Cambridge nor hold public office until 1828 when the so-called Test Acts were repealed. As a result, Bowring began work in his father's business at 13 and made his way in trade, moving to London in 1811. He was gifted at languages and was sent to Spain and Portugal in this decade to conduct business negotiations for his employers who supplied British forces on the Iberian Peninsula. In 1817, he established the first of a series of unsuccessful businesses, this one involved trade in herrings and wine. In 1820, he published the first of a series of collections of poetry from European countries, *Specimens of the Russian Poets*, which was followed by similar volumes of poetry from Holland, Spain, Poland, Serbia, Hungary and Bohemia. In the same year he also met, and became a devoted acolyte of, Jeremy Bentham. In 1827, his company collapsed and he, by now married with six children, was in financial trouble. In 1828, he began in government service investigating accounting practices in Holland. In 1830, he was appointed secretary to a government commission on public accounts and the next year became commissioner himself, investigating trade between Britain and France (along with George Villiers, the later Lord Clarendon). In 1831, he stood for parliament, unsuccessfully, but was elected in 1835. He lost this seat in 1837 and was subsequently sent to Egypt and the Ottoman Empire on government business before becoming an MP once again in 1841. The issues he stood for included, in the words of Gerald Stone in the *Oxford Dictionary of National Biography*, 'abolition of corn duties, a more humane application of poor relief, the extension of popular education, revision of quarantine regulations, abolition of flogging in the army, the suppression of the opium trade, and the worldwide abolition of slavery'. He was also a keen supporter of the introduction of decimal coinage: Alabaster read his *The Decimal System in Numbers, Coins and Accounts* of 1854. In the 1840s, Bowring made a series of large and unsuccessful investments in ironworks and railways that left him, in 1847, in serious financial difficulties once again. It is generally thought that this is why he took up an offer to be consul in Canton from 1849 to 1853, and then plenipotentiary and chief superintendent of trade in the Far East and governor, commander-in-chief and vice-admiral of Hong Kong from 1854 until 1859. He retired back to Britain on a pension and unsuccessfully stood for parliament once again in 1860. In the last decade of his life, he was active in the cause of prison reform.

Bowring's governorship is generally held to have been only moderately successful. A genuine reformer, he underestimated the power of the large business houses and the uncooperativeness of much of the existing bureaucracy. In addition, he was not particularly successful in his liaison with the Foreign Office, reputedly annoying them with his disinclination to make decisions on the ground and referring back to London for advice. His sincere commitment to utilitarianism led him to attempt a 'necessary humanising of the administration towards the Chinese', in Endacott's words, but this was not a position welcomed broadly by the non-Chinese population of Hong Kong.[27] Perhaps the blackest mark on his record was allowing the *Arrow* incident to escalate into war on his watch. When he left Hong Kong in 1859, 'the foreign community showed their hatred and contempt by ignoring him, but the Chinese said farewell with presents and other indications of their high opinion of him'.[28] In the diaries, Alabaster only ever speaks of Bowring with admiration.

Although he was born in Ireland, William **Caine** (1799–1871) was from an Indian Army family and had lived in India from infancy. Following family tradition, he joined the so-called Cameronians, the 26th Regiment of Foot. Serving in the Iberian campaigns, Ireland and India, the regiment was sent to China in 1839. Caine took part in the capture of Zhoushan (Chusan) and was appointed its chief magistrate. On the de facto seizure of Hong Kong in 1841, he was made magistrate of the new territory, becoming chief magistrate, provost marshal and sheriff on the signing of the Treaty of Nanking in 1843. He, therefore, represented, in one person, the judiciary, the police and the prison service, despite being, in Endacott's words, 'as ignorant of British law as he was of Chinese laws, customs, and usages'.[29] In 1846, Caine became colonial secretary, a post he held until 1854. When Bowring was appointed governor that year, Caine was made lieutenant-governor. This represented a new division of power in the colony. Previously, the governor had been in charge of both domestic Hong Kong administration and the diplomatic and trade posts associated with China. Thus, Caine was intended to take control of the colony itself while Bowring dealt with matters of foreign affairs. This situation held for a little over a year until June 1855 when Bowring took back both roles, after he had raised objections with Lord Palmerston, the new prime minister. Caine applied unsuccessfully for the governorship of the Straits Settlements in 1858 and

---

27 Endacott, *A Biographical Sketch-Book*, 43.
28 Endacott, *A Biographical Sketch-Book*, 44.
29 Endacott, *A Biographical Sketch-Book*, 62.

retired in 1859. However, before his retirement he took the opportunity to launch a bitter libel case against his old enemy, William Tarrant, editor of the *Friend of China*. He died in England in 1871. His last years were by far the longest time he had ever spent in his home country.

Caine was, therefore, crucial in Hong Kong's life from its establishment as a British territory until 1859. He lived there for 18 years in total, and had served with four governors and two administrators before that. It is hard to overestimate his influence on the early period of the Hong Kong's British history. Despite their disagreements over their roles in Hong Kong's administration, Bowring apparently did not lack respect for Caine, although he characterised him as being from 'the old – the very old – school'.[30]

Henry Fletcher **Hance** (1827–1886)[31] arrived in Hong Kong in 1844, aged 17, and was appointed to the Civil Service on the recommendation of the then governor, Sir John Francis Davis. By this time, he had been educated in both England and Belgium and taught himself botany. In 1854, Hance was transferred to the Superintendency of Trade, where he was Alabaster's superior. His career in the Consular Service was, however, not spectacular. He was at the British Consulate in Canton at the time of the Second Opium War, losing many books and plant specimens in the burning of the foreign factories. In 1861, he was appointed vice-consul at Whampoa, a position he held until 1883, except for a few short periods as acting consul in Canton, including one from 1883 to 1886. He was transferred to Amoy as acting consul in that year but died not long afterwards. Thomas Wade, his long-time colleague, explained the trajectory of his career by noting that 'there was no inducement to him to study the language', and that while he was a more than capable diplomat, knowledge of Chinese became more and more a requirement for advancement as the years went by.[32]

Wade continued by noting that Hance's 'leisure was devoted to his favourite pursuit, Botany', and it is this for which he is best known. It is no exaggeration to say that during his life Hance was *the* authority on Chinese plants. He corresponded assiduously with the greatest botanists in

---

30 Quoted in Endacott, *A Biographical Sketch-Book*, 65. On Caine, see also Christopher Munn's entry in Holdsworth and Munn, *Dictionary of Hong Kong Biography*, 57–58.
31 On Hance, see Patricia Lim's entry in Holdsworth and Munn, *Dictionary of Hong Kong Biography*, 173, as well as that by R.K. Douglas, revised by Lynn Milne, in the *Oxford Dictionary of National Biography*.
32 See Hance's obituary by Francis Blackwell Forbes in *The Journal of Botany, British and Foreign* 25 (1887), 1–11, especially the citation of Wade's correspondence to Forbes, 3.

Europe, in particular those in charge of the Botanic Gardens in Kew, and was awarded an honorary doctorate by the University of Giessen in Hesse, Germany, in 1849. This university was a centre for the new natural sciences during the nineteenth century and is famous for its botanic gardens founded in 1609. Among his various other honours and fellowships, Hance was elected a member of the Deutsche Akademie der Naturforscher Leopoldina in 1877. Over his career, he published more than 200 scientific papers in the major botanical journals of his day and also created a herbarium of over 22,000 specimens, which he bequeathed to the British Museum.

Alabaster Diary, Volume 1

1854[1]

August

4. Left England in the *Indus*, Captain Soy, for China.[2]

5. 3.10. Ushant[3] – looming in distance.

8. Finisterre[4] – a high peak.

9. Rock of Lisbon.[5] [sketch]

Terifa[6] (noticed). Wall round town. Batteries. Lighthouse. Polaccas.[7] Round towers. Hills in furrows.

Straits of Gibraltar. Africa N. Spain south. Telescopes wanted. Ships all around us. Villas. Hills wreathed in clouds. Azure skies. Olives. Small light houses.

Ape's head.[8] Top wreathed in clouds. Very splendid.

Luminousness in the sea increasing the farther S we went.

Clearness in the sea quite like glass.

---

1 A mistake for 1855.
2 The *Indus* was a P&O paddle steamer launched in 1847 specifically for the Southampton to Alexandria route.
3 Ouessant, an island off the coast of Brest.
4 Cape Finisterre; Fisterra, on the north-west coast of Spain.
5 Cabo da Roca, the westernmost point of Portugal, adjacent to the city of Lisbon.
6 Tarifa, the southernmost point of Spain on the Straits of Gibraltar.
7 A variety of triple-masted sailing vessel common in the Mediterranean.
8 Probably a mistake for the peak known by most mid-nineteenth-century English-language sources as 'Apes Hill' on the northern coast of Morocco, now Jbel Moussa. One tradition regards Gibraltar and Jbel Moussa as the Pillars of Hercules. See, John Purdy, *Sailing Directions for the Strait of Gibraltar and the Mediterranean Sea* (London: R.H. Laurie, 1841), 7.

8.[9] Cape St Vincent revolving light.[10]

Trafalgar.[11] [sketch]

9. Gibraltar. [sketch] Like a lion couchant with guns peeping out everywhere. Covered with shrubs. Houses all about it. Surrounded by ships joining the mainland. Things noticeable: Moors, Jews, Arabs. Portugueze Grapes. Elliot's monument[12] where he is represented as weak in the back. Buglers. Shops in the real Turkish style. Talking guide. Mists over the rock. Segars.[13] Boatmen. Boys. Women. Mules, donkeys, horse, &c., &c.

13. Zembra Island.[14] [sketch]

Pantalaurea[15] [sketch]

Malta. Square towers all round. Immense batteries near entrance. Moorish arches. Towers. Large buildings. Priests 1/3 of population. Boats. [sketch] Windmills [sketch] with 5 sails. Schools. Officers. Hotels. Portugueze women with mantilla and gossiping in churches. St John a most magnificent cathedral paved with marble mosaic tombs of Knight Templars. Handsome plate. A magnificent statue of the baptism. Some very good pictures. A magnificent ceiling. English chapel with 8 tombs. Lazzarone[16] smoking.

19. Alexandria.[17]

20. Cairo

21. Suez a beastly, dirty, hot, choleraic place. Beastly rooms. Beastly dinner and worse soda water but some very good bathing. Dusty. Sandy. All our luggage arrived on camels & we had great fun in each separating his own. All the camels lay down to be unloaded.

Aden.

---

9   This entry and the next appear to have been added after the previous two, to add details forgotten on the day.
10 Cape St Vincent, Cabo de São Vicente, the south-westernmost point of Portugal.
11 Cape Trafalgar, Cabo Trafalgar, to the Atlantic side of the Straits of Gibraltar.
12 George Augustus Eliott (1717–1790), governor of Gibraltar, when it was besieged by French and Spanish forces (1779–83). The monument Alabaster would have seen was removed to The Convent, the governor's residence, in 1858, when it was replaced by a bronze bust. Both monuments are still extant: the original in the cloisters of The Convent, the bronze bust in the Botanical Gardens. See Pepe Rosado, *The Convent: An Illustrated Guidebook* (Gibraltar: FotoGrafiks Design, 2012).
13 Cigars.
14 Off the coast of Tunisia, in the Gulf of Tunis.
15 Pantelleria, in the Straits of Sicily.
16 Scoundrels, rogues.
17 Travel from Alexandria to Suez via Cairo was overland until the Suez Canal was opened in 1869.

Point de Galle.[18]

Penang. A rainy day but jolly fun. As soon as we got on shore, off we set in carriages to go to the waterfall but our carriage soon lost the others & losing its way I, **King** and Sturrough[19] had a most exciting walk through brushwood, over hedges, along by streams, over a stream up to our knees in mud & altogether in a beastly mess till we got to the mountain which is covered with nutmeg trees & after a jolly climb we saw a splendid waterfall. Nutmeg trees. [sketch] Chinese shops. Cheap pineapples. Mangosteens. Ladrones.[20]

September

15. Mallacca.[21] Apparently little doing.

Glassy sea. Flying fish.

Singapore.

Hong-Kong. My destination at 1 am on Monday morning.

October

14. Began my diary. Stopped at home and did almost nothing which was shameful. Received an invitation to breakfast with the Governor.

15. Heavy rain beginning about 2 am. Began to read Davies' book. Marcus Antonius was the first who sent an embassy to China but it failed.[22] Mail day. Got some berries of the *Croton sebiferum* or Candleplant.[23] Went to see some ivory and silver ware. Remarkably cheap and good. Only 5 dollars for a filigree silver cardcase. Did no work. Am getting on well at the office. Having to do duplicates rather than triplicates.

---

18   Galle, Sri Lanka.
19   Probably W.A. Sturrock who worked for F.D. Syme & Co. in Amoy, later becoming a partner in Boyd & Co. in the same city.
20   Southern Chinese pirates, known by the Portuguese term.
21   Malacca, on the western coast of the Malayan peninsula.
22   John Francis Davis, *The Chinese: A General Description of the Empire of China and its Inhabitants* (London: Charles Knight, 1836), 11.
23   Now more commonly known as the Chinese tallow tree.

16. Office. Heard that **Caine** had been to King's College. Went to the mainland with **Leonard** and our party and had a bathe. Leonard dined with us. We breakfasted with the Governor, who as usual received us well. New Government House[24] is very handsome inside and looks like a Governor's house, though I am sorry to say **Sir John** looks not like a Governor.

17. Great news. The Calcutta mail came in today. The Russians have sallied out at Sebastipol[25] & been repulsed with 4000 killed. Sveabourg[26] has been bombarded and the town and harbour been smashed and perhaps the batteries. Riga has been smashed at. Supplies are cut off from south part of Sebastipol which must now surrender. The Queen has been to Paris.[27] The Empress is *enceinte*.[28] Parliament is prorogued.[29] Sir de Lacy Evans[30] has brought in a bill to take all the regulars from Hong Kong, &c.[31] The sea of Azof[32] and the White sea[33] have been cleared of the Russians and there have been great successes in Asia. Vivat Regina. When we got the news there was immense excitement to get a paper. The *Invincible*, British Ship, ran down and sank a Yankee Clipper laded with coolies and got into Hong Kong with 10 feet water in her.[34] Went to the bowling alley[35] in the evening and now to bed.

18. Got up at 5 o'clock and went with **Adkins**, King & Leonard to bathe. A bad bottom full of rocks. Cut myself awkwardly on return. Inspected the wreck of the *Invincible*. Her bowsprit and foretopmast gone. Dr Dempster[36] is gone to Macao so I shall have to wait. 100 or more soldiers are going home. Got various grasses. Hong Kong abounds in unnamed and unclassified

---

24 Completed October 1855.
25 Sevastopol, Crimea.
26 Suomenlinna (Sw. Sveaborg), Helsinki, formerly a fortress built on an island in the Helsinki harbour.
27 Queen Victoria was in France from 17 to 28 August 1855.
28 Eugénie (1826–1920), wife of Napoleon III, was pregnant (*enceinte*) at the time with Napoléon, Prince Imperial (1856–1879).
29 14 August 1855.
30 Sir George de Lacy Evans (1787–1870), MP for Westminster.
31 See Hansard, 14 August 1855, 'Conduct of the War'.
32 Sea of Asov, north-east of the Crimean Peninsula, connected with the Black Sea through the narrow Strait of Kerch.
33 The White Sea, connected to the Barents Sea in far north-eastern Russia.
34 The clipper *Invincible* collided with and sunk an American clipper, the *A. Chesebrough*, two days out of Hong Kong and damaged herself, and, with the *A. Chesebrough*'s crew on board, was helped back to Hong Kong by the *Lookout*, another American clipper. See Octavius Thorndike Howe and Frederick C. Matthews, *American Clipper Ships, 1833–1858, Volume 1* (New York: Dover Publications, 2012), 368.
35 The bowling alley was in the original building of the Hong Kong Club.
36 Dr James Carroll Dempster came to Hong Kong in 1854 as a staff surgeon with the Army Medical Department. He was seconded to the Hong Kong Government as colonial surgeon and left for India in 1857, later spending time also in the Crimea and in New Zealand.

grasses. I have some thoughts of collecting and writing a book about them myself. Must go to Wade and get a teacher.[37] **Woodgate** says he thinks we shall be out of office in 3 months.

19. Up at five and off with the others to bathe. Did not go in. **Tatham** of Armstrong and Lowndes[38] went with us. My foot too bad to bear a boot. Dr Dempster came and gave me a prescription for some pills. The *Spartan* has come in. Got several new grasses. Hong Kong is very rich in grasses from the bamboo to diminutive meadowgrass. The seed of one sort like a fox's tail of others like a feather. Some all downy and nearly all of them handsome. Crammed at radicals. Leonard came in the evening.

20.21. Got lazy and did not do it yesterday. Went to office but did little work. Got a 38 page despatch about Benevindo[39] to do. In health am a little better. Today went out for the day with Leonard, Tatham, Adkins, King, **Forrest** and myself. At first they could not get a Sampan but I started off and got one. About 7½ we started, taking chaou chaou[40] with us and four guns and two revolvers for fear we should meet pirates who swarm all round Hong Kong. We landed at Saisan,[41] had a jolly breakfast and afterwards went shooting in those cursed paddy fields where you have 5 inches of uneven ground to walk on and 5 feet below you, mud, mud, beastly mud. We (or rather they) shot here a dove, a shrike, a ricebird, two sparrow. Afterwards coasting along after a place for dinner. We could not find one for some time as there was a fearful surf everywhere. At last we did land through the surf by means of jumping. Had our dinner and some champagne and off we set home as it was getting dark, singing songs and enjoying ourselves, and arrived home after adding a heron to our bag. Noticed on our way lots of shells and that Hong Kong is decidedly of volcanic origin. The Harbour seems to have once been an immense crater.

---

37   On Thomas Wade, see Introduction.
38   A mistake for Armstrong and Lawrence.
39   Known generally as Bemvindo, and also Vulpino, see below. Identified by John King Fairbank as Benevindo da Razor Baptista in *Trade and Diplomacy on the China Coast: The Opening of the Treaty Ports, 1842–1854* (Cambridge, Mass.: Harvard University Press, 1953), 345.
40   Food.
41   This is probably a mistake for Saiwan, specifically the place sometimes known as Siu or Lesser Saiwan. 'Saiwan is seven miles from Victoria, a little to the south of the Lymoon pass, which separates Hong Hong [sic] on the north-east from the mainland … [the hills above Saiwan Bay are] cut into terraces, rising behind each other, near their base, for the cultivation of rice', John Kinnis, 'Contributions to Medical Military Statistics of China', *The Transactions of the Medical and Physical Society of Bombay* (1847–48): 3–34, 26.

22. The *Tartar* is in and the *Winchester* is expected in tomorrow. Adkins, Forrest and King went after a pheasant but did not catch it. Had a false alarm of the mail. Albany[42] is going on very slowly and I – lazy, sleepy & stupid – feel all my ambition oozing out and beastly avarice coming in. O Lord! I beseech thee gard me from avarice.

23. Mail not in. Am awfully tired of office but this afternoon I put on a spurt and did a good deal. Have in fact nearly finished Benevindo, that beastly Portuguese who licked[43] a Chinaman. Beastly manners which made Meadows[44] forget himself and lick him in return for which, as is quite right, he now pays the penalty in loss of appointment.[45] Tatham and Leonard

---

42 The Albany Building, which was being renovated as accommodation for government officials. It stood on what is now a playground at the top of the Hong Kong Zoological and Botanical Gardens. Built in 1844, it was demolished in 1935.
43 Beat, thrashed.
44 J.A.T. Meadows (1817–1875), at the time acting vice-consul in charge of the British Consulate at Ningbo.
45 Meadows was suspended but later informally taken back on as interpreter in Ningbo. He was reinstated to the Consular Service as interpreter in Shanghai, and in 1861 resigned to go into business in Tianjin. Robert Hart (1835–1911), at the time student interpreter at the consulate at Ningbo and later, famously, head of the China Maritime Customs Service, described the original incident in his diary:

> Christmas Day. Monday, 25 December 1854 … There I was sitting writing a letter to Hughes, when I heard some terrible screams; after listening to them for some time I became alarmed and went to see what was the matter. At the Doorkeeper's room I found all the men assembled; and on asking Anqua the matter, I learned that his Brother-in-law (one of the consular people) – a lad about nineteen years of age had been beaten by <u>Vulpino</u>, a Portuguese. The chap was brought out to me, and truly he looked rather the worse of [sic] the blows he had received; his forehead covered with black lumps – one of his ears quite black – his nose bleeding – his lips swollen – and his hand cut. He gazed with a very vacant stare, that was quite ridiculous; meanwhile Anqua's wife continued to howl and stamp on the floor at a great rate. I then went in search of Mr Meadows, whom I found in company of Mr Marques. As soon as they separated I told Mr Meadows what had occurred; upon which he returned to the Consulate, examined into the matter, told every man in the place to don the Consular Cap, and arm themselves with sticks. At the same time he buckled on his sword, and stuck a double-barreled pistol in his belt. He then, followed by the Servants, went to the house at which the Portuguese was stopping. I followed in the rear and remained outside the house; but hearing some scuffling inside, I got rather excited and rushed in: there I found Vulpino, lying at the foot of the Stairs, holding to the Banisters, while the Chinamen pulled him from them and belaboured him with their huge clubs; the poor fellow was suffering very severely, so I put a stop to the beating: he was then lugged off (in his shirt and trousers) to the consulate; but as he now and then made resistance he got some more blows, so that I again had to interfere. Indeed, he might have been very severely injured had I not been there, as Mr Meadows was very much excited. Brought to the Consulate, he was tied to the post and received five thirty (35) [sic] lashes of a good rope from Anqua who certainly laid them on 'with a will'. I then got the flogging stopped. Mr M. was so excited that I think he did not think <u>how</u> the man was being used. The man was cast loose; he then said to the Consul – 'Mr Consul, may I go?' – 'yes,' replied Mr M. 'Thank you' and with a graceful bow he took his departure. The Chap did not seem to care a fig for the drubbing he had got when it was finished. He <u>yelled</u> while being flogged; but did not shed a tear. This man has often maltreated Chinamen. Shortly afterwards Mr Marques

came in and dined with us, Adkins and Forrest being out. The Russian prisoners breakfasted with the Governor. Tatham licked Captain King's[46] cooly. Expect a row. Found that the opposite shore is lined with shells. Another day wasted.

24. Mail expected in. Went to office. No news much. **Cooper** is given up.[47] Noticed a file of ants. They had made a regular road across the road and under the direction of their queen were going to and fro.

25. There was a fearful row last night between some Yankees and Englishmen but our Jacks licked them. The *Winchester* and *Pique* came in this morning while we were bathing and now there are going to be some courts martial held. The insurgents are collecting at Lintin[48] and are expected to take Canton. If they do, it will be a jolly opportunity for Sir John. Went to the bowling alley in the evening. A certain drunk Yankee yclept[49] Captain Taylor[50] cursing and swearing, &c., most amusingly. King is whistling so I shall leave off.

26. The mail in just. As we were going to get into the water we heard *Fort William* fire so off we set, racing like mad, but with all our efforts we were nearly last. We just heard that The Malakoff[51] had been taken & off we

---

came up to complain of this affair; but tho' many words were spoken no resolution was arrived at … These Lorcha men are very troublesome; and whatever conduct they may be guilty of, Mr Marques wd not, cd not, and dare not punish them. It was on this account that Mr Meadows took the matter into his own hands. But what the upshot of the whole may be, it is difficult to say. It may in its consequences be rather serious. Mr Meadows says that if he cd not have brought the fellow to the Consulate, he wd have shot him. I was rather against this line of conduct; and endeavoured to dissuade Mr M.: but he had previously made up his mind to act in this way if a Portuguese would strike one of the consular servants.

Katherine F. Bruner, John K. Fairbank and Richard J. Smith, eds and narratives, *Entering China's Service: Robert Hart's Journals, 1854–1863* (Cambridge, Mass.: Council on East Asian Studies, Harvard University, 1986), 95–96, doi.org/10.1163/9781684172627. Mr Marques was the Portuguese consul. Bruner, Fairbank and Smith describe Anqua as 'the Consulate factotum', 57.

46 Captain King of the 59th Regiment of Foot was aide-de-camp to Sir John Bowring.
47 In April 1855, the *Sybille*, the *Bittern* and the *Hornet* were dispatched to investigate Russian activities in the Sea of Okhotsk and on the Russian coast at de Castries Bay. Cooper must have been seconded as an interpreter on this expedition.
48 Now, Nei (or Inner) Lingding Island, in the mouth of the Pearl River, west of Hong Kong. The insurgents were likely members of the Tiandihui or the Heaven and Earth Society, whose uprising in 1854–56 is usually called the Red Turban Rebellion. See Frederick Wakeman, *Strangers at the Gate: Social Disorder in South China, 1839–61* (Berkeley: University of California Press, 1966); Jaeyoon Kim, 'The Heaven and Earth Society and the Red Turban Rebellion in Late Qing China', *Journal of Humanities and Social Sciences* 3, no. 1 (2009).
49 Archaic, 'called'.
50 I have been unable to identify this Captain Taylor.
51 The Malakoff redoubt was captured by French troops on 8 September 1855 and presaged the taking of Sevastopol the next day.

came. Went to office. Adkins and Forrest got some letters but I and King got none at first. At last, Woodgate brought me some and King brought me another & afterwards I got the *Illustrated*,[52] so now I am jolly. All at home have been ill but are getting better. **Henry** has been to Paris and **Charly** has been to Hastings where he has found Henry's certificate. Sebastopol is in flames. The Queen has been to Paris. The Empress is *enceinte*. Riga and Revel[53] have been bombarded. Edkins, King, Tatham, Leonard and Forrest have gone out & I am alone.[54] Forrest is going to Siam & government is going to provide lodging for Student Interpreters which is jolly. I have so many things to read that like a cat in a tripe shop I know not what to begin on. We had splendid saluting this morning because of Sebastopol. All the ships fired a broadside.[55] The *Styx* has come in.

27. Went bathing as usual. At the office we had more work than usual. A memorial from Lord Shaftesbury[56] and an answer to it from Lord Clarendon[57] have come in & had to be copied. We had to take some home & I have just finished my share. The opium trade is truly a gigantic evil and one which will, if not stopped in time, ruin 1st China then India and damage England much. Some damage it has already done. If it be put down suddenly, ruin will attend on many. The first houses[58] will break and China like the West Indies go to the dogs, but if it be done gradually, it will not be so much felt and in 10 years the exports from England will be 10 times what they are. If we continue the trade we dishonor ourselves, disobey our God, impoverish and demoralise China & India, which we are doing rapidly. If it be stopped gradually, in 10 years China & Chinese trade will be twice as flourishing as it is now, but we must expect a row for the merchants

---

52   *Illustrated London News*.
53   Alternative name for Tallinn.
54   Joseph Edkins (1823–1905) was a long-time missionary with the London Missionary Society and later worked for the Chinese Customs Service. He was one of the most learned foreigners in China during the nineteenth century.
55   See *China Mail*, 1 November 1855, 2:
     On Friday last, the British Men-of-war in harbour were adorned with flags, and a great firing of guns took place, in which the Spanish steamer *Jorge Juan* joined. The cause of their rejoicing did not at once appear, and has not yet been satisfactorily explained … But in the course of the day we learned that the rejoicing was on account of the fall of Sevastopol, of which fact the Admiral has especial information, which it would perhaps have been advisable to communicate to the public by a more intelligible medium than the cannon's-mouth.
56   Anthony Ashley-Cooper, seventh Earl of Shaftesbury (1801–1885), the well-known politician and reformer. In 1855, he had sent a memorial to Lord Clarendon on the evils of the opium trade.
57   George Villiers, fourth Earl of Clarendon (1800–1870), foreign secretary (1853–1858 and, later, 1865–1866 and 1868–1870).
58   'Houses' here refers to mercantile houses, those privately owned businesses involved in the import and export trades.

are powerful & a rash stoppage would raise a commotion not only among the merchants but among the Chinese. To be continued. Forrest has won a pony at a raffle.

28. All the others went out to shoot and I stopped at home. Went to church. Had a war sermon.[59] Came home bringing some magnificent grasses and had some fritters. Put things to rights. Read the newspaper. The others came home after wading up to their knees and above in the paddy fields & killing some sandpipers, snipe & a kingfisher. Had dinner & then they went home. I hear that Forrest has called us 3 in a letter 'the greatest bears he ever saw'. Well, Mr Forrest, take care.

29. Have felt wretchedly ill all day but did a good bit of work at office. Noticed the drying the flour (& bleaching it) in the sun. The flour is spread in large round pans and left out in the sun. Still bothering with the Shang-hae duties.[60] It seems to me that the merchants are in the wrong decidedly. When Shang-hae was taken the Custom House was stopped which the merchants considered equivalent to a release from all due duties but Alcock, rightly judging these duties payable by Treaty, made the merchants give bonus requiring them to pay the duties if it was decided so by H.M. Govt and he was right for he was bound by the Treaty not to give up the ships' papers till the duties were paid and if the provisional system had not been made, all trade would have been stopped by the Chinese Government who indeed would have done so if it had not been for the P.S. so I think the merchants fools and scamps. Fools because they could not see how advantageous it was to their interests to pay, for the Chinese will always now distrust them & in case of a similar occurrence again the Consul will not dare to make a P.S. & trade will be entirely stopped and ruin will ensue to many rogues because they kept not to their bonds.

30.31. Two days have passed almost without an event. Yesterday King was taken bad with diarrhoea, which is now departing slowly. Forrest is busy about his departure for Siam. I am getting up my working powers as fast as

---

59   A sermon that discusses Christian responses to war, in particular ideas of 'just war', duty and conscience.
60   The payment of customs duties in the treaty ports was dealt with under the Treaty of Nanking. After the occupation of the Chinese city in Shanghai by the so-called Small Sword rebels in 1851, the operations of the government-run Customs House ceased. Rutherford Alcock (later Sir, 1809–1897), British consul in Shanghai at the time, instituted a system whereby departing captains would leave a promissory note with their respective consuls for duties to be payable when a new customs authority was established. This was the Provisional System, or P.S., that Alabaster refers to. See Fairbank, *Trade and Diplomacy*, 410–38; Bruner, Fairbank and Smith, *Entering China's Service*, 161–68.

I can. I went to hear the band play where I was amused by drunken jacks. Had a look at the making of a China mattress. [sketch] Must get models made of their machines.

November

1. Thursday. The *Powhatan* went out this morning for Yankeeland and saluted the *Macedonian* & was saluted. There have been 12 courts martial and the assistant surgeon & a lieutenant of the *Winchester* are dismissed the service. Pay day. Had our pay to pull. Home dollars[61] are brutally inconvenient. Only think a fellow has to bring a month's pay home in a handkerchief. Forrest busy packing up ready to go to Siam and as King & Forrest are away, I have rather more to do at the office.

2. Great News. General Keenan the American Consul is arrested and it is likely to give rise to great events.[62] I will give all I know. A Yankee captain 1st flogged a British seaman on board his ship. We send to arrest the

---

61 At this time, the silver dollar was the standard currency throughout Asia, and in many other parts of the world. Originally Spanish – the famous 'pieces of eight' – by the mid-nineteenth century, most silver dollars in circulation were Mexican.

62 The *China Mail* reported this case in its issue of 25 October 1855. According to that account, the captain of the US Ship *Reindeer*, E.W. Nichols, had severely beaten a carpenter on the ship while it was in Hong Kong harbour. After a complaint was submitted to the police office on Monday 22 October, the police had rescued the carpenter and summonsed Nichols to appear in court. The case was held the next day and Nichols was found guilty and ordered to pay a fine of $50 and give $25 compensation to the carpenter. Nichols refused to pay and was to be taken into custody. Keenan, the US consul, had been in court throughout and had repeatedly challenged the court's jurisdiction on the grounds that the offence had occurred on a US ship. Keenan accompanied Nichols to the jail, the judge having declared that if Nichols refused to pay the fine, he should be imprisoned for one month. On reaching the jail, the two men:

> proceeded to move down the hill, upon which the Usher arrested Nichols by seizing him by the collar, but was pushed on one side by Mr Keenen, who, exclaiming 'Mind whom you are playing with,' proceeded with Nichols at a rapid pace followed by the Usher Martin to Messrs De Silver & Co.'s whence they took a boat and went on board the U.S.S. *Powhaten*, outsailing the Usher and his assistants, who pursued in another boat.

Obtaining a warrant, Martin went on board the *Powhaten* to either retrieve Nichols or the money for the fines. The captain, McCluney (elsewhere spelled M'Cluney), did not admit that Nichols was on board, and let Martin know that he considered the court proceedings illegal and would resist any attempt to claim British jurisdiction over US ships in Hong Kong harbour with force. The *China Mail* concludes: 'Such we believe to be the facts of the case, in which our saucy cousins have acted somewhat ungraciously as well as illegally'. In the next issue, dated 1 November 1855, it was added that the fines had been paid but Keenan was summonsed to appear before the magistrate. Not appearing, a warrant was issued for his arrest. The *China Mail* of 15 November 1855 reports that Keenen did in fact appear before the assistant magistrate on 13 November and was bailed to appear in the Supreme Court on charges of 'rescue of a prisoner, with assault, and assault and battery'. The Supreme Court case was set for 29 November, but all charges were dropped before it could sit. For a full accounting of the case using Keenan's correspondence and placing the affair in the context of longstanding discussions over questions of jurisdiction, see Amelia Kay King, 'James Keenan: United States Consul to Hong Kong' (MA thesis, North Texas State University, 1978).

captain and ask for a summons from Keenan, which he pooh poohs us out of. Well, we seize the man & bring him on shore where he is, by stratagem, rescued by Keenan and carried on board the *Powhatan* where we sent for but could not get him. Consequently we summon Keenan, which summons he says he shall not regard and consequently he is nabbed today. As there is sure to be a fearful row, perhaps a war, I put this down. America has little or no navy or army but she is rich and would prove an awkward enemy, especially if France turns false. Went on board the Siamese bark *Castle* with Forrest's luggage, and such a beastly hole I never saw. Stinking, dirty and disreputable. The crew half Chinese who all wore beastly ugly turbans & Malays who are a much handsomer race than the Chinese & who have splendid black hair. The bark is a rum looking thing something like this shape [sketch] & was originally built for a junk. Sir John went on board the *Winchester* today and a salute was fired. King is much better.

3. Forrest went off today to Siam. Went on board his ship again. Leslie's[63] dog followed us into the boat and came home with us as if we were his masters. Forrest's cabin is a most fearful hole, 5 ft by 4 at the outside. Chinese children seem happy little animals, petted by their elders in every way. They seem a merry set. One little one this morning aged 2 was being led about by his elder brother this morning as I was waiting for a boat & was shown as a great curiosity myself, whereat he squalled vigorously. Had to send all our boys away because they won't say who stole the biscuits, to my great sorrow.

4. Went to church. Made up my accounts. Went for a sail. They are getting on slowly and badly at the Albany.

5. Had rows on rows. It appears that Forrest has received money from us to pay our expenses & then gone off without doing so, so we have had to fork out again. A press of work at office. A day passed without an idea.

6. Went to office & afterwards walked to East Point. Really. The Chinese boats on the water. These are miraculous. Imagine thousands of boats all moored together. The rice is almost ripe and harvest will soon be here. Went to Leonard's this evening saw Tatham & τίνα Rogers.[64] There are at present in Hong Kong no less than 4000 rebels.[65]

---

63 T.C. Leslie, a merchant with Dent & Co.
64 τίνα: Greek *tina*, 'that'. Rogers is likely Alexander Roger, merchant's clerk, Dent & Co.
65 The rebels were likely Red Turban insurgents fleeing the purge that took place after the defeat of the rebellion.

7. Went to office as usual. Got a cocoon. All the insects here seem endued with great powers of weaving silk. In evening, went to Royal Asiatic Society.[66] Sir John read a paper on Siam with whom our trade was once so great that 50 English ships were engaged on the Menam River.[67] The monkeys there are very fierce. In fact, Bell & Hunter once shot a young one in its mother's arms, which so exasperated the monkey as to make Bell & H. run for it.[68] In Cochin China they are much the same. Bats, monkeys and marble seem the chief productions of Cochin China where they have a north east & south west monsoon like us but contrary in their effects. The museum is in very bad condition & has very little in it. Dr Harland[69] looks a clever man. Calm, slightly nervous but knowing much. Adkins would come home early so I could not stop.

---

66   The Hong Kong Branch of the Royal Asiatic Society was formed in 1847 but was defunct by 1859. It was reformed in 1959 and continues to exist.
67   The Menam River is the Chao Phraya. Bowring's talk – he was president of the society at the time – was reported in the *China Mail* of 22 November 1855.
68   Charles Bell, a student interpreter, accompanied Sir John Bowring to Siam when he negotiated the treaty with that kingdom in 1855. Bowring left him and Forrest there to learn Thai with a view to them serving in the new consulate. Bell resigned in 1857 and two years later died of 'jungle fever' while looking for gold. Hunter is likely Robert Hunter, Jr, private secretary to the Siamese king, who died in 1865. He was the son of the Scottish businessman, Robert Hunter (1792–1848), who was resident in Bangkok from 1820 to 1844. In Sir John Bowring's *The Kingdom and People of Siam* (1857), he quotes from 'notes on an excursion to the city of Pechaburi', 'from a gentleman, now resident in Siam'. Given the content, this gentleman was likely Charles Bell himself:

> At the mouth of the river, myriads of monkeys were to be seen. A very amusing incident occurred here. Mr. Hunter, wishing to get a juvenile specimen, fired at the mother, but, unfortunately, only wounded her, and she had strength enough to carry the young one into the jungle. Five men immediately followed her; but ere they had been out of sight five minutes, we saw them hurrying towards us, shouting, '*Ling, ling, ling, ling!*' (*ling*, monkey). As I could see nothing, I asked Mr. Hunter if they were after the monkey. 'Oh, no,' he replied; 'the monkeys are after them!' And so they were – thousands upon thousands of them, coming down in a most unpleasant manner.

69   Dr Aurelius W. Harland (1822–1858) was a medical doctor. During his 14 years in Hong Kong, he was resident surgeon of the Seamen's Hospital and colonial surgeon. He carried out the first operation in Hong Kong using anaesthesia. He was also the long-time secretary of the Hong Kong Branch of the Royal Asiatic Society, a fervent naturalist and great friend of Hance. He studied Chinese and published studies and translations of Chinese medical texts. He died in 1858 of 'congestion of the brain' that was associated with a 'remittent fever' he first acquired treating Chinese seamen. E.J. Eitel wrote of his death that: 'No event in Hong Kong was mourned so generally and so deeply as the death of Dr Harland'. His younger brother Edward was one of the founders of the great Belfast shipyard of Harland and Wolff. On Harland, see Christopher Munn's entry on him in Holdsworth and Munn, *Dictionary of Hong Kong Biography*, 175.

8. Grand Cricket Match. All China against the 59th.[70] All China was thoroughly licked. Got away from office early. Wrote some letters. My foot is bad.

9. Bought several catties of lead for bullets. The Governor is going to pay our rent for us till the Albany is ready. Quid est jollium.[71] Nothing else to put down save that we played whist this evening. Got an immense spider. His body about 1½ inches long. All yellow & black. Fearfully wet. Pouring as it pours in Hong Kong. Only did a little work. Not very much but yet a little. Some more student interpreters are coming out.

10. A cold day. Had a fire. They tell me the thermometer is at 75 but non credo.[72] Adkins and Tatham went out shooting. Shot but little & got covered with mud.

12. Getting ready for the mail. No news. Adkins & King are gone out while I remain at home writing letters, &c., &c. Verily my diary getteth dull.

13. Went out. Bathe and in the afternoon out shopping. Bought a paperknife to send home by Captain Jones.[73]

14. Busy packing up a little box to send home, writing letters, &c. Am still unwell but a little better than I was. Have not sent much home. Wrote 11 letters. Quid est jollium.

15. The mail went out today having on board Bourbuillon, late French Plenipotentiary in China.[74] He had a salute of 17 guns & a band & Sir John saw him off and all was grand & just as it should be. Had a walk near the Happy Valley though why they call a racecourse surrounded by cemeteries

---

70 The *Overland Register and Price Current* (15 November 1855) reported on the game:
On Thursday, the 8th instant, a Cricket match came off between the 59th Regiment and the 'All-China Cricket Club,' in which the latter were defeated in one innings by a majority of 53, an event imparalleled in cricketing annals in China, and which we never wish to see dittoed.
71 Latin, 'How very jolly'.
72 Latin, 'I don't believe it'.
73 I have not been able to identify this Captain Jones.
74 Alphonse de Bourboulon (1809–1877), minister plenipotentiary for France from 1851 to 1855 when, as Alabaster notes, he returned to France. He was sent to China again in 1858 as envoy extraordinary, establishing the French embassy in Peking. He left China for the second time in 1862, travelling overland. See Patrick Taveirne, 'The Religious Case of the Fengzhen District: Reclamation and Missionary Activities in Caqar during the Late Qing Dynasty', in *The History of the Relations between the Low Countries and China in the Qing Era*, ed. W.F. Vande Walle and Noël Golvers (Leuven: Leuven University Press, 2003), 369–418, 385–86.

the Happy Valley I don't know. Valley of the Shadow of Death[75] would be much better. Here comes a burial party of soldiers. On this side you see crosses & urns. On that, tombs of miserable Chinamen & perhaps, in those bushes, some haggard, miserable, unshriven, childless coolie is giving up the ghost. And here, in the midst, are all the vanities of the world. All the vices & few of the virtues of mankind. When one sees in imagination the wretched vicious man – pallid, haggard, tall, thin, with gleaming eyes, straight hair, his clothes all dirty & devilish smile upon his lips, time is fleeting, ne'er returning. Oh alas. Time to waste, there is none.

16. Went to office early. Felt deuced seedy. Had a row with Adkins in which, as usual, he made a fool of himself. (He is perfectly welcome to read this as well as any other private letters I leave about.)[76]

17. Went to the Governor's to breakfast. Consul Alcock was there. He is an oldish, clever, and what the ladies call 'a nice man'. Sir John let fall a hint about his opening China. I enjoyed breakfast very much & begin to like the Bowrings very much.

18. Stopped at home and was singularly happy. Read all my letters. Put several things to rights & though all the others had gone out shooting, made myself singularly jolly. King came home about 5½ sweating fearfully and brought two additions for my collection. Adkins is out still. After waiting dinner till 9½ I found he had gone to Leonard's, which discomposed me for a time. Dr Dempster came this morning & has given me some physic & I have found out that the Chinese give their gods a nimbus. The number and variety of spiders here is marvelous. Almost as curious as the ants, who make regular roads to my certain knowledge & very good roads too. Read my letters this morning. How beautiful are **Aunty's**. So full of love and affection. What mother could be more affectionate than me?[77] Who could have denied herself more? Oh Aunty! thou art matchless among women & Oh **Uncle**! who could have taken so much trouble? Have denied himself so much? Have loved me as you have done? & my manly brother Henry & earnest Charly & you little **Percy**, how I love you all! Absence from home, how it makes one regret home's pleasures! How it strengthens your love! Oh Lord! I pray thee grant that I may find everyone well and happy! I beseech thee! How pleasant it is to build castles in the air, to fancy your

---

75 'Valley of the Shadow of Death' comes from Psalm 23 in the King James version of the Bible: 'Yea, though I walk through the valley of the shadow of death, I will fear no evil: for Thou art with me.'
76 The sentence in brackets is crossed out, but still legible.
77 'Than me' is probably a mistake for 'to me', or 'than her'.

return, to hope that next mail will tell you that your estates are recovered & that you are able to go home.[78] How you revel in the thoughts of such great happiness. It has often struck me that building castles in the air is a very profitable thing. It bouys you up under adverse circumstances when you would otherwise sink. But enough of this, let's to hard facts. I saw the pheasant and the Governor today. I feel strange this evening and seem to have a sad presentiment upon me. (My presentiment came to nothing.)[79]

19. Went to office, & after office went for a row. The first boat refused to go & ran, but we got into another & chased it. When two of them jumped overboard and the third got into a junk, another boat refused to take us so we gave orders to a policeman to take him up but he got off. But we hope will be nabbed some time.

20. Woodgate's Birthday. He gave King a basket of Pummelows. We set about thinking of how jolly it would be to walk back to England.

21. A Dutch Steamer came in today from Japan with a Dutch embassy & par consequence there was saluting.[80] In fact Stirling[81] seems to take delight in saluting & does little else. A pouring rainy day. Ce que c'est?[82] Very unseasonable. Did a little work this evening. 2 extras are coming to office.

---

78 The 'estates' were in North America, straddling the borders of the USA and Canada on Lake Superior, which was Chippewa (or Ojibwe) land. In 1832, Mary Alabaster, Chaloner's grandmother, had bought the deeds to two tracts of land (for 20 pounds) that had originally been signed in 1760. The seller, Miss Ann Jones, had received the deeds as an inheritance; her grandfather, Robert Jones (1704–1774), had acquired them on the death of Sir Samuel Touchet (1705–1773), one of the partners in the Lake Superior Company, in partial payment of an unrepaid loan. Whether the deeds were real, whether they would be recognised by either the US or Canadian authorities, and thus whether they were worth anything at all, were open questions. To investigate matters fully, Chaloner's father James made a journey to North America in 1837, during which time he consulted with lawyers and others, and sought out records that may have proved the deeds' worth. Although he returned disappointed, holding the view that no more funds should be expended on the claims, he did manage to negotiate an agreement with various parties, especially the lawyers, to share any proceeds should they be held to be valid. In the end, nothing came of them, but Alabaster's remark indicates that he, at least, still held out some hope that he would come into money in November 1855 and be able to cut short his career in the Consular Service. For a full account, see John S. Alabaster, *An Alabaster Quest*, to which I am indebted.
79 The sentence in brackets is in smaller script and was obviously added later.
80 The steamer was the Dutch naval vessel *Gedeh* under the command of Captain Gerhardus Fabius (1806–1888). With him on this journey to Nagasaki was Johan Maurits Count Van Lynden, an adjutant of the Dutch King. A painting of their meeting with Nabeshima Naomasa 鍋島 直正 (1815–1871), the daimyō of Saga Domain in Kyūshū, is held in the Maritiem Museum Rotterdam, see www.geheugenvannederland.nl/en/geheugen/view?coll=ngvn&identifier=KONB11%3AP1794.
81 James Stirling (later Sir, 1791–1865) was at this time rear admiral and commander-in-chief of the East Indies and China Station of the Royal Navy. He had founded the Swan River Colony in Western Australia in 1829.
82 French, 'qu'est-ce que c'est?', 'What is going on?'

Quid est jollium. My ideas all the morning centred on walking home. If one had money & companions it would be jolly but, as it is, is nearly impracticable.

22. A cold day. On way to office stopped at a washerman's & saw him ironing. He took some water in his mouth, squirted it out all about & then ironed the thing with a sort of saucepan filled with a charcoal fire. Did a little work at office. The Dutch embassy very uncommunicative, so it is supposed they have not succeeded. A threatening letter sent to Canton. Went to the Albany where they are progressing favourably. Wretched Indian women about in evening. Went to Leonard's passing a gambling house which was tolerably full. One fellow holds up any number of fingers suddenly and another shouts out what number he thinks it is, so it is a tolerably noisy game.[83] Came back with Leonard (after seeing Tatham and young Armstrong[84]) in a boat. Wrote for Dr Dempster.

23. A really cold day. Saw Dr D. who gave me some physic. As usual, went to office late. The Chinese government have prohibited the use of lorchas[85] by natives, which I do not suppose will have much effect. Did a little Chinese. Find it rather hard. Went out for an evening stroll. Met several policemen with swords and bayonets. Only think of that in England. A pirate ran through the harbor the other day with a prize in tow.

24. A tiger has been seen on the other side. Worked hard at the office. Leonard came to dinner. The *Encounter* has come in.[86]

25. A splendid day. I, Adkins and Tatham went out in a boat. Saw the *Sybill* come in & after, a splendid sail through beautiful scenery till we came to a jolly bay where we landed.[87] Passed through a field or two where they were reaping and threshing rice, for no sooner do they cut a sheaf than they come & knock the rice out of it & attracting numbers of fokis[88] round us, on we

---

83   This is *huaquan* 划拳, which is still very popular as a drinking game.
84   Possibly the John Martin Armstrong listed in the 1855 Jury List as working for Armstrong, Lawrence & Co. However, Alabaster's reference to him as 'young' Armstrong might mean that he was either the son or younger brother of this Armstrong.
85   A variety of boat commonly seen in southern Chinese waters that had a Western-style hull but a junk rig.
86   The *Encounter* had been in Hakodate (or Hakodadi as it was rendered) in Hokkaido, which had been opened to foreign trade in 1854 under the Convention of Kanagawa.
87   The *Sybille* had also been to Hakodate.
88   'Foki' appears to be an obscure word for men hired by families who required extra labour. See Barbara Ward, 'Kau Sai: An Unfinished Manuscript', *Journal of the Hong Kong Branch of the Royal Asiatic Society* 25 (1985): 27–118.

went over hills & valleys & a magnificent cover.[89] On we went scrambling & it really was jolly. We started[90] a pheasant, a hawk & last a woodcock. As I had been walking through cover till thoroughly tired, I let Adkins and Tatham go after him & sat down pro tem,[91] whereupon the boys came up and sat down by me & felt my clothes & laughed, felt again & so on, just as you hear of savages doing, only these were very polite. Then we went into a temple of the Queen of Heaven[92] in which were 4 images, offerings, loads of lanterns and banners, a drum, & a very good bell. One finds the drum & bell in all joss houses.[93] [sketch] Then we went & chinchinned[94] the natives, who are a jolly polite set. One wanted me to smoke his pipe & we had a long conversation by signs. Then after some practice with my revolver at a hat & more chinchinning we came home. The scenery today was really jolly. Hills & dales covered with vegetation. The sea peeping in at odd corners. Here sugarcanes, here cacti & a blue, blue sky overhead. It was splendid. Mem:[95] a very good boat. Tatham stopped for dinner. Leonard came. King dined at Woodgate's. Beauty of Chinese scenery in its irregularity. Made an old Chinaman fire a gun. Such fun when he drew the trigger back. He jumped but he took kindly to beer. [sketch] Chinese plow. Lindsay[96] and party came back after shooting 3 pheasants in a week's shooting & seeing 2 deer, which excited one fellow so much that he let fly with N° 3 shot at 2000 yards distance.

26. 2 Portuguese have come to office. I have got a jolly little Chinese pup, which I shall call Smoke. I have won a bet. Joined in a lottery & altogether am going fast to the dogs. Quid est horridum.[97] The mail is due & due & due but is not in.

---

89 'Cover', here, is hunting terminology and refers to undergrowth that may conceal game.
90 Startled.
91 Temporarily, for a while.
92 The Queen of Heaven (Tian hou 天后 or Tin hau in Cantonese) is Mazu 媽祖.
93 Temples; 'joss' comes from the Portuguese *deus*, 'god'.
94 Greeted.
95 Memorandum.
96 It is unclear which Lindsay this is. There is no Lindsay listed in the Hong Kong Jury Lists for 1854–58. The 1859 Hong Kong Directory, which lists 'foreign residents' of all the treaty ports, also has no Lindsay. Lindsay & Co. was, of course, a major mercantile house; however, in this period it was led in China by H.H. Lindsay's nephew Robert Antrobus.
97 Latin, 'How very horrid!'

27. I have just been out on a false alarm of a mail, which is not in yet. We are getting the arrears up fast at office. Finished the abridgement of Staunton's account of Macartney's embassy.[98] It contains much information but it is horrid to think that an expensive embassy like Lord Macartney's should have accomplished nothing. I do not like the abridgement. It is badly written & leaves one in uncertainty whether Lord M. did kotow or not, i.e. the most important thing in the whole affair is left out.[99] It is now cool weather. Our pups have taken to howling by night.

28. Went for a sail round the ships before breakfast. Did a lot of work at office. Went up to the Albany which begins to look very jolly. The mail is not in yet.

29. Had an amusing row at office. The Portuguese[100] shut the door so I opened it. He shut it. I opened it. Whereupon he, in a wax,[101] shut it. I quietly went and opened it, whereat he flew at me 'Will you shut thaat door?' 'No.' 'Why for you no shut that door Mr Hantz?' (Mr Hantz takes no notice.) P. gets black in the face. 'If you had asked, I would have left it open.' 'Askkk Youu?' 'Yes.' 'Will you shut that door? (looking as if he would eat me). Well, I no can write. I will tell Mister Woodgate,' & so it ended & tomorrow I suppose he will. The mail not in yet.

30. The last day of the month. The mail not in yet. Adkins has a lot of letters of Cromwell time, which I must write to Uncle about. No news except that Bowring has written a jolly blowing up letter to the Viceroy about Ejin,[102] which I hope will have some effect.

---

98 Sir George Staunton, *An Abridged Account of the Embassy to the Emperor of China, Undertaken by Order of the King of Great Britain from the Papers of Earl Macartney* (London: John Stockdale, 1797).
99 The 'kowtow' (*koutou* 叩頭) was a formal bow made by kneeling and knocking (*kou*) the head (*tou*) on the ground. A kowtow of nine prostrations was required at an audience with the emperor. On his 1793 embassy to China, there was considerable fractious negotiation over whether Macartney would have to perform the kowtow when he met the Qianlong emperor. Macartney insisted that he would only genuflect as he would to his own sovereign, George III, but the Chinese side insisted that this was inadequate and compromised on the number of prostrations, reducing the requirement to just one. Nonetheless, it is now accepted that Macartney did not kowtow – partly as his gout and generous girth would have made it practically impossible – but in Alabaster's time there was still some doubt.
100 Several Portuguese worked in government offices in Hong Kong at this time, but none in the Superintendency of Trade.
101 In a rage.
102 Foreigners, literally 'barbarians', *yiren* 夷人. Ye Mingchen (葉名琛, 1807–1858) was the viceroy of the Liang Guang, or the two provinces Guangdong and Guangxi.

December

1. Saturday. Payday. Received a gorgulious sum but alas, like all human delights, it will quickly melt away. Oh mail! when art thou coming in? Already a fortnight beyond your time! Went out and about in a boat taking Smoke with me. Pitched him in. He kept up jollily & looked as miserable as a wet dog generally does. Ran into lots of lankar boats.[103] Adkins is fearfully savage about the dogs.

2. Sunday. Finished *Gil Blas*.[104] It really is a splendid book but yet I think it too long and near the end its wit diminishes. Le Sage was a splendid writer & his mode of writing afforded him many opportunities for displaying his capabilities but story on story becomes, in the end, troublesome and fatiguing. Thus in *Gil Blas*, though you laugh heartily at some places such as the False Flatterer, and his sly hits at the doctors against whom he seems to have a particular spite, the aguazils,[105] and all hypocrites and imposters & gain much information seeing the instability of human affairs, yet it seems dull near the end. I have read few books I like better and it is one I would put in the hands of every child, as from it you get amusement, instruction & good writing at once. The mail came in just as we were in the middle of service.[106] *Fort William* fired & as soon as service was over, I & Adkins got a boat & went off to the *Norna*. She brings news of the taking of Sebastopol but with little honour to us. Still, the forts on the North are to be taken. However, Russia has lost a good deal, among other things 70 ships, stores innumerable & men by millions. Frederick of Prussia is after the Princess Royal, confound him.[107] For my part, I think we have enough Germans already & a Jew is Lord Mayor.[108] They ought to have had lots of old hats all over the coach & the Knights should be represented by 'Old Cloes' instead

---

103 I have been unable to identify what kind of boats these are. To speculate: the word 'lançar' in Portuguese means 'to throw' and is used in the term to 'throw the anchor'. Anchor-boats were small craft employed to carry the anchor of larger ships to the point in a harbour where it was to be fixed.
104 *Gil Blas* (1715–35) was written by Alain-René Lesage (or Le Sage, 1668–1747). Tobias Smollett's (1721–1771) translation into English of 1748 was widely reprinted in the nineteenth century.
105 Officials.
106 The church service.
107 The Princess Royal was Victoria (1840–1901) who married Emperor Frederick III of Prussia. He proposed to her in 1855, they were betrothed in 1857 and married in 1858. The eldest daughter of Queen Victoria, she was the mother of Kaiser Wilhelm II.
108 Sir David Salomons, first Baronet (1797–1873), became Lord Mayor of London in 1855.

of being Men of Straw.[109] The difference of China and England first struck me forcibly today, for here I went to church under a broiling sun, while the same time last year I went over roads hard with ice and muffed up in a great coat. Leonard came. Adkins has gone to Woodgate's to dinner and I suppose I shall go next Sunday. My letters not yet out.

3. I got my letters and some of my papers last night but after I had read them was too lazy to do any more. Wonders on wonders have happened. Louisa and Josephine King are both going to be married. Henry has given up engineering & is fagging[110] Chinese for love of me. Aunty, Uncle & Percy are better & Louisa Meyer is grown a whopper (quid est horribile).[111] Charly & everyone have been to Herne Bay. A box is or was coming out but has not arrived & Elizabeth Poulton, whether my cousin or my grand neice, is dead. Admiral Stirling is made Rear Admiral of the Red.[112] **Payne** & oh misere! Glynes, inimitable Glynes, are coming out. Glynes, whom I abominate. There is going to be a biannual examination of all us buffers which will keep us up to the scratch. Had a thundering salute about the taking of Sebastopol.

4. Woodgate absent from office. Am reading my papers. Not very much to interest one. Leonard & Tatham came this evening after which we slippered the dogs for howling. Saw preparation of chaou chaou for coolies next door. It merely consisted in chopping up greens, fish's guts, &c. & boiling them. Chinamen are jolly cooks out of beastly materials. They make jolly meals.

---

109 In the mid-nineteenth century, one of the professions Jews commonly pursued was the buying and selling of second-hand clothes. The street-cry of 'old cloes' let people know they could sell their old clothes, which were then resold at markets such as Petticoat Lane. See John Mills, *The British Jews* (London: Houlston and Stoneman, 1853), 264–65. It was customary to knight lord mayors of London. See Alfred B. Beaven, *The Aldermen of the City of London, Henry III - 1908, with Notes on the Parliamentary Representation of the City, the Aldermen and the Livery Companies, the Aldermanic Veto, Aldermanic Baronets and Knights, Etc.* (London: Eden Fisher & Co, Ltd, 1913).
110 Working hard at.
111 Louisa and Josephine King were obviously friends of the Alabaster family. In a letter dated 15 May 1857, Alabaster admits to his Aunt that 'I am still in love with L.M. just as bad as before but have not written, wanting space'. Not long afterwards, on 24 August 1857, he updated his aunt with the news that he had ceased his formal interest in Louisa: 'I have written to Mr. Meyer approving of the destruction of my epistolary communications, for I quite agree with him that it is inadvisable to fetter her with any engagement.' See John S. Alabaster, *Correspondence*, 17. The Meyers family were friends of the Alabasters.
112 See above, footnote 81. The rear admiral of the Red Squadron outranked the rear admirals of the White and Blue squadrons, and was one step below the vice admiral of the Blue Squadron.

5. Nothing of any note. I read Oakley[113] till I could read no more. Another lawyer has come to Hong Kong. Agi[114] has not come back. Did not waste this day.

6. The *Styx* and *Rattler* are going home. A French embassy is going to Siam. I am getting on tolerably with Chinese. The Albany is finished but I do not like it much.

7. Woodgate asked me to dinner tomorrow. The *Dolphin* has come in. The *Styx* has gone. The band of the *Sybille* played today. It is a jolly band & the amusement was heightened by some jacks who were drinking & singing. A mounted policeman passed. The image of Don Quixote. Saw Lawrence.[115] Was introduced to a certain Mr Tate.[116] A conceited ass of considerable information. Lots of people about. Miss Pearce & Miss Drinker.[117]

8. Dined with Mr Woodgate. He has a very jolly house but very lonely. Captain Stewart of the *Nankin* and Captain Watkins[118] were there to dinner where I had some jolly beer. Captain Watkins is a jolly, sensible old fellow who has a great deal of sense in him but Captain Stewart is a tough, obstinate, surly old fellow. After dinner, the captain of the *Sybille* came in & gave one an opportunity of seeing a French sea captain.[119] He was rather a swell. Very talkative but rather a nice fellow. Sir John is going to Foochow &

---

113 Horace Oakley (1818–1875), one of the original 1843 appointments to the Consular Service, was first assistant in the Canton Consulate from 1845 to 1857, retiring on the grounds of ill-health, which Coates says was alcoholism. He was granted a pension of 90 pounds.
114 Agi appears only once more in the diaries, on 30 December, as 'Mr Agi'. The present entry would imply that he was a lawyer, as would the later one in which Agi threated to sue Alabaster. Unfortunately, I have not been able to identify him.
115 Probably George Richard Lawrence, the son of Frederick William Lawrence, the principal of Armstrong, Lawrence & Co.
116 Joseph Priestly Tate was a mercantile assistant at W.H. Wardley & Co.
117 Miss Pearce was presumably the daughter of Richard Pearce (d. 1871) of Dent & Co. and Miss Drinker, the daughter of Sandwith Drinker (d. 1858) of the mercantile house Rawle, Drinker & Co.
118 Thomas Vernon Watkins (d. 1870), at this time Hong Kong harbour master and marine magistrate, ultimately rear admiral.
119 Confusingly, there were two ships named *Sybille* in Hong Kong waters at this time. The first, under the command of Commodore C.G.J.B. (Charles) Elliot (b. 1818), belonged to the British Navy. The second, under Captain de Maisonneuve, belonged to the French Navy.

Woodgate as soon as his back is turned to Macao. There was a determined attack on Murrow's house the other night.[120] It seems the skins taken at Urup[121] supposed worthless are worth $400 each. Woodgate is a brick.

9. Went out with Adkins, King and Tatham to our old place. The hills were covered with mist so we spent most of the day in the boat. The bottom of the water was covered with most magnificent corals – red, yellow, green and white – & we had some fun catching sea slugs. A black hairy beast 7 or more inches long which, when you take it up, emits a white substance as sticky as

---

120 Mr Murrow is likely Yorick Jones Murrow of Murrow & Co. Lloyd Edward Murrow, presumably his son, worked for him as a clerk. The *Overland Register and Price Current* (15 December 1855) reported the robbery under the headline 'Dashing Burglary':

> About 10 p.m. on Friday Evening last, Mr Murrow, having retired to his bedroom, was roused by hearing a knocking and altercation at the door leading from the Road to his Compradore's room: rising at once and feeling convinced of the character of his visitors, he quickly ran down stairs and succeeded in making fast, with the aid of his coolies, the already half opened door, he then – not having any ammunition – dropped from a small window in the side of his house, and hastened to the nearest Police station to give the alarm.
> The thieves, finding Mr Murrow's door closed against them, immediately went to the door of Messrs. W.H. Wardley & Co.'s house, and under pretence of having a letter and parcel 'from the Club' to deliver to Mr Tate (the only Foreigner in the house) they succeeded in obtaining an entrance, and they immediately cut down the coolie at the door. Leaving four of their number in the passage to prevent communication with Mr Tate (in bed up-stairs) the remainder crowded into the coolies' rooms and with their knives and spears wounded several coolies and held the rest at bay. With pick-axes they burst open two slight doors separating the Compradore's rooms from the coolies' rooms, and with the same effective tools they knocked a hole in the side of the money chest.
> While this was proceeding below, (with the utmost speed and with a frightful noise of crashing wood and shrieking coolies) Mr Tate, who unfortunately was quite unarmed, ran to the head of the stairs, and on making his appearance found a man waiting below with a long gun in readiness – finding what was the matter he called from the Verandah for assistance, and hearing voices in the distance was emboldened to run down stairs with a stout stick – just in time to see the whole gang in full retreat to the westward – one of whom, turning round, fired his gun, the ball from which however, missed its mark considerably, and pierced the verandah. Attention was then imperatively demanded in the extinguishing of large quantities of smouldering paper, &c., which the villains seem to have lighted to increase the confusion. The whole passed in a very short time, the thieves not above four minutes in the house. The robbers had no clothing on except their jackets – were many of them painted or masked; – all carried knives, and spears, and some pick axes of large sizes, some of which latter they left behind them. The police were soon on the spot and a pursuit was commenced which however was unsuccessful seeing that the gang appear to have taken one road (that towards Aberdeen) while the police in the first instance took the lower road toward the stone quarries.
> The amount of money taken was fortunately not much – about $1,150 and a considerable quantity of Chinese clothing being the whole booty. The whole robbery appears to have been well planned, and to have been the result of careful previous observation – and the quickness with which they attained their object and decamped, is really wonderful.

On Murrow, see Christopher Munn's entry on him in Holdsworth and Munn, *Dictionary of Hong Kong Biography*, 331–32.

121 One of the Kuril Islands (also known as Commander Island), on which Russians hunters had killed fur seals since the eighteenth century.

glue. Then, after chasing & shooting a teal, we came home & I had a good row till I was tired & came home so tired I could not sit up to write my diary & my hands were blistered. The *Nankin* went out.

10. Woodgate ill with ague & absent from office. Oakley of course immediately cut & I did nothing all day but read an old paper of 1842 – the time of the Chinese War – out of which got considerable information. After office went to look at curios and in the evening Leonard came. He is horribly ill. The *Hindostan* in which I came out, 1st came out in '42 when it was something out of the common.

11. The *Sybille* fired a salute which startled me excessively. A wet, misty, windy day. Did scarcely a stroke of work at office. Came home in a boat. Saw such a jolly joss – a paper junk – the boatmen would not let us take it.

12. Wednesday. Woodgate came back. Did considerably more work at office. Went to Leonard's and had a jolly row home. Wrote letters. Oakley has applied for and is likely to get the Vice-Consulate of Whampoa. A Chinaman came to office today & the following colloquy ensued. Woodgate: 'Well, who are you?' Chinaman: 'Me Lorchaman.' W: 'But what's you name?' C: 'Yes,' & so it went on. Have written to Henry, Charly, Percy, Uncle, Aunty & Cabban.[122]

13. Thursday. King is going to Foochow in a few day's time for which I am both glad and sorry. Glad for his sake and sorry for mine. It revives all my home wishes but I must make my mind up to this sort of thing. Had a boat home. Saw 24 hawks at one time over the harbour & the Shanghae Steamer was being towed by boat across. A junk has been robbed of 25,000 dollars just outside the harbour. Adkins went to a performance by the privates of the 59th. It was very badly done. King dined at the Governor's and I spent my evening at Leonard's.

14. Friday. A wedding passed by while we were at breakfast. 1st came two fellows carrying lanterns, [sketch] then musicians, then 4 lanterns all gold & jolly, then a lot of fellows in red, [sketch] with cymbals and boys dressed in spangles carrying bells [sketch] & last a gilt & painted chair, making a fearful row. Went to office early. Commodore Elliot is dead from wasting away & is to be taken on board the *Macedonian* tomorrow. A shell & some

---

122 Charles Cabban was a fellow student at Oxford of Alabaster's brother Charles.

powder blew up today, killing a Chinaman and wounding an artillery man. Wrote another letter to Henry and one to Aunt Kate. Adkins is writing to Forrest.

15. Mail went out. Commodore [Elliot – crossed out] Abbot[123] was carried on board the in a grand procession. First went:

Soldiers

Band playing dead march in *Saul* [124]

3 marines   Herse   3 US marines

Yankee Sailors

Governor & Admiral

Nobs of all descriptions

Minute guns firing.

The marines were the ugliest dressed & most inefficient men I have ever seen but the officers are a good looking set. Tatham, Leonard & a τίς[125] Vandercuyp[126] have all been here & L. & T. are going to sleep on rough shakedowns. Little Smoke is getting intelligent.

16. Sunday. At 2 a.m. started 4 of us for duck hunting & after 2 hours pulling, arrived at our destination. Here we anchored & made ourselves comfortable, when by the phosphorescence in the water, a boat was seen advancing. Jimmy hailed it. No answer. Hailed again & again. No answer. Jimmy: 'I think that pirate boat.' 4 guns and a revolver pointed. Last hail and it turns out to be a fishing boat. At 5, day began to break & I woke the others. 5½, some ducks flew close by. 6, got a fishing boat and after some ducks. Breathless excitement. All the heads ducked down & every now & then taking a look. On we go. Nearer. Nearer. Stop. Bang! Bang! & off

---

123 Commodore Joel Abbot (1793–1855) was the head of the US East India Squadron when he died. The *Overland Register and Price Current* (15 December 1855) reports that:

    We regret having to announce the death of Commander-in-Chief of the United States Navy in these seas, which event took place on the morning of the 14th instant. Time does not permit us to give any lengthened notice of the deceased officer. We shall merely state that he was sixty two years of age – that he died a Christian's death, with all that peace and serenity of mind that might be expected to follow a consistent and intelligent Christian life. He was much esteemed by the officers and men serving under his command, and those who most intimately knew him loved and esteemed him the most. The remains of Commander Abott [sic] will be conveyed from the residence of Robert P. de Silver Esq., United States Naval Store Keeper, on board the *Macedonian*, this afternoon to be conveyed to the United States for interment.

124 Oratorio by G.F. Handel (1738).

125 τίς: Greek, *tis*, 'who?'

126 This is likely Antoine Wonter P. Kup, listed as a merchant's clerk working for Lawrence & Co. on the Jury List for 1857 and 1858.

goes the first gun I ever fired. Bang! Bang! Bang! go the other guns & lots of feathers tell a tale. Till 8, dodging after duck. 8, breakfast. Smashed an egg in my hand. 8½ to 10, going after ducks, which we did not get. 10, got some lines & set out fishing. 10.10 to 11, sailing under a splendid breeze. Here we go, cheerily. Is it not jolly? Whrr, whrr. 'There goes our mast.' 'Well, haul it in!' So it is & all's well. Whrr & it is out again. 'Well, let us go home.' Here we go at a jolly rate. 'Let's land on the other side.' 'Very well.' 'What jolly scenery.' 'Look at the *Sibylle*.' 'She is an old tub.' 'Confound these barnacles.' 'Well, come on a jolly little walk.' 'Look at those hawks!' Bang! Bang! 'He's hit.' Here is a feather, there is a dog. 'Shoot him!' Too far back to the boat. Jimmy sails it. Don't we walk along? Drop Tatham. Drop Leonard. Lie down home. Bathe and dress, fresh as a lark. Here is Tatham & Vandercuyp with whom I begin conversation. Hot all the year round in Batavia. Dinner & then awfully tired & so good night.

17. Monday. The *Bittern*, renowned in piratical warfare, came in bringing poor Cooper.[127] He looks fearfully ill. Never was a fellow so changed. He is horribly seedy & has got 6 [month's – crossed out] week's leave. Went to bowling alley this evening. Old Vandercuyp is a regular Dutchman. You could tell him by his breeches, by his cap, by his tout ensemble. All Germans have a peculiarity about their caps. They are all pressed down in front and pulled out behind. [sketch] They all have it & they all smoke & are philosophically and pigheadedly disputatious. How strange it is here. Everyone goes armed in England, no one here.

18. Tuesday. Went to office to read. Did not do too much today. The gun sepoys were practicing today & we stopped to see the soldiers doing pidgeon.[128] They are advancing rapidly to perfection and instead of doing pidgeon in the barracks come out and form squares & all sorts of things.

19. Wednesday. Saw Cooper at office today. He looks much better than he did. He is stopping with Dr Harland. The *Chusan* came in. Molesworth[129] is dead. The Russians have been defeated. The Regatta came off today.[130] A horrid affair. The French licked us fairly & the Yankees unfairly, nasty

---

127 See footnote 47.
128 Hong Kong pidgin, 'work', 'occupation', 'business'; from which, pidgin (or pidgeon) English.
129 Sir William Molesworth (1810–1855), British politician and, at the time of his death, colonial secretary.
130 The full results of the Regatta – run by the Victoria Regatta Club – are given in the *Overland Register and Current Price* on 15 January 1856.

beasts that they are. They got a light boat – more like a gig[131] – to go against ours & won but their other boat – built like ours – came in last. Jardine's boat came in 1st of the China boats. No cup will be given this year. King tried to badger me into an argument about fishing this evening & would not leave off till I lost my temper.

20. Thursday. Went to office early. 2nd day of the regatta. A much better day than yesterday. The *Seroon* won the cup & the *Pique* beat the Frenchmen. It was rare to see Moisoneuve[132] exhorting his men like a father and his children & they all were such theatrical looking coveys & put themselves in such attitudes. One fellow came to the side & ejaculated, 'Helas!'[133] in such a way it was astounding. Then there was a match which the French won & a race for smaller boats in which the *Pique* was 1 & Yankees last & a Chinese boatrace. This is the one no.478 beat and it was a splendid race. What a fearful pace our boats go. 10 miles an hour & heavy looking boats, they look. Saw Wade & Dr Johnson.[134] Vansittart[135] is an energetic looking thin man always bobbing about.

21. Friday. Last day of the Regatta. Got out at two. There was an exciting yacht race & the *Pique's* pinnace beat the *Sybille's*. The *Pique's* marines too beat the *Sybille's* marines and altogether the *Pique* has licked the *Sybille* hollow. Then we had two Russian boat crews against each other. They are fine fellows but not so strong or clean as ours & did not row nearly so well. Saw Commodore Elliot.[136] He is a little man with a hooked nose but looks cross. Am getting in condition for work, both at office and Chinese. King is gone to Antrobus's[137] ball tonight.

---

131 A small, light and fast boat with four rowers and a coxswain typically used to transport the captain between ships or from the ship to the shore.
132 Albert Louis Marie René Pougin de la Maisonneuve (1813–1903), French naval officer, at the time a second-class midshipman.
133 Alas!
134 Rev. John W. Johnson (1819–1872) was an American Baptist Missionary Union missionary based in Hong Kong from 1848.
135 Commander Edward Vansittart RN (1818–1904) of the *Bittern*, famous in 1855 for pursuing and sinking many pirate ships on uncharted, shallow waters in the Pearl River Delta. He retired as a vice-admiral in 1879.
136 See footnote 119.
137 See footnote 96.

22. Saturday. King came in at half past two, very much delighted with his ball. We have all received invitations to the Governor's ball. Went up to the Albany. The other end is being cleared out & we have at length got the cooly to leave the windows open & the place begins to smell savory. Did a good bit of work at office & took my 4 gallons of Chinese.

23. Sunday before Christmas. Went to church to hear a bad sermon, which I could not attend to. Went to Leonard's who is laid up with fever & read *David Copperfield*. How fierce Dickens is about his childhood. Had a Chinese conjurer who did some clever sleight of hand tricks, especially balancing a bamboo. Putting my tinbox to rights & found a photograph of Uncle's. Quid est jollium. Took Smoke out. He follows well. It is fearfully hot tonight.

24–25. Last night I forgot to write my diary but did nothing except work & go up to the Albany, but today I have done much. 1 in the morning, the boy sends in a most gorgeous cumshor.[138] A cake (rather queer tasting) covered with sugar and flowers and altogether gorgeous & a basket of oranges. We went to church & I felt as if I was in church & I thought of Aunty and Uncle. Oh, how I wished I was home. This is the 1st Christmas I have spent from home & on the whole I have enjoyed it. After church we went and saw Leonard. Was introduced to Rymers & Calders.[139] Leonard is better much. Then we had a very pleasant walk up to a bungalow. It is very pretty place indeed but the bungalow is falling to pieces as no one lives there. Came back to dinner. Had a splendid turkey but such a plum-pudding! Half a dozen plums in it & I was unable to drink the queen's health for laughing. Then round a fire we sat & as usual argued till we began to make Smoke stand with his forepaws on a bottle when I thrashed him for obstinacy, for which I am sorry & then we had a laugh at King making his bed & now to bed. Oh Lord! I pray thee grant that next Christmas day I may be merry at home. Grant that Aunty and Uncle are and may continue well, as also all my friends, relations and enemies. Amen. I don't know how it is. I do not fell inclined to go to bed. I want to go home and see them & I shall very soon run away home if I don't feel more comfortable here. Oh Lord! I pray thee grant me industry and talent but above all knowledge of you and thy ways. Amen. Grant I may become a man. Self-reliant. Loving my neighbours as myself.

---

138 Usually 'cumshaw', a thank you gift or, sometimes, a bribe.
139 Edward Reimers (who was, at this time, honorary consul for the Hanseatic City of Hamburg) and Joaquim Vieira Caldas both worked for Dent & Co.

26. Jolly fun. I feel to be a schoolboy again. We are tonight determined to move tomorrow morning & amidst all our confusion old King has been performing all sorts of antics, making me split with laughter. Cooper came in tonight. He is nearly all right. One wears a silver band when at a consulate. Went up to the Albany and had a pretty walk thence. I am very jolly & intend getting a teacher.

27. Got up at 5 & by 8 everything was moved. It was jolly up at the Albany early this morning & it was good fun for King got out of bed, called everyone fools & mad for getting up at an ungodly hour. We have a jolly view of the harbor & splendid breeze. Went to Leonard & Tatham & Lawrence came this evening. They are too fast. Am very sleepy.

28. Got up tolerably early this morning & went half way up the Peak this evening. Tatham, Lawrence & Cuyp came up this evening. Tatham is a great deal too bad. I begin positively to dislike him. Have done a very little Chinese today & hope on the 1st to regularly begin. Am getting mean, stingy and vicious, which is a nuisance but I hope it is only a temporary affection. There is a splendid new midway up the Peak & I sat me down & fancied I was a weary traveller. I hope I may some day be a wise and great man, though at present I be mad, for mad I am to all intents and purposes.

29. A fearfully cold day. Invited Cooper to dinner but he did not come. Woodgate is ill. Leonard is very ill. The Governor is ill. The *Hornet* has sailed under secret orders and I am horribly cold.[140] Did some Premares[141] today.

30. Sunday. Woodgate came as we were at breakfast in an unfurnished room & post prandium in comes Mr Agi whom I gave a fearful blowing up & turned out of the house. He swears he will sue me, which I must confess though I shall most likely win it, I should not like. Went to church & heard a good sermon. Saw the 1st junk I have seen in Hong Kong harbour come in this afternoon.

---

140 *China Mail* reports that the Hornet left on 'a cruise'.
141 The *Notitia Linguae Sinicae of Premare*, translated by J.G. Bridgman (Canton: The Chinese Repository, 1847) based on the work of the Jesuit Joseph Henri Marie de Prémare (1666–1736).

31. Monday. The last day of the old year. The mail came in bringing Payne with it. An inevitable war with America & little news from England or home. A parcel has come out but when I shall get it I do not know. All at home are well comparatively. Percy has got a dog. Today ends a memorable year in my life. I am supporting myself for the first time. I have seen many strange countries & am settled far away from England among a strange people far, far away from home. O Lord! I beseech thee grant next year may be better spent than this.

Finis

Alabaster Diary, Volume 2

1855[1]

January

2. My diary of this year is begun badly because not begun on the first of January. Because I have no object of engrossing interest, because my accounts are not settled & because I have no teacher. Last year was a great & memorable one in my life. I hope that this will be a greater. Yesterday being the first I went to the office till one, to Leonard's and to the Governor's ball where notwithstanding I made no attempt at dancing I was very happy. The lights of the officer's uniforms, the pretty ladies but above all the amusement of seeing people was great. From Sir J. to the middies,[2] each afforded a laugh or instruction. From bullying Dr Parker[3] to eccentric Dr **Hance** you gained knowledge was equally obtainable.[4] You saw how bluster carries one on & how modesty keeps one back. After great fun at supper[5] and great enjoyment on my part, we came home at two this morning. Caine was back to office today, after which we went to Leonard's and have this evening been vainly endeavouring to elucidate the accounts.

---

1 Mistake for 1856.
2 Midshipmen.
3 Dr Peter Parker (1804–1888), American doctor, Presbyterian minister, medical missionary for the American Board of Commissioners for Foreign Missions, and later diplomat, in China. At the time of this diary entry, Parker had just returned to Hong Kong from America in order to take up the position of 'Commissioner of the United States of America to the Empire of China', establishing his legation in Macao.
4 As written in the manuscript.
5 Before 'supper', 'dinn' (i.e. 'dinner') has been crossed out. Alabaster here shows his consciousness of using the word more associated with the upper classes.

3. Another day wasted. I am getting very lazy and Wade is not back. The *Bittern, Coromandel* & *Hornet* are all in – the *Coromandel* with 2 junks & a lorcha. There was a most determined attack on Jardine's the other night by pirates who fired regular volleys at Jardine's sepoys killing one and wounding several. Went for a row among the junks which are beastly tubby things. Saw Leonard who is nearly well. Fighting with Paine I have got a fearful blow on my thumb, which is horrible stiff. Paid the servants & sent the House Coolie off. My plum pudding came. Outside it is fearful but looks jolly inside & dear Aunty had put a lot of macaroons in which are all spoilt & some jolly filberts[6] & one of our venerable pears.

4. Went to office early and today I did the last arrear dispatch. After office we went a good way up the peak & then took to rolling stones down the hills. They went down with a fearful bang. This evening we eat the plum pudding. It was very good indeed. Payne was complaining of lumbago & King said, 'Oh yes. I can easily imagine it. I sometimes have it slightly here,' touching his leg.[7]

5. Went to office early instead of Adkins & worked tolerably hard. We are finishing off despatches at a slapping pace. Wade is not back yet, for which I am sorry as I feel workable. I wish I could go & see some jolly old Chinaman who could not speak a word of English for 6 months. It would be immense advantage to me. The great guns in the battery were firing today. Some of the shots went very near. After office we went to see Leonard and Tatham came in & took the others to look at a centreboard[8] which we shall not buy. Ating[9] went away today on sick leave.

6. Sunday. I regret to say Sunday misspent. I did not go to church. I did nothing. I am wasting time fearfully & am thoroughly ashamed of myself for so doing. Leonard and Tatham came this morning & had some rifle shooting & King entered church in a distingué manner. Skimmed *Martin Chuzzlewit, Oliver Twist* & *Nicholas Nickleby*.[10] The 1st and 3rd are very good but the 2nd I don't like.

---

6   Hazelnuts.
7   Lumbago is pain in the lumbar region, or lower back.
8   A sailing boat with a removeable centreboard rather than a fixed keel.
9   Probably a mistake for Atim, below.
10 All by Charles Dickens: *The Life and Adventures of Martin Chuzzlewit* (1843–44), *The Adventures of Oliver Twist* (1837–39) and *The Life and Adventures of Nicholas Nickleby* (1838–39).

7. This seems doomed to be a misspent year as another day is wasted. I did 1½ hour of Chinese this morning but that is all. Adkins went to office at 8. All the reports of merchants de opium are coming in pitching into Ld Shaftesbury.[11] Made a fizgig[12] for first time in life & bought a Chinese pack of cards in which there are 30 pairs and you pair out. Much ingenuity is displayed in the construction of them. Sic diem peregent.[13] Atim[14] left for Macao today.

8. Went to office early & after went curio hunting with Payne, Lawrence & Adkins. Saw some nice shells. Went to Leonard's. There is some talk of a rising of the coolies.

9. Read in Wade's room till 12. Wade has a jolly lot of jolly books. There are only 16 more enclosures[15] to do & then there is some chance of soon getting out of office & then we shall begin Chinese with a vengeance. Wade is not back even yet nor have I begun my letters or am I getting on well with Chinese. Went for a row this afternoon.

10. Another day added to those wasted ones of this year. I am wasting an immense lot of time. Wade is not back nor does there seem much chance of his coming back. Went to see the soldiers put up their tents. When the word of command is given, No. 1 & 2 will hammer in the pegs, No. 3 & 4, &c. raise tent. All the soldiers immediately knock each other over & in about 7 minutes up rises a tent. 'Get in your tent!' Not a soldier is to be seen. 'Pack tent!' Lo, the tent is down, the pegs are out and all is packed in a bag & marched off & off we go too.

11. We are getting up arrears at a fearful pace at office & what is better at the end of this month I and Adkins get out of office. Bell is going to be made 1st & Forrest 2nd assistant in Siam.[16] Wrote a letter to Miss White.[17] A fearful gonging is going on.

---

11   Attacking Lord Shaftesbury. See Volume 1, footnote 56.
12   A small firework.
13   Sic diem peregerunt, Latin, 'Thus, they pass through the day'.
14   I have not been able to identify Atim. The 'A' is a typically informal mode of address that, as in this case, precedes a person's given name.
15   Enclosures, here, are documents included in the same envelope as an item of diplomatic correspondence, either between consulates, or with the Foreign Office in London.
16   This actually took place when C.G. Hillier arrived to take up the position as first consul in June 1856. Hillier died four months later from dysentery.
17   I have not been able to identify Miss White but she was evidently a friend in England.

12. Wade came back today bringing two teachers, Miaou & Siang, both very dirty – especially Miaou – who however to atone for it has a magnificent pronunciation & quite puts Siang, an ex-mandarin, in the shade. Well, today they came & are to live in our house. King & I received them & we had a little conversation in which I was quite astonished by my knowledge. However, as Cooper was come to dinner we knew not how to get rid of them but at last we got rid of them with Cooper's help. Cooper dined with us & told us about Forrest who it seems was a fearful liar. We spent a very pleasant evening. Adkins and Payne dining at Woodgate's but that is not the chief news. Robertson[18] has advised the forcible seizure of Chusan & from various things I spect[19] a row as Bowring backs him up.

13. Got an abominable cold. Did not go to church. Wrote letters and was about to commit a great sin but did not. Put my accounts in order. The *Vandalia* came in. Leonard, Tatham & Lawrence came. Leonard is a nice fellow. Tatham is a blackguard and Lawrence is nearly as bad.

14. Wade got us some books but has as yet only given us one. Written by a Manchu of the Canton garrison. Had a read with the teacher. It was capital fun. Wrote letters & finished them all up, viz. Aunty, Uncle, Charly, Henry, Percy, Miss Cox[20] & White. Rather a waste day.

15. Rubicon is passed and I am not sorry for it. I entered not far into the stream, for though pleasure follows perseverance yet pain stops one at the outset, and when long expectation has weakened you, you stop soon & by degrees you enter into the pursuit. Chinese is a difficult language there is no denying, but still in time or as my teacher says, 'man, man'.[21] I hope to overcome the pains and difficulties which are so apt to repel a beginner & though grinding there is no doubt at first is far from agreeable but after a time you get to like it and work away with a will, and when you begin to diffuse what you have till then retained, how great is your delight. Then do you feel the man. What you have toiled for is gained and you are happy. When will this day come for me? When shall I be illustrious? Ah! When? But the instruments for this? When you meet with sharpness and intelligence, hesitate not to turn it to your own account. Linger not because it is of low

---

18 Daniel Brooke Robertson (1810–1881), consul in Shanghai (1854–1858).
19 Suspect.
20 Like Miss White, I have not been able to identify Miss Cox.
21 Chinese, 'Slowly, slowly'.

condition. Out of dross cometh gold.[22] Sic tantum.[23] At a sale today the others have been expending largely for mess[24] & thereon I have had rather a stormy discussion with no result & like all young housekeepers pay more at a sale than at a shop.

16. Very seedy and sleepy. Beautiful walk. Got *Sacred Edicts*.[25] Leonard came dinner.

17. Another lazy day. Must look out. Adkins is working madly. Do not intend to work too much though. It is again determined to send King to Fuhchow in the *Antelope* next Sunday. Tatham has sold Bluff for biting him to Leonard who with Roger[26] came this evening.

18. Had a narrow escape of my life this morning. Adkins had been firing his revolver & not knowing a barrel was loaded, playing with the trigger, fired the bullet passing close by me & afterwards through two partitions. King is to go per *Hornet*. Went with Payne to call upon the bishop.[27] It is rather a nice place but the bishop is a great muff & expects to be toadied & thinks we don't know all about primitives & phonetics.[28] Have had a mat which makes my room jolly. Adkins is madly working.

19. Dies memorabilis.[29] Exit from office where we were told today that we in future were only to come on Mondays which is jolly and will give us lots of time for Chinese. I hope I shall keep up with Adkins at least & I will try to beat him if I can. King is definitely to go per *Hornet* on Tuesday & Payne, Adkins and Tatham go excurtionising tomorrow. All the blacks are going to be turned out behind. Mem: clouds like cotton wool covering mountains.

20. Sunday. Went to Church. The bishop preached. Adkins, Payne & Tatham went out shooting but shot nothing. Staid at home & muddled. I seem to have a faculty for putting things tidy yet am always untidy. However, it gives me great amusement & a muddler I suppose I shall remain for ever & anon. Tomorrow I begin work. Hurrah! How jolly it will be.

---

22 The vocabulary and tone of this passage are reminiscent of Bunyan's *Pilgrim's Progress*.
23 Latin, 'How is this so?'
24 The eating arrangements for a group of people.
25 William Milne, trans. *The Sacred Edict; Containing Sixteen Maxims of the Emperor Kang-He* (London: Black, Kingsbury, Parbury, and Allen, 1817).
26 Alexander Rodger, at the time a merchant's clerk at Dent & Co., where Leonard also worked.
27 George Smith (1815–1871), the first bishop of Victoria (1849–1865).
28 The two components of Chinese characters. 'Primitives' are known now as 'radicals'.
29 Latin, 'a memorable day'.

21 First day out of office. Had 7 hours work at Chinese & at 4 went to Wade who helped me over certain difficulties & then we went to Tatham's & had a sail in the centreboard. It is a jolly boat. Was introduced to Armstrong & Lawrence senior[30] who is a sensible fellow. When we came home Woodgate came. Horribly angry because King had not called upon him. However, King came home in time to make it all square & we went off to the *Hornet* whence we brought off two oldsters & had a walk. Brought them to our place & had a pleasant evening.

22. King went today.[31] It is strange how messes break up. Ours though only of 4 month's duration has had three changes. We sadly miss King. He was a jolly fellow & a clever fellow & I have often looked to him with confidence, while now I am left to my own resources. A French corvette came in today & there was as usual saluting. Atim came back. We went to Leonard who is still ill. Went to Wade & am very sleepy.

23. Got my 8 hour's work but somehow I am not in trim & do not work well while I am about it. Adkins is working like blazes & Payne is doing nothing to benefit him. Had a little writing today among other things & found it deuced hard. The *Bittern* went out for Foochow today & the *Vandalia* took away Dr Parker under fearful saluting. Went to Leonard's who is still ill & Lawrence & Tatham came up pistol shooting. Our houses are assessed at $600 which I think is too much. Heard a rum anecdote. As Payne was crossing the desert a fellow traveller called out to some staid old buffers, 'Look at that camel. He's of a different breed. He's got some brown under his tail!'

24. Did my work and played chess with Payne. I have not yet got deeply interested in work though I hope to soon & then I shall go ahead. I like the *Shung yee*[32] but the *Tseen Tsz*[33] is beastly & how I shall learn it by heart I don't know. Next door is being repaired & it is very cold. Payne is jealous of our working and tries to stop it by, 'Don't works', &c.

---

30 This Armstrong is the father of 'young Armstrong', who Alabaster had already met. See Volume 1, footnote 84. On Lawrence senior, see Volume 1, footnote 115.
31 King departed for his post in Fuzhou.
32 *Sheng yu* 聖諭, the Kangxi emperor's *Sacred Edict*. See above, footnote 24.
33 *Qianzi* 千字, commonly *Qianzi wen* 千字文, the *Thousand Character Classic*, a children's reading primer.

25. Got my full 8 hours which was a great thing though I am not able to work well and steadily yet. Old Miaou protested I was doing too much – that one only wanted to be able to speak, writing being no use. There is some truth in this & I must learn to speak first, but then I shall try to write. He was very talkative & told me all sorts of things. A regular wet day now. The hill is enveloped in mist. Now it is quite fresh & clear & now it is raining cats and dogs. Payne had to go to the office. Had a tumble coming back from a walk to office. Adkins is gone to the Uniao Joviale to see the *Sibylle's* men act.[34]

26. The mail is expected in today but it is not come. This morning it was misty but this afternoon fine. Did little work. Went to the town. Payne got a flute & a canary & is very musical & the Bishop came. He is very polite & the room was in an awful mess but *maski*[35] that Payne bolted to dress & Adkins out of the house & I had the pleasure of receiving him. However, at last Payne came down & Adkins in and we received him in (a most curious) state. Am improving in my chess playing but am ill & fear it will be a bad illness, which God forbid.

27. Sunday. Payne woke us up early with a false alarm of the mail so Adkins & he went up to the gap[36] & I accompanied them half way. After breakfast as we were going to church we met Leonard & Tatham & consequently turned back but went in the afternoon to hear a long but uninteresting sermon & then home where we found Payne, Leonard and Tatham revolver practicing & from that they & Adkins went on to jumping & leapfrog. Only fancy, in the 19th century Her Majesty's subjects playing leapfrog on a Sunday afternoon. Well, I see no harm in it but I wish Tatham could control his tongue as he goes on. The other day it seems one of the bulls smashed a house on the other side as they were practicing & a jolly rising is contemplated by the Chinamen. It is found out that they mean if not

---

34 This was likely in the Club Lusitano, one of the two Portuguese clubs in Hong Kong at the time. Nicholas Dennys wrote in his *The Treaty Ports of China and Japan* (London: Trubner & Co.; Hong Kong: A. Shortrede & Co., 1867) that 'there are five clubs in Hong Kong, viz. – 2 English, 1 German and 2 Portuguese: – one of the latter containing a well constructed little theatre and concert room' (p. 14). On naval theatricals from a slightly earlier period, see Gillian Russell, *The Theatres of War: Politics, Performance and Society, 1793–1815* (Oxford: Oxford University Press, 1995).

35 Hong Kong pidgeon, 'no matter', 'anyhow'.

36 Victoria Gap, the space between Victoria Peak and Mt Gough, now the terminus of the Peak tram.

prevented to set fire to Taiping shan³⁷ – their own quarter – & while the soldiers and sailors are putting out the fire to attack the merchants' houses. Saw Mrs Winchester³⁸ – a stout tall lady – at church. The mail is not yet in.

28. Thanks to the Lord my disease turns out to be only a little relaxation. Dempster came and I have to wear a sort of belt. The sepoys are having a house built for them & then we shall have possession. A naval officer was robbed near our place the other day at 1 o'clock & it is not safe to go out alone unarmed. Went to office. Robertson is still sore about the Inspectors.³⁹ It is now fate and I am tired.

29. Went up a ravine and had a bath in fearfully cold water.⁴⁰ The hills here, if seen at a distance, are brutal but when you get to the ravines they are beautiful. Did Chinese all today without making much progress. Old Miaou is going to get me several things. Had a row with a stationer who wanted to overcharge me. Went up a ravine with Payne & after dinner, thinking that there was a reception at the Governor's, we went there & were ushered into a room, when after a short time we discovered that there was a grand dinner and no reception. So after waiting a long time, away we came.

30. Went to the Governor's to breakfast & saw Mrs Winchester. Enjoyed myself very much indeed. The more I see of the Bowrings the more I like them, especially the old lady. It was a reception, it seems, last night but they were late at dinner. However, it is all right now. After breakfast, as luck would have it, in comes the mail – the *Cadiz* – and off to it we go. No news & no Glynes. Then to office where I got a Medhurst⁴¹ & some letters for Adkins who has had, I am sorry to say, some bad news. Home, tiffin, work at Chinese. Stanley's book is colloquial, it seems.⁴² Letters. Aunty is better.

---

37 The area on the upper slopes of Sheung Wan where Chinese people lived in Alabaster's time.
38 Jane, née Black (1820–1867), was the wife of Charles Alexander Winchester (1820–1883), originally a naval surgeon who transferred to the Consular Service in 1842 as medical officer in charge of Hong Kong. He served in many of the treaty ports in China and then in Japan and retired in 1870. During the period covered by the diary, he became vice-consul in Canton.
39 The inspectors of customs, associated with the Provisional System, see Volume 1, footnote 60.
40 Glenealy Ravine or Elliot's Vale, covered over at the end of the nineteenth century, and now simply Glenealy.
41 From the context, probably W.H. Medhurst senior's *English and Chinese Dictionary* (Shanghai: The Mission Press, 1848).
42 Henry Stanley, trans. and ed., *Chinese Manual: Recueil de phrases chinoises, composées de quatre caractères, et dont les explications sont rangées dans l'ordre alphabétique français* (London: Harrison and Sons, 1854).

Uncle has better hours but worse pay. Henry is cramming like mad. Charly is at Brighton. Percy is a jolly little fellow. Sarah Poulton is going to be married. Aunt Kate is better & that is all.

31. Last day of the month. Have not done much but yet have made a little progress. Today had a jolly morning at the *Shung yü*[43] & a jolly bath & a grind at Lord Stanley's book and Wade came & blew up the teachers & seemed dissatisfied & Leonard came & has a new cold, poor fellow & I & Payne went & brought Tobler[44] to dinner & we had rather good fun. Forrest wrote today about his tailor's bill saying that Mr C. Bowring would pay it & so ends the month.

Januarius peregit labores
Elsi qius est que shores
debet ut tu celorequies
atop of your bedes[45]

February

1. Truly was Time depicted with wings for he is flying at an awful pace. However, though slowly, I am I think making a little progress. Just as I & Adkins were getting on jollily with the *Shung yü* a note comes wanting Adkins at office and I am wanted tomorrow. However, Wade is going to speak about it. Did a little work this evening & all together, though I have not nearly done all I wanted, yet I have done a little. I have no time for reading. The *Sybilles* have gone and the *Macedonian* is going.

2. Bathed and worked til 4. The *Sybill* has returned with Dent, 1st Lieutenant, dead. Went out after 4 o'clock & got some beautiful japan[46] boxes very cheap – 5, one inside the other – for $5. Payne got some bronzes & Adkins 2 swords. Things are fearfully cheap because of the new year & crackers are abundant. Worked this evening and now to bed.

---

43 Rendered, above, as *Shung yee*. See footnote 31.
44 Julius Tobler, clerk at Bover Bros & Co., Ningbo.
45 Quasi-Latin, 'January's labours have passed/ And so those on these shores/ Should quickly go to your rest/ Atop of your beds'.
46 A kind of black varnish.

3. Sunday. Sat in flannel nearly all day in an awful state of laziness. Leonard came to our shop and we to his. On the road whither we saw some drunk Chinamen. The first I have seen. Dent on the *Sybill* is not dead. I am always horribly premature. Did my accounts. Find to my joy I have about 80 dollars in hand.

4. Awfully cold day. Went to office. Sir John is going to Japan in June. I hope I shall go too. They are talking of wanting us another fortnight at office, confound it. Just to make us forget all we learn. Did some *Shung yu* with Wade & in the evening with my teacher. Tatham and Tobler came & the *Sybille* went.

5. Great pidgeon. The Chinese New Year's Eve, Shrove Tuesday, &c., &c. Had to go to office. It is an abominable shame. Wade is ill. Then I and Adkins had a walk in the town where we saw great preparations. Everyone in their best clothes & gorgeous to a miracle & all the places had josses & we went into two respectable places. At the first there were a lot of fellows, Howqua[47] among them & they had a table with a red cloth over it & pork & beautiful pyramids of cakes, &c., &c. & they asked us to sit down but we declined & crackers kept on going off, not like English crackers but jolly large ones with hundreds of bangs & every boat had red paper on it & an old workman brought a tray with a cooked cock, &c., &c. on it & burned some paper & poured liquid into little cups & bowed & then went away & we went into another house & they offered us cigarettes & Adkins had one & we saw several muzzy[48] Chinamen and it was jolly & then we came home, crackers still going on & fired off some crackers & then Payne dining at Duncanson's.[49] I and Adkins went to the Governor's reception where there were lots of ladies none of whom I knew however & a Siamese nobleman who seemed very much out of his element & had a Portuguese Interpreter & the Admiral[50] who as well as his secretary are jolly looking fellows & Lane[51] who is a young and clever looking fellow & I was again

---

47   This was Wu Chongyue 伍崇曜 (1810–1863), the son of the more famous Howqua, Wu Bingjian 伍秉鑑 (1769–1843). Howqua was a rendering of *haoguan* 浩官, 'Great Officer' and was an informal designation for the head of the merchant house known as the Ewo Hong (or Yihe hang 怡和行).
48   Tipsy, drunk.
49   At this time, Edward Ford Duncanson (1833–1899) was a merchant's clerk at Gibb, Livingston & Co. Later in life, he became a director of P&O, the London and County Banking Company, and the Hong Kong and Shanghai Bank.
50   James Stirling, see Volume 1, footnote 81.
51   Odiarne Tremayne Lane (1834–1856), a cousin of Sir John Bowring who came to Hong Kong as his private secretary before moving to the Canton Consulate. He was killed when a wall collapsed and fell on him.

asked to ride in the races & Colonels Caine & Graham[52] & Caine[53] & Captain Watkins & lots of fellows & I spoke to Sir John about the office but it was no good & home we came. Everywhere is illuminated & the Chinese, determined to do it in style, have set fire to one mountain & made immense fires on two others & crackers &c., keep on going off & it is jolly. The Chinese rockets are beastly but there is a sort of thing like a small canister of powder which makes a fearful row & though the reception was rather slow, yet I am jolly, jolly, quemadmodum[54] jolly. Saw Lawrence senior. The cad was in an awfully loud coat & also two of the Three Graces – two horribly ugly old women – & now I am going to bed to try to sleep.

6. Chinese New Year. A lazy day. Did no work. Payne went to office where Wade was not & then had a jolly row from East to West Points & then a walk through the town. All the Chinamen in their best clothes dressed awfully splash and walking about in their best, giving cards & bowing like blazes and the streets paved with crackers. It was good fun to see all the little buffers dressed in red & pink & all sorts of gorgeous array & chinchinning like blazes or crackers & all as pleased as punch & we shelled the sepoys with a new sort of firework & then home after a sail in Lawrence's centreboard. After tiffin, up come the two Lawrences, Tatham & Leonard & we have rifle practice & then fireworks & then the Lawrences and Tatham depart, we agreeing to go down after dinner to see the fun in the town. But after dinner it began to rain & as these philosophical Chinamen will put it off till tomorrow, we did not go but had jolly fun pegging[55] crackers. Leonard & I against Adkins and Payne in which we got the worst. It seems that though in anticipation of an attack the troops were patrolling all night & all the men of wars' men were on shore. Two attempts were made to fire the town. The *Pique* went out today for practice.

Mem: new rockets without sticks & self propelling shells

Mem: Japan

---

52 Henry Hope Graham (1808–1886), served in China from 1852 to 1859. From 1857 he was a member of the Hong Kong Executive Council.
53 This repetition occurs in the manuscript.
54 Latin, 'how extremely'.
55 Throwing.

7. Got up horribly late. Did some work. Went to Wade's. Wade not at home. Then to Tatham's & Leonard's & then home in the evening. The 2 Lawrences, Tatham, Leonard come up and we have crackers, rockets, clucks,[56] new sort of Catherine wheels, magazines which make as much row as an 18 pounder & a jolly pelting match & now we must settle down to work. Deuced hard. Had an invitation to breakfast from Colonel Caine for Saturday. When in at Leonard's, Calders came suddenly in. He is a rum buffer.

8. Rather a better spent day than yesterday. This morning Adkins & I got the pronunciations of all the first chapter of the *Shang yu*. In the afternoon till 3½ I did that & various other pidgeon & then we went to Wade & had a jolly half hour's work and in the evening we had the teacher in and had an hour & a half of conversation, in course of which we heard of a jolly little dog belonging to the emperor which lights his pipe for him[57] & today I enquired about all the student interpreters. Lane will learn it in two years more. Jones[58] never. Adkins in three years. Cooper in three years. King from impediment never. P.[59] never. I think this plan of having conversation a jolly one though awfully tiring.

9. Got up at half past 7. Did a little work and then to Colonel Caine's to breakfast & it really was a capital one. Lane was there as well as Messrs Scharf & Walkinshaw[60] and another fellow. Caine is a rum old buffer, a great epicure & altogether an Indian Colonel, who I believe are the jolliest fellows going. Did some Chinese after our return, Lane coming with us & in the evening old Miaou taught me chess. It is very unlike the English though it has the same number of men & squares & tho' the chief object is to take the King & so give checkmate – & the Chinese say 'chang'[61] when they check

---

56 Presumably a type of firecracker.
57 This was a Pekingese. The first five Pekingese dogs in England had been taken from the old summer palace in Beijing when it was attacked in 1860. One was presented to Queen Victoria, who named it Looty.
58 Charles Treasure Jones (b. 1838), at the time a student interpreter who, like Alabaster, arrived in Hong Kong in 1855. He had a 12-year career in the Consular Service before being dismissed for misappropriation of funds. Proceedings against him for embezzlement and for bankruptcy in Shanghai were both unsuccessful. For a time, he owned and edited newspapers there. He later emigrated to Sydney where he was twice more declared bankrupt. In 1898, his estate was 'released from sequestration' and his debts paid.
59 Payne.
60 John Scarth and William Walkinshaw were both merchants at Turner & Co. at this time. Scarth was also author of *Twelve Years in China: The People, the Rebels, and the Mandarins* (1860) and three short books with the title *British Policy in China* (1860–61).
61 *Jiang* 將.

you – there are only 6 pawns & the board is divided into two by a river which elephants cannot cross. There are 6 pawns which advance one step a time till over the river when they can go either straight forward or sideways, horses or knights who move like ours, two sz[62] who move 1 step like bishops & who are limited to 5 squares, 2 seang[63] or elephants who move as bishops but only 2 steps at a time, 2 paou[64] who move as rooks save not being able to take a piece unless there is another between them, & kuen[65] who move exactly like rooks, & one mandarin or king who moves one step at a time & another peculiarity is that the pieces are put on the corners not on the squares. I fancy it is easier than chess as I learned it so easily but it is rather a jolly game and I rather like it. Wade has after all his talk only written one chapter of the *Shangyu*.[66]

10. Sunday. Leonard came to try his gun. Went to church where the bishop delivered an impressive sermon. Came home. Had a jolly climb up to a ravine but did not go so far as the others. Came back and wrote letters to Henry & Uncle. More chess & now to bed.

11. A tremendous wind. Very cold & raining. Went to office as usual on Monday after which had a little conversation with Wade who gave us a short examination in which I do not think I came off worst. Wade appears riled about the queries I put. I don't care. I thought I was right. Came home. The Shanghae Mail came in & the *Barracouta*. Had a game at chess with Payne with whom, like a fool, I have entered upon a match of 11 games & afterwards had two games with the sinsang,[67] one of which I lost & the other won. Kings cannot be face to face nor can they or the 2nd bishops move out of the enclosure. He says it was invented by Chaou Kwangyin[68] who lost Hwashan by it. There has been an amusing tho' serious emeute[69] in the North. The Manchoos have double pay of the Chinamen & the military

---

62 *Shi* 士/仕.
63 *Xiang* 象/相.
64 *Pao* 砲/炮.
65 These pieces are commonly called *ju* 車/俥 in Mandarin. It may be that 'kuen' is Alabaster's attempt to reproduce the Cantonese pronunciation of this character, 'Geoi' in first tone. The apparent differences in these two romanisations are reduced by bearing in mind that, in the romanisation system of Mandarin, Alabaster was using 'g' sounds rendered as 'k', while 'k' sounds were rendered as 'k' followed by an apostrophe.
66 Wade's work on the *Shengyü* or the *Sacred Edict* appears in his *Hsin Ching Lu* (see Introduction). Alabaster is correct in his assertion: only the first section of the *Shengyü* appears in Wade's primer.
67 Chinese, *xiansheng* 先生, 'teacher'.
68 Zhao Kuangyin (927–976, r. 960–976), that is Song Taizu, the first emperor of the Song dynasty, who (it is said) lost Huashan or Mt Hua to the Daoist sage Chen Tuan (d. 989) in a chess game.
69 Uprising.

chest being nearly empty, they determined to bring the Manchoos down to Chinese pay. This, on payday, caused a row in which 3 Manchoos are killed. Thereon, the Tartar General demands 10 Chinese to revenge it on. The Governor General, to decide how many he shall give, reviews the armies and after it says the Manchoos are not better than the Chinese, whereon the Manchoos kill him & the Chinese kill the Manchoo general & the military treasurer, a Manchoo & the Manchoos kill the criminal judge, a Chinaman, & then there is a general row which is said to threaten the Empire.[70]

12. All the morning it rained & we had to go to office where I did more work than usual. We are to go every day till the mail goes. Came home. Did some work finishing my vocabulary of the 1st Chapter[71] & then I & Payne went to the reception. No one there but Mr & Mrs da Silver,[72] the Attorney General[73] & the family but I had a very pleasant evening & did not waste it entirely. Mrs Da Silver I am sure I know. She is a pretty woman & I am sure I know her. Sir John and the Attorney General were talking to each other, so Miss Edith sang & Mrs da Silver & Mrs Winchester & Payne & Lane & it was very jolly & as seeing that I have no chance of getting on here & besides wish to go to Japan I began operations in a conversation with Miss Bowring who I like very much.[74]

13. Had to go to office again, confound it. From Wade's report the Chinese rebellion is dying out but there is other news. Winchester comes down to Canton. Morrison[75] goes to Ningpo. Wade doing his pidgeon here & Gingell[76] is thinking of cutting the service. Hughes came down today. According to his account they are rather fast at the Consulates but have lots of time for Chinese. Hughes is a jolly fellow from what I have seen

---

70   I have not been able to identify these events.
71   See above, footnote 65.
72   This was likely Robert P. de Silver, from Philadelphia, the first US consul to Macao. In 1854 he decamped to Hong Kong and started a family business, De Silver & Co. His wife's name was Emily Bob. See Vincent Wai-kit Ho, 'Duties and Limitations: The Role of United States Consuls in Macao, 1849–1869', in *Americans and Macao: Trade, Smuggling and Diplomacy on the South China Coast*, ed. Paul A. Van Dyke (Hong Kong: Hong Kong University Press, 2012), 143–52, 144–45.
73   Thomas Chisholm Anstey (1816–1873), the controversial attorney-general of Hong Kong (1855–1859). See Peter Wesley-Smith's article on him in Holdsworth and Munn, *Dictionary of Hong Kong Biography*, 6–8.
74   Edith Bowring (b. 1831) was the seventh Bowring child.
75   George Staunton Morrison (1830–1893). Son of the famous Robert Morrison (1782–1834), he later became consul in Nagasaki.
76   William Raymond Gingell (1817–1863). Evidently, Gingell did not 'cut the service' as he was appointed first British consul in Hankou in 1860 and died there in 1863.

of him. A sharp nose, a fresh face and curly hair. Payne tried to punch my head today & cut his fingers for his pains. Won 2 games of chess in my match tonight.

14. Went to Wade today to complain about going to office. He is making a jolly vocabulary among other things. It is to be a splendid one. Hughes is a jolly fellow. Had, like a fool that I am, a row with Payne. Wrote a letter to Aunty & now to bed.

15. At office. All the morning I was in a fearful rage but we are to be out again on Monday. The mail went today. Sent letters to Aunty, Uncle, Henry, Percy and Aunt Kate & Katy. After office went down town & got paper, &c. Hughes is a rum fellow but has been rather fast. All the evening we were singing.

16. At office as usual. Vansittart has been slogging the pirates like fun. Had a walk with Adkins partially up the ravine & afterwards Leonard, Tatham & Lawrence came up & we had cards in the evening. What a fool I am wasting all my time. Hang it.

17. Adkins went out shooting with Caine and **Repton** and 30 or 40 coolies at 4 o'clock in the morning & came back with a bag of a pheasant and a partridge. Leonard came to breakfast and after we went out behind shooting and walking. I rammed a wad down each of Payne's barrels & there he was, fuming and swearing like blazes. He really could not think how it was it would not go off & I set him to reload it and prime it & had some prime fun. Lawrence came too. I, like a fool as I am, indulged in a swear against that damned beast Hance before Hughes. It will all get to his ears.

18. Went to office, nominally for the last time. Got a jolly little dog – half English. This evening had the teachers in and had a confab with them.

19. The first day of the Hong Kong races.[77] Worked all the morning with Adkins & after tiffin went to the races with Adkins & Leonard. Thousands of Chinamen were there & jacks & soldiers & as they were the first races I had ever seen, I was deeply interested. Stewart in the Artillery won two races. A fellow in Jardine's another. Little Birge[78] another & one of the

---

77 The Race Meeting was extensively reported in the *Overland Register and Price Current* (15 March 1856), the previous edition including tips from 'Chanticleer', 'Wong-nei-chung Foxes', and 'A Man in the Corner'.
78 I have not been able to identify Stewart or Birge.

officers another. Chumly[79] though a good rider could not dodge it. There was only one episode, viz. a horse ran away & a drunken jack caught it & rode it full tear round the course. Such lots of kept women were there, some dressed in English style & looked very jolly & altogether it was a jolly day though I did not feel as excited as I thought. Jacks & soldiers near the end being drunk were rather disgusting.

20. A splendid day though rather hot. Worked away jollily. Am nearly square. Second day of the races. Did not go. Stopping at home & finishing the 2nd chapter of the *Shang yü*. Went to Wade but Wade was not in so home we wended, stopping by the way to look at the washerwomen beating the clothes on smooth racks & scrubbing them with brushes. In our bathing place up the ravine there are fish. I intend to go & get some of them. Had a jolly walk with Adkins & we found a splendid shady place where we sat down.

21. The last day of the races. A capital day. I have made up my mind to waste no more days yet a while this morning worked in an unsatisfactory manner. Did a little *Shang yu* & this afternoon went to see the races. Had capital fun. There were lots of people. Saw Leonard & Tatham. One rather good race for the Canton Plate & a jolly match between Oysters and Hot Cockles,[80] one being nowhere & the other brought in by his pony, but best of all was the race for the native purse. All Chinese riders. One was pitched off hand.[81] Two came in all proper, one winning by 6 or 7 lengths. One was ignominiously led back & the others either bolted or stood still.[82] One of the riders was on lots and preciously rum he looked & after that there were foot races & wrestling between jacks. Various strange sayings coming out: one fellow going up to another said, 'Yes, we've had a little go. We'd a dozen of brandys & a dozen of ale between colas & various things of the sort' & has[83] we came home we heard talking. Some fellows off the *Pique* holding forth about Petropaulski:[84] 'Why d'y'see, the French admiral was going in, so we

---

79 At this time, Francis Chomley (1822–1892) was a mercantile assistant at Dent & Co. Later, he became a senior partner and was the first chairman of the Hong Kong and Shanghai Bank. He was also a member of the Hong Kong Legislative Council.
80 This race was actually the China Stakes, and the horses concerned were Amoy Oysters and Hot Coppers, *Overland Register and Price Current*, 15 March 1856.
81 Straight away. The *Friend of China*, 15 March 1856, reported that: 'Three or four riders dismounted involuntarily during the race.'
82 'This usual amusing race which was to have been in heats was unexpectedly terminated in the first, by no one coming in except one out of a lot of 8', *Overland Register and Price Current*, 15 March 1856.
83 As.
84 Now, Petropavlovsk. See Introduction.

goes up into the riggin' – they made us man the riggin' – to give him 3 cheers & do y'see, he turned back & wouldn't go in & we were between 4 batteries. We lost 46 men first shot. 360 in our company. When we came back we were only 300 & the bloody old admiral[85] shot himself, fear the Roosians should do it,' and totocheyangti shte[86] tending to show disgust at their leader & allies. This evening had a long confab with the teachers & now I lazily am going to bed. The teacher says the Russians pay tribute & that the English did the same sometime ago. The *Coromandel* came in. Ta tsoleaou te shte wopuchilaou[87] – goodnight. One race was capital, Magniac[88] winning it. 'Off they go.' 'No chance for grey. Brown will have it.' Once round, brown will have it. 'Yes! Ten to one on brown! Who will bet against brown?' Twice round, brown is sure of it. 'Yes! No, yellow will! Brown for ever.' Three times round, this is a long race. 'Brown! Hurrah, hurrah, hurrah! No, yellow! Ay! No! Yes! Brown, forever!' Round the corner, brown first. 'Hulloh! Grey first, by jingo! Ahahah! Cleverly done.' 'I'll wrestle any man. I'll take the black man. I dearly love a black man. I've been in Afrika, in Asia, anywhere you can name. How d'ye know to call a fellow? Fukky is a blaguard[89] name.' It properly means fu-ki,[90] which is jack, d'y'see?

22. What a blessed fool I am this evening. Because Payne made himself disagreeable to me, I must needs do to him. I really must learn to control my temper. It is getting unbearable. Played whist & wasted my time. The *Coromandel* it seems smashed 5 out of 25 Junks seen cruising about by a shooting party.[91] The *Winchester* went out to practice & I & Adkins, after twice seeing Wade & spending a day of hard but unsatisfactory labor, we went up a jolly ravine where there are many jolly things – animal & vegetable – to be seen & now to bed at 11¾ pm.

---

85   Admiral Price, who committed suicide the morning the fighting began.
86   Chinese, 'Duoduo zheyangde shide 多多這樣的是的', 'And a lot more like this'.
87   Chinese, 'Ta zuolede shide, wo bu zhiliao, 他做了的是的我不知了', 'What they did, I'm not really sure'.
88   At the time of the diary, Herbert St Leger Magniac was a mercantile assistant at Jardine, Matheson & Co. He later became a partner in the firm and from 1862 was Danish consul in Guangzhou (1863–1877).
89   Blackguard.
90   Hong Kong pidgeon, possibly, Fa-ke, 'American', from Cantonese *faa-kei* 花旗, 'flowery flag', the US flag.
91   Reported in *China Mail*, 28 February 1856.

23&24 24. Sunday. Yesterday & today are so mingled that I scarcely know when yesterday ended & today begun. However, it is great news. The brutes have tried to burn Hong Kong for plunder.[92] Yesterday we worked much as usual and had a climb up the ravine & the *Winchester* was firing & Adkins & Payne went to dinner at Repton's & came home today at 12½. I was sitting up doing Chinese till 1 & Adkins & Payne were getting to bed when we hear the bugle at the barracks & Payne rushes in crying fire & we rush to the window. All the sky is lighted up. Flames are seen & it is evident there is a fire, so we quickly arm & put on great coats & off we go, Hughes refusing to get up. As we near the town we see it is a tremendous fire & as we get farther in there is immense confusion. All the Chinamen armed with swords & rushing to & fro, some with their property yelling and shouting at everyone & thieves trying to take it away & regular row & fearful smoke and flames. In Gough Street we find a policeman with musket & bayonet vainly endeavouring to stop a fellow bolting with a bag of rice & we help him & pass on. No troops here yet. No sailors & the flames bursting out on all sides. Only 5 or 6 houses alight yet, but those blazing fearfully. Other houses blazing now. Here is a police engine. Work it! Here come the Spaniards. Fine fellows. First on the field. Here come the soldiers & the engineers & everyone. Everyone here, no one head. Sir John running about everywhere. All the officers not being as yet able to do anything. We look about us.

---

92 The fire was reported in the *China Mail*, 28 February 1856:
> An alarming fire broke out in or close by the Western Market about midnight on Saturday last, which destroyed nearly a hundred houses, with property estimated by the Superintendent of Police, it is said, at about $20,000; but how he fixes on so low an amount, we cannot imagine, as one firm alone, the Chaeng-Ty Hong, lost upwards of $12,000. A stiff breeze was blowing at the time, which, with the wooden verandahs erected in defiance of Government proclamations, may account for the extent of the conflagration.
> As was to be expected, the men-of-war's-men under Commodore Elliot and his officers, were conspicuous for their activity. The Spanish war-steamer *Reina de Castilla* sent fifty men with an engine, which did good service; and the soldiers worked well, but might have behaved better, and been kept more under control; while Tam Achoy's engine (American-made) worked admirably under the direction of Mr G.L. Haskell. There was of course the usual amount of drunkenness – and of plundering, in which some of the Native police took an active part; which more and more tends to shew the necessity of a Special Constabulary force to act upon such occasions; for civilians alone are capable of distinguishing the thief from the honest man saving his property.
> To prevent the fire spreading further to the westward, it was found necessary to blow down some houses, and though every warning was given, and effort made, even to the employment of force, to drive the Chinese from the spot, eleven men were buried in the ruins, of whom four were got out alive. Of the seven killed, only three have been claimed, the others probably having been thieves engaged in pillaging the houses.

The fire was also reported in the *Overland Register and Price Current*, 15 March 1856.

Here's Ricketts,[93] Caine, Repton, Oakley, Pereira,[94] Leslie. Everyone going to pull that house down. 'Put the rope through the window. Hurrah! Pull away!' I haul away. We all haul. It shakes. Hurrah! It bends down. It is a rotten place. 'Throw out the bed, the chairs, everything! Hurrah!' It has broken out up there. The P&O sheep are all loose. The soldiers are working. 'We want hands. Would you send the sailors?' 'Can't you use these Chinamen?' 'No, they won't work.' 'Well, all right.' I lose Adkins & Payne. Go to Oakley. Dodge about. Plundering going on like blazes. There tumbles a roof in. 'Look at that flaming street. Is it not grand? Have you seen all the Chinamen saving their property?' 'Lotsee!'[95] Some Chinamen are working.' Armstrong is directing a hose. 'Oh! Here you are! Did you see that cat jump from one burning house to another?' 'No.' 'Let us help Armstrong.' All the merchants are here. The Fokis begin to work. 'Haul away!' 'Send the water in!' 'Can't get through there.' 'Get a long hook.' Adkins & Payne rush in, haul away, smash down some woodwork, haul away some more. 'I am ducked!' 'So am I.' 'Never mind.' Here the water comes down my back. 'Haul away!' 'There is an opening!' 'Pump! Pump!' 'Smash that glass in the way!' 'Let us go down this street.' 'Hoof up!' 'I can't stand this. It's awful. I shall be stifled.' 'Come back!' We get a drink. They are going to blow up a house. Houses are being pulled down. Bang! There is the explosion. 'Let us come round and see.' We lose Payne. 'Oh! Here is Hussam.'[96] Well, how does it go on. They are getting it under. Lots of people are standing about quietly chatting. 'It is not so bad as that in '51.[97] We shan't have another yet awhile.' Here is Tait:[98] 'Oh, have you heard a lot of Chinamen were blown up in that house?' They are getting them out. Here comes a poor fellow with both legs broken & his head damaged. 'Let us come & see. We may be of use,' says Adkins. So off we go, Tait with a sword by his side. 'Oh, I can't stand this. The smoke is awful. It is suffocating.' All the rice bags are lying about. They dig out one dead. Those brutes, the Chinamen. They treat it like a bit of wood. A policeman is plundering. A sailor who was blown up too is helping to get another poor fellow out. He is out. 'How many were

---

93 There were two John Ricketts in Hong Kong at the time, father and son. John Rickett senior was the principle marine surveyor of the colony and a justice of the peace; his son worked at the Pacific and Oriental Steam Navigation Company. It is unclear whether Alabaster is referring to one of these (and mistakes his name) or both (with odd grammar).
94 Edward Pereira, like Leslie, a merchant at Dent & Co.
95 Hong Kong pidgeon, 'Look at that!'
96 There were several people named Hassum (not Hussam) in Hong Kong at this time: Jetha, Purdhan, and Mitha, all of whom are listed as 'clerk'.
97 A fire on 28 December 1851 razed the Sheung Wan market and killed 30.
98 Probably Joseph Priestly Tate, see Volume 1, footnote 116.

therein?' '5.' 'Why, 6 have been got out.' & then home we come at 4½ & don't get up till 11. Awfully hungry. Leonard is here. He slept through it all as did Tatham. Pereira, Calders,[99] Leslie & some one else got their fire engine out without waking him. 200 or more houses have been burnt. The cause is supposed to be incendiarism. Adkins behaved jollily in going up through stifling smoke & stamping a nascent fire out. No European houses were burnt. All the soldiers' bread and lots of stores were however. We go with Tatham to see the ruins. Many people there. In many places it is still blazing. We go to the Chaouchaou house, next door to the blown up house. The keeper tells us he lost 3 or 400 $ by thieves, that the blown up men were thieves & he thinks there are more under the ruins. It was splendidly blown up, no two bricks stopping together & it saved the town. The ruins smell horribly. One house I helped to pull the front off early this morning had got lathes[100] over it by night. Leonard lost & offered a reward for Bluff, who was at Tatham's all the time. King's brother[101] is going to be married to Miss Sullivan.[102] Quid mirabile[103] & I am very sleepy.

25. Went to office. Scarcely anything to do. The mail is expected tomorrow & De Silver's traps are to be sold & he has made a catalogue. Quite a miracle of bad spelling. Mohogony. Pilgrams of the Rhine. Botony. Mcdougly for Macauly, &c., &c. Am going to get one or two things. Had a walk with Adkins. Took Polly & ducked her. She is a jolly little dog if she would only follow. Had two games at chess with Payne. One a draw. One he beat me. Hughes wants to furnish the house handsomely. I don't. There is all the difference. Had a talk with the teacher.

26. Worked Chinese unsatisfactorily. Payne went to the sale. I went to Wade & to Leonard's. Leonard came to us. Carels[104] & singing & I am going to bed dissatisfied.

99 Joaquim Vieira Caldas, see Volume 1, footnote 139.
100 Laths, roof frames on which tiles and slate are fixed.
101 King's brother was Charles John King (1831–1886), who was a merchant in Shanghai. In 1860 he went into partnership and founded the house Chapman, King & Co., with major interests in machinery and wharves. King was also the first chairman of the Shanghai Gas Co.
102 Fanny Rosina Sullivan (1836–1900) was the daughter of George Grey Sullivan, who had died in 1853 while in office as consul in Amoy. King divorced Fanny in 1863. Subsequently, she married Cornelius Thompson of the Admiralty.
103 Latin, 'How extraordinary'.
104 Carols.

27. All the morning worked unsatisfactorily at *Shungyu* with Adkins, we neither being in trim. We did not get on well. After tiffin worked at phrases & made a good many. In fact I have 73 to clear off before Saturday so I must look sharp or I shall not do them. Payne came in having bought a lot of things which I refuse to pay for & tho' it is a great bore must refuse to pay for as it was against my will they were bought. Had a game with Payne at chess, which I was fool enough to draw & afterwards learned to play with Chinese cards & had had a game with the teacher. Then conversation & now to bed as soon as I have done a little more pidgeon. Another Chinaman still alive was dug out of the ruins today & two of the sepoys behind with their wives have been put in quod[105] for stealing wood next door which they did. Pr. et armi.[106]

28. Botheration. The 3 weeks are near an end & I have done nothing today. I first had a game at chess with Payne & so did not begin work till 10½. At 1½ left off tiffin.

Went with Adkins after the things got at the sale which we could not get. Then up the hill some way where I had a jolly blow & then Tobler came to dinner & Vingt-et-un[107] & so sh puh to tsoti.[108]

29. Bitterly cold. I am getting slovenly & lazy. Adkins was out with Lane all the morning & I did talk pidgeon & now to bed it being horribly cold. Wade is ill.

March

1. Another month begun. Did Chinese. Went to Tatham's. Had a sail. Wore my pin. Got some of the things from De Silver's. Came home. Seedy and stupid. Read *The Great Hoggarty Diamond*.[109] It was bitterly cold and ∴[110] Captain Cowper[111] is absent we can't get our pay.

---

105 In jail.
106 Latin, short for 'prudentia et armi', 'wisdom and strength'.
107 The card game known in English as 'twenty-one', closely related to pontoon and blackjack.
108 Chinese, 'Shi bu duo zuode 是不多做的', 'I didn't do much else'.
109 *The History of Samuel Titmarsh and the Great Hoggarty Diamond*, by William Thackeray (1848).
110 Because.
111 William Cowper (d. 1856) of the Royal Engineers, at the time acting as surveyor general, dying on 26 December, while dispatched to Canton. He 'was superintending the pulling down of some Chinese houses outside the factory, when one of them suddenly fell on him, from which he sustained such extensive injuries as to cause his death in less than three hours'. Henry Stooks Smith, *The Annual Military Obituary for 1856* (London: Longman, Brown, Green, Longmans, and Roberts, 1857), quoting 'Admiral Seymour's Despatch'.

2. Sunday. With Payne, Adkins & Lane I went to the other side & spent a jolly day. Adkins & Tatham had guns. It was about as hot as it is on a hot summer's day in England. It was jolly and woody. Very pretty & quite at times reminded me of old England. Saw 4 tree & one proper pheasant. Had a jolly sail and capital fun. A book in my pocket & while they beat, I lay me down to read & it was fearfully cold coming back & I slept all the evening on our new couch, which is very hard. Hance called during our absence & Lane came to dinner. He is a jolly clever fellow & I am disgusted with myself. Hughes is a beast & a fool I am. Satis Ming cubandum est mihi nam malleum non est.[112]

3. Got up late & lazy. Had breakfast & in came Lane to invite us to the Governor's today. Went to office. No work, so back we came. Went again to get our pay. Back again without it. Went out fishing as tho' my fishing days were not over. Caught naught. Dressed & to the Governor's where I had the pleasure of escorting Miss B. into dinner, getting me on my wrong side of course. It was a tolerable dinner & I & Miss B. somehow kept on laughing at each other. After the ladies had been gone 2 minutes, in we went & the other 3 went to billiards, I like a fool stopping to hear attempts at singing & finding myself detrop.[113] At last, we came away. Sir J. still working. Snow the other day. I forgot to mention, it froze on the Peak for the 1st time known.

4. Got up late worked Chinese. Hughes won't have the rocking chair & so Payne has to keep it. Mess this moon swallows all my salary et mes depenses. Presque tous mes epargnes et je n'ai que cinquante risdales[114] pour faire les depenses dumois prochain mais ne craignez rien. J'ai persuade (au moins je le cras) les autres a donner une somme certaine au comprador. le nuit ci il y a un bruit d'un feu mais ee n'est que rien l'Eglise Francaise etait encendie et voila tout nous avons receves ce jourer nos salaries[115] & now to honest English. Read an account of the English sailor shot by a policeman who was generally well behaved. Only 3 or 4 cases of drunkenness on duty having

---

112 Latin, 'It is enough that Ming is lying to me seeing that it is not a bad thing!' I do not know who Ming was or what this refers to.
113 Superfluous, unnecessary.
114 Rijksdaalder, rix-dollar, a Dutch minted silver coin that circulated in their colonies and beyond.
115 French, 'and my expenses. Almost all my savings and I have only fifty risdales to make the expenses of next month but do not fear anything. I persuaded (at least I believe it) the others to give a certain sum to the comprador. In the night there is a sound of a fire but it is nothing. The French Church was fired and voila we all received our salaries today'.

been reported. There was a false alarm of the mail. Adkins & Lane went up the Peak. Went to see Wade. He is very bad indeed & here comes an ebullition.[116] Hughes is an unmitigated beast.

5. Worked, walked & wasted time as usual. Worked morning till 1 from 10, afternoon 2¾ to 6¼. Walked from 1½ to 2½. The mail is utterly given up. Wasted the evening playing Vingt-un. I won immensely but am glad to say really that we got in a muss[117] about paying & so nobody paid at all. Hughes makes cocksure of going to Pekin & is going to stay at home ill which will be a nuisance. Nai maski wor so yaou yer puh sh cheko chipa ta sh wormun seang neen shu.[118] My teeth have now been on edge 2 days.

6. The mail not in even yet. Went up to the gap & as we took it easy it was a jolly walk & when you got there & on one side saw the ships & town of Hong Kong & on the other side the sea & islands innumerable, coupled with a delicious breeze & a smell of hay it was jolly. Met Leonard up there. Dempster came to Hughes who will have to lay up. Worked at *Shung yu*. Quarreled with Payne as usual. Went to Wade who is still very ill & who was full of all sorts of dodges & very talkative which I was glad of. Had our usual confab. The teacher told us about the Chinamen fancying eclipses to be caused by a dog eating the moon & therefore they beat gongs.[119]

7. The mail is supposed to have gone down on the Pratas.[120] Had a row with Payne in which for once he certainly was wrong & got in a rage & so till tiffin did nothing. Scarcely after tiffin went out a little way with Adkins & Payne. Came home. Worked. Went to Wade. Non vidi.[121] Came home. Someone off the *Winchester* buried. Worked. Dinner. Payne said rather a good thing. We were talking about wine, beer, &c., &c. At last Hughes said, 'Well, I think Adam's ale is best.' P. then said, 'Who is Adam? Is he an Irishman?' Adkins dined with Colonel Graham & lots of others. Capt. Bushe[122] &

---

116 An angry outburst.
117 An argument.
118 Chinese, 'Nai maski wo suoyao ye bushi zhege jiba. Ta shi. Women xiang nianshu. 乃 maski 我所要也不是這個雞巴. 他是. 我們相念書', 'And in any case I don't want this kind of crap. He is a dickhead. We want to study'.
119 A widespread and longstanding element in Chinese mythology, often noted by Western observers in the nineteenth century, including Samuel Kidd (1841), G.E. Morrison (1895) and Arthur H. Smith (1899).
120 Pratas Islands, in Chinese the Dongsha islands, about 340 kilometres south-east of Hong Kong.
121 Latin, 'I didn't see him'.
122 Charles Kendal Bushe, at this time captain in the 59th Regiment. He was a grandson of the lord chief justice of Ireland of the same name.

an other went out duck shooting & at the 1st discharge sent a duck gun of Gibbs,[123] value £140, into the water. C'est tout.[124] Won my match with Payne, he only having won 1 game, 5 or 6 draws & 7 my winning.

8. Another week is gone like blazes & little or no work done in it, tho' mail is supposed to have gone down & the *Lancefield* is said to be outside. Worked this morning. Tiffin. Went out. Dempster came to see Hughes. Worked. Went to Wade who truly thinks we are very idle. Down to Tatham's intending to bathe. Don't do so. Bring Leonard up with us. Play Vingt-un till we are all getting savage. Work & now to bed.

9. Got up rather late & felt very jolly. Went to church where the bishop preached & then we went for a long row about the harbor. Came home & found Leonard who going for quills[125] in a boat saw 5 pirate junks blazing into 2 others. His boatmen were funky[126] but he went in. The *Barracouta* went out & we had a thunderstorm. Some of the flashes very vivid & now to bed very tired & sleepy. Leonard is sleeping here.

10. Just as we were in the middle of breakfast off goes the guns & all go up tho' it rains like blazes. Leonard is second on board. It is the *Norna*. The *Pera* broke down at Lisbon and so it is so late. I have an awful lot of papers including *Punch's Almanack*[127] & what is better, letters. They are all well tho' Aunty has had to nurse her cook thro' a dangerous fever. Dined at the Meyer's on Christmas day.[128] Charly at Brighton & Percy at Hammersmith. Henry has been to a ball at Hammersmith at the Dunlop's & Ada fancies herself in l.[129] with me. What fun! I shall immediately begin a correspondence with that amiable little girl. Uncle has left the Mill & Mary P., the Travers.[130] Henry is determined to come out here. I am awfully popular at home. Old Jelf[131] has sucked in my letter. Luckily it will be a lesson to me – tho' in future. He was awfully pleased with it & sent it to Aunty for perusal. There is a rumour too that there is peace & now I have been doing Chinese & that is all the news.

---

123 Probably Hugh Bold Gibb, senior partner of Gibb, Livingstone & Co., later chairman of the Hong Kong Chamber of Commerce and a member of the Legislative Council.
124 French, 'That's all'.
125 The use of bird's quills as writing instruments was outmoded by this time (Alabaster's diary is written with a metal-nibbed pen). Instead, quills were filled with gunpowder and used as fuses.
126 Frightened, panicky.
127 *Punch's Almanack* was an annual spin-off publication of the magazine *Punch*.
128 See Volume 1, footnote 111.
129 'In love'. Ada was Ada Dunlop, see below.
130 I have not been able to identify Alabaster's references here.
131 Rev. R.W. Jelf was the principal of King's College (1844–1868).

11. Col. Sibthorpe[132] & Rogers[133] & Cubitt[134] are all dead. Worked at Chinese till 12 & then had to go to office. This mail brings important news. Parkes has brought out a wife. Hague[135] has resigned & Sinclair[136] is to be Consul at Ningpo. Meadows comes out in April. Woodgate is Secretary. Caine is first & Hance 2nd Assistant, so there is a vacancy here again. I have written lots of letters today. To Dr Major,[137] Watley,[138] Cabban, Aunt Kate, Katy, Ada Dunlop & that is all. Had a jolly bathe this morning & tho' I have not done much, have passed a jolly day. *Punch's Almanack* is inimitable. It is so like nature. I wish I could draw like Phiz.[139] Wrote a verse letter to Ada D. Full of humbug.

12. Got up early. Was headachy. Went to office. The rain pouring down cats & dogs. An immense quantity of work at office. Had to stop till 5. Oakley is to be proposed as Vice-Consul Siam.[140] Went down to Tobler to get Adkins. Watch cleaned. Came home. Cards & now mulligrubs[141] and bed feeling that tho' I worked at office my day was otherwise illspent as I have done little or nothing in other respects.

13. Got up tolerably early. Worked Chinese. Had to go to office at 9 & scribbled away at a railroad pace till 4½. Did a jolly lot. There is something satisfactory in working hard. Am going to make a summary of all my letters. It is a dodge of Hughes's. Had the teacher in & talked. He says some hanging is going on in this neighborhood & wrote a lot of letters after it. I shall send away a very heavy mail this time. Rather cold.

14. Awful work at office. Parkes is to take charge of Canton Consulate. Aspinall[142] bolted down here from Shanghae & was sent back again this day. Had a bathe in the evening. The old teacher gave us a long exhortation,

---

132 Charles de Laet Waldo Sibthorp (1783–1855), ultra-Tory MP for Lincoln.
133 Samuel Rogers (1763–1855), poet, banker and art collector.
134 Thomas Cubitt (1788–1855), London master builder.
135 Patrick Hague (1817–1878) was one of the original appointments to the Chinese Consular Service in 1843, when he was 26. He retired as Ningbo vice-consul for health reasons in October 1855 with a pension of 193 pounds.
136 Charles Anthony Sinclair (1818–1897), an 1843 appointment, had a long and distinguished career in the Chinese Consular Service, serving mostly in Fuzhou from where he retired as consul in 1886.
137 Dr John Richardson Major (1797–1876), first headmaster of the King's College school.
138 I have been unable to identify this Watley.
139 Hablot Knight Browne, cartoonist and illustrator (famously of Dickens's novels) who also drew for *Punch*.
140 This appointment never occurred. He retired later in 1856, see below, 8 August 1855.
141 Out of sorts, either due to low spirits or stomach ailments.
142 W.G. Aspinall (1822–1879), merchant with Aspinall, Cornes & Co. in Shanghai and later Yokohama, where he is buried.

which was received with roars of laughter, not to use printed paper for bumfodder[143] & went thro' the motions. Woodgate came back today. He tells me that Wade expects me to do great things one day. Adkins is keeping a strict eye on my progress. Have written all my necessary letters already. Caine is a humbug.

15. The mail went. Hughes breakfasted at Government House. Winchester came down from Ningpo. He is a rum, small, perky, pompous little man. Office till 12. Bilious & lazy. My little dog is ill with I know not what. Had a walk up to the first peak & stopped there watching a hawk hover & then down like a shot. A day wasted in toto. I am a humbug. That is a fact. I wish I was not but I am. Leonard & Tatham came up & T. & Adkins had a bit of a quarrel. Played cards, &c.

16. Sunday. Got up very late indeed. Only just in time for church. On the road whither the Governor's carriage passed me & I, of course, in duty bound saluted & was much amused by Mrs Winchester taking it all to herself. The singing was excellent but my attention was rather distracted by a draft O'Dell[144] preached after tiffin. I put out summer things & dodged about till 4 when we went up to the peak or rather the others did, for I stopped at the first peak after a foolish tiff with Payne. It is strange. I am getting very touchy. It is very foolish. I was jolly on the peak for some time waiting for them but it getting cold I came down leisurely and near the bottom was overtaken by them & we found Leonard at our house. This evening, as well as I could, I read Staunton's *Embassy* for I am fully sleepy. Adkins & Payne have discovered a fellow student at King's, who had a brother killed in the Crimea, dressed as a sailor. They tried but could not get an opportunity of seeing him. My little dog is still ill.

17. How the time slips on. 'Tis like a dream. To office today went I & work did I there. Enough for 10 men & 'twas jolly. Oho! Yes, jolly. Oho! for them & after office was over, I with Adkins to Tatham's did go. A boat then we took & off we did go, down to West Point where there was a very jolly place to bathe, the bottom being sandy & very jolly & a jolly rock whereon one could dress & be divinely happy. Well, we had a jolly bathe. 'The first kick was brickish,[145] my booys.' Well then, home we came & Payne dined at Woodgate's & came home excited and muzzy but Woodgate has a plan

---

143 Toilet paper, thus 'bumf'.
144 Rev. M.C. Odell arrived in Hong Kong in 1849 to work in St Paul's College and, by 1853, he was also acting colonial chaplain. Later, he served in Malta as a military chaplain and in 1878 he was the minister of the All Saints Military Church in Aldershot.
145 Excellent.

for establishing a mess for all the Civil Service. He and Captain Watkins wishing to live up next door. Major ____ in the Ordnance, Mercer[146] & Wade all being willing to join us. In fact we might get a gorgulious mess without much expense or bobbery.[147] Went to Wade today. As usual he is full of his crotchets[148] but I am in hopes he will do something at last which will help me on just a little. Nye Brothers have failed to the amount of 1,500,000[149] & it is an awful smash but the worst of it is it will bring down so many others. Small ones.

18. Woodgate is gone to Canton. The criminals are pardoned & Bowring answered our letter by writing to Colonel Graham who has spoken to Capt. Cowper. Worked Chinese till 3½. Went to Wade with Adkins. Wade has finished the 1st chapter.[150] Then we went out & bathed. It was jolly. 'Oh, that kick out is splendid.' Home, Leonard promising to return with us in the evening. Hughes. First he resisted in reading aloud & then in monopolizing the teacher. To my infinite disgust.

19. Did Chinese as usual & was rather jolly in the morning & Old Chu, a new teacher for Adkins arrived. He speaks for all the world like Mrs Marsh[151] & Seang has returned. Hughes brought a thing partially in Bowring's hand altered by himself, which it seems I have misinterpreted. But be it as it may, I flew out in a passion & we have not spoken since tho' I shall make up if possible tomorrow, warning him not to do it again. Bird[152] is up & Leonard came so we wasted the evening at cards. It has one good effect tho' i.e. I hate them like mad.

---

146 William Thomas Mercer (1822–1879), a notable government official throughout this period, began his career as private secretary to Sir John Francis Davis, his uncle, when Davis became governor in 1844. By 1854 he was colonial secretary and auditor-general but despite essentially running the government for periods during the 1860s, his ambitions to be made governor of Hong Kong or the Straits Settlements were stifled. He retired on medical grounds in 1867 and returned to England. On Mercer, see also Christopher Munn's entry on him in Holdsworth and Munn, *Dictionary of Hong Kong Biography*, 320–21.
147 Commotion, squabble.
148 The *Oxford English Dictionary*'s delightful definition: 'A whimsical fancy; a perverse conceit; a peculiar notion on some point (usually considered unimportant) held by an individual in opposition to common opinion'.
149 Nye Brothers & Co., an American trading company based in Canton, collapsed on 11 March 1856.
150 See above, footnote 65.
151 Mrs Marsh was a Hong Kong milliner married to Henry Marsh, farrier.
152 Alexander Bird (1812–1860), appointed in 1843, and at this time vice-consul at Whampoa. In Bowring's words, he was 'an honest but irascible man whose lack of suavity, deportment, discretion, and self-control had inflicted much disagreeable correspondence on his superiors'. Quoted in Coates, *The China Consuls*, 113.

20. So closes another day. This time last year I was in London & Ada Dunlop and Katy were at our place & I was at home & a schoolboy & now I am in China and I suppose a man. Tomorrow is Good Friday & to think how happy I was last year with all my friends around me makes my throat come up in my throat and I wish I could cry. It would be quite a comfort. Oh, I wish I were home. I am sick of Hong Kong. Shall I ever see Aunty again? I hope so, but it is awful to be out here afar from all I hold dearest in the world. I remember last year perfectly, even to buying figs to solace myself & talking to Mrs Somebody whom I stood in intense awe of – somewhat abated it must be confessed by my appointment – & whose dog I fondled & where I blushed up to my ears hundreds of times & my march for the original bunshop & getting I know not how many Chelsea buns & all sorts of things & coming home & finding Ada & Katy W. almost makes one cry out, 'Hang it all!' Oh, when shall I be home again? I've a good mind to run away for Hong Kong is beastly. I have made up with Hughes & am glad of it. It has cost me a struggle & it was only at the last minute I did so but somehow I did not like to carry it on till Good Friday & I am glad I have not. The sepoys are all going tomorrow & the females have had a most curious dance consisting of stepping backwards & then forwards, bowing low & clapping the hands as they go round, one singing & the others joining in chorus & there were many satirical comments upon us which I have no doubt were very witty, only we did not understand them. The teacher has got a lot of the things for me, viz. the chessmen which Adkins says are very good but which I think might be better & 6 pictures, each being 4 fables & it is quite jolly to have them all round my room & he has got one copy of the book on agriculture and weaving which is a jolly book. Had a read with the teacher & was confirmed in my idea that working at the tones is rot, for as I found with Summers,[153] if I understand the thing and read as if I were talking not reading a lesson I pronounce the tones sufficiently correctly. At least the teacher says so, yet I could not tell the tone of a single character perhaps & I believe we have the tones just as much in English but are sensible & don't bother about them.

---

153 Rev. James Summers (1828–1891), was appointed professor of Chinese at King's College, London, in 1854 having worked at St Paul's College in Hong Kong from 1848. The author of primers on Chinese, he later learned Japanese and moved there in 1873, helping to establish English-language teaching in Japan. His notable students included Nitobe Inazō 新渡戸 稲造 (1862–1933) and Tanizaki Jun'ichirō 谷崎 潤一郎 (1886–1965).

21. Good Friday without buns passed in a semi-unjolly way. The sepoys have all left and so now we have lots of outhouses which is a great comfort tho' this is counterbalanced by the loss of their protection. Someone now is in the verandah. Friend or foe I know not tho' I shall soon. He is just now I fancy by Hughes' room. In the morning Adkins & Payne went to church. The sepoys having previously left & I had in my shirtsleeves composed myself to work when in come Leonard, Tatham & Weevle[154] or some such name & there is practicing with rifles for a few hours & when at last numbers of wonderfully good shots have been fired, we have tiffin & then go out for a bathe. Adkins is out of sorts & would not bathe & Tatham when undressed & in the water thought it too cold but I had a splendid bathe. It was awfully jolly. So, so jolly in fact that I actually threw myself down in shallow water & wallowed in the sand & then home we came & after dinner everyone was cross & sleepy & when I came up we found a rat in my room & chase him but don't get him & now here I am frightened by strange noises wanting yet not liking to go to bed.

22. Up late but had a bath and all day was uncomfortable and seedy. It is abominably oppressive. In the afternoon went out for a swim. Came home. Adkins & Payne have now gone down to the town. Rats are running about my room & I am heavy with sleep. It seems we are to have a peace. If so something will be done in China. Old Payne has just come home having left Adkins behind acting very improperly. It will be very amusing tomorrow.

23. Lazy. Did not go to church in the morning. Sat & talked. Tatham dropping in in the afternoon, sailed & bathed. Payne got a dog. A mastiff.

24. Old Payne stopping at home with the fruits of indiscretion at present in their primary stages. Did the consular books. Some Chinese. Hughes has thanked Sir John for the exit of the sepoys & I & Adkins are mentioned in Wade's report as having made but little progress being much interrupted by office work. Tatham & Leonard came in & disputed about the *Praya*[155] & *Wild Dayrel*.[156] The presents for the King of Siam have been mostly spoilt or lost tumbling overboard.[157] A nasty, wet, foggy, windy, beastly day.

---

154 Probably A.W. Wheely, mercantile assistant at Dent & Co. where Leonard worked.
155 From the context, this *Praya* was likely a ship, but I have not been able to identify it.
156 The *Wild Dayrell* was an opium clipper of 253 tons owned by Dent & Co. and built in 1855.
157 King Mongkut (1804–1868, r. 1851–1868) corresponded with Queen Victoria and with British and French scientists. In 1856, Queen Victoria sent a large number of gifts, most of which perished on the way, especially the scientific diagrams and the 'charts of the Indian and Chinese seas'.

25. A smart fall of rain. Payne stopped at home. Adkins had to go to office at 1 & his teacher paid me a handsome compliment by saying he understood my Chinese tho' he did not Adkins & he said I should learn it in a year at the most. I hope I shall but fear I shall not or anything like it. If I do however it will be immensely jolly & I should like above all things to catch up. Hughes went to the reception. Captain & Mrs King there & Tate. Lady Bowring ill. Tate full of the attacks on him. There was an attack on the *Hussar*[158] last night. Sir J. took me aside at going away & just as I thought something important was coming out, he told me he had received Hughes's letter & would always be happy to do anything to make us comfortable. Adkins has been dining at Repton's.

26. Adkins went to office. Awful cram is now all the go. Adkins is cramming madly. So is Hughes & I am trying to but cannot tho' I try. However I have done something today. Caine is going home most likely & then is going to Amoy. Geo. Morrison coming here & a lot of changes par consequence. Two pirates were hung this morning.[159] Leonard lame & I have had a hard day.

27. Adkins was at office again. It is an infernal shame. Worked away myself & tomorrow I shall also have to go. First of all today the French ships came in i.e. the *Virginie* & *Sibylle* and of course were saluted & their admiral came & Sir J. was bawling for the guard which came not & then the *Nankin* came in with a fearful amount of sail set & now a steamer. Perhaps the mail is in. There is bad news too today. There is a fearful fever among the Chinese which kills them after a few hours at the rate of 100 a day.[160] I hope none of us will get it.

28. An awfully hot day & I rather seedy in consequence. Woodgate came back blowing up as usual to Hughes. 'Great disgust' & 'ought to be a drill sergeant,' 'great bear,' &c. broke upon my ears & afforded me great amusement & then we went to Wade who seemed to think we were not going on as we ought & Caine came & said the mail was in sight & so off we set to Leonard's who believed not & then to Tatham's. Adkins however got among a lot of fellows, none of whom believed it & luckily, for it turned

---

158 The *Hussar*, built in 1852, was a clipper owned by one of the companies of American Frederick T. Bush, who had been US consul in Hong Kong from 1844 to 1848.
159 *China Mail*, 27 March 1856, 'Two men convicted at last Criminal Sessions of Piracy and Murder, were hanged within the Magistracy compound yesterday morning at daylight'.
160 Probably cholera, this outbreak being part of what is known as the 'third pandemic' that began in 1852.

out to be a hoax & we had a row right round the *Virginie*. She is a fine frigate & then in the evening I & Hughes had a race smoking for $1 & he beat me hollow but I considered I won my dollar for it made him awfully uncomfortable.

29&30 30. Sunday. Last night I wrote nothing, simply because smoking against Hughes for double or quits of our late wager. I beat him, it is true, tho' by an awful exertion having beaten him I felt sick & catted[161] horribly, just being able to totter outside. Nothing happened worth noting, save my dog evinced signs of intelligence & Adkins was offered the 4th Assistantship by Woodgate. I shall be horribly jealous, I know. Today, Sunday, I have not spent so well as I might, for this morning instead of going to church I went partially up the ravine & got two very curious animals or rather water insects. Adkins tiffining at Dent's & after tiffin, bang goes *Fort William* & off start I & meet Woodgate who tells me Glynes is coming out by the mail & that I am to fetch him off, so I get a boat & start off & meet Adkins in another, so in a most tempestuous sea I get into his boat. All the houseboats are out when down goes *Fort William's* flag[162] & in steams *HMS Encounter* thus selling all Hongkong[163] & so I came home & read Uncle, Henry, Charly & Percy letters. They are really beautiful many of them & I wish I could act up to them & then I read Gutzlaff's first voyage[164] wherein he makes out Chinese sailors a most depraved set, but that on the whole the Chinese receive you well & medicine seems to be about the only thing they respect us for & they are always wanting to detain missionary doctors.

31. It seems the mail came in last night after all & I was agreeably surprised this morning by having 3 letters brought to me. One from Aunty & Uncle, another from Henry & Charly & another from Cabban. Aunty tells me all the home news & is a jolly letter. Uncle among other things tells me of the death of Captain Criddle[165] & Henry's being likely to join me on this side of the water & saying 'My box &c. is started.' Charly is better & writes that at Oxford they enquire after me & also that Cabban is not

---

161 Vomited.
162 As a salute to the *Encounter*.
163 Alabaster's meaning is unclear. Perhaps the house boats approached the *Encounter* selling all manner of goods to the sailors.
164 From Charles Gutzlaff, *Journal of Three Voyages along the Coast of China, in 1831, 1832, & 1833; with Notices of Siam, Corea, and the Loo-Choo Islands*, or its precursor volume, *Two Voyages*. The former was reprinted many times.
165 Captain Criddle was evidently a member of Alabaster's uncle's family. A Captain John S.H. Criddle, resident of Ryde on the Isle of Wight, and formerly of the Indian Navy, is reported to have died on 10 January 1856, aged 68. See *Allen's Indian Mail*, 5 February 1856, 84.

popular for reason of his coolness & impertinence. He is trying against Charly for the Clarendon prize. Then comes Henry's. Clarendon[166] has given 4 appointments to K.C.S.[167] & he is sure of one & is consequently full of excitement about them & Jelf has told him to thank me for what my fraternal justly designates a wretched letter & last of all an yepistle[168] from Cabban in which, poor fellow, he says my brother is his only friend, truly & sincerely & that he has got a scholarship at Queen's & implores me to write. Especially, too, he lets fall hints & fears which I will investigate. Jones is going to Ningpo & Woodgate told us to tell Payne that a friend thought he did not look very ill. Did a little Chinese.

April

1. Wet, drizzly & brutal. Stopped at home & did Chinese. Worked hard but did little. However, there was great news at the office. Geo. Morrison is to be 1st Assistant here. Caine goes to Amoy, Hance 2nd, Hughes 3rd & Gregory[169] is coming from Foochow causing a vacancy there as 4th & Adkins, it is said, is to go to Canton. I would much rather they would send Payne & that they would dismiss me to Foochow. **Mongan** too is 2nd at Shanghae, so now Cooper, King & Adkins & Jones are the only ones between me & an assistantship. Went this evening to the Governor's reception. Had an adventure in my first ride in a chair i.e. an upset. It is very jolly being carried, however I like it better than an omnibus & when one got there, there was a dinner party, so I had to do the agreeable to Miss Bowring & another lady & afterwards they came out of dinner & the Governor spoke to me of course & then I had a confab with Colonel Graham & Irving[170] & the Bishop told me he had intended to ask me & Payne to dinner but Mrs Smith had been ill. The French admiral is a jolly looking old fellow & so is Stirling who is going home. Alcock was there & lots of people. These soirees at present are very slow ∴ I know scarcely anyone but I hope they will soon become more agreeable to me.

---

166 Clarendon was in charge of the appointment of student interpreters.
167 King's College School.
168 Epistle.
169 William Gregory (1830–1916) entered the Consular Service in 1854 as a student interpreter, ultimately retiring at 60 as consul at Yichang. Coates describes him as 'a tubby, sloppily dressed little man who was well enough liked personally but who was an exceedingly ineffectual consul', see Coates, *The China Consuls*, 275–76.
170 Probably a mistake for J.J. Irwin, colonial chaplain (1855–1867).

2. Got up at 5½ as is now my wont. Got my pay. Worked Chinese. Have had many beautiful ideas all of which I forget & now sleepy & tired I go to bed. Woodgate & Capt. Watkins came up this afternoon.

3. As usual I have had several things today to be ashamed & sorry for. We had a few hours this morning at Chinese when a letter came & called us to office for an appeal by Wilkinson Dent[171] had to be copied for transmission to Shanghae & I had an awful lot & Payne saying something that irritated me I gave him the lie[172] & afterwards & threatened to thrash me if I did not apologise, which of course I refused to on compulsion but have done this evening & I will try to keep out of such scrapes in future & afterwards played at cards & lost a dollar & an evening.

4. Had a day at home & did a little work. That is to say I expended many happy hours but got but little benefit therefrom. It is horribly disheartening, just as you are cramming up a thing, to find it bad & wrong. It is abominable. If Wade goes on with what he is doing it will be a great thing but will he? There's the tug. The orthography he was so full of seems quite thrown overboard. Old Hughes has a notable scheme for going to Peking i.e. get a note from Meaou to say he speaks well. I was very much amused when I heard it. Old H. does not know I know it. Henceforward we are going to manage by a compradoreship.

5. A muggy beastly day. Everything damp. Beastly. Brutal. Abominable. Working away at Chinese. Ill tempered as the deuce. Hot and sleepy all day, nearly swearing at old Meaou. So has passed today & at last the mist is clearing away & so am I.

6. Sunday. Got up late. My window had blown open & filled my room with mist and moths. Got up and sauntered about till tiffin then read a little of Gutzlaff who is very entertaining indeed & Leonard dropped in & we talked till dinner & then we sat outside, the fireflies dancing about & looking very pretty indeed with their clear green light. We caught one and I was surprised to find it was only about the size of a common fly with a small yellow transparency behind in which was a bright light. We also killed a centipede [sketch]. A horrid looking thing. The French ships left today for the north & the *Coromandel* had to go after them. The weather was very fine today.

---

171 Wilkinson Dent (1800–1886) was one of the brothers who ran the merchant house, Dent & Co.
172 To accuse someone of falsehood, to call them a liar.

7. Got up latish. Have done little or no work. Went to Wade's teacher. Leonard, Tatham & Lawrence came. Leonard in Canton one evening was chasing a firefly & after a long chase it, as he thought, settled so at it he went. Took his cap off & let fly at it & to his astonishment knocked sparks out of it when on nearer inspection he found he had hit a respectable Parsee slap in the face as he was enjoying his weed & laughed so awfully as not to be able to apologize. The *Bittern* came in. Read the final letters of Sir J. & the Admiral. They soap[173] each other abominably & now early to bed & I hope early to rise tomorrow.

8. Got up late. Bathed, &c. Adkins went to office. Worked with Meao who is ill & went to sleep in the afternoon. Seedy myself. Fear Payne has given me a touch of his complaint. I hope not. It frightened me considerably. Bought a rocking chair & settled with Payne and afterwards Leonard & Vingt-un. Came up & so to bed.

9. Adkins went to office & I, seedy, could not have the teacher for he, like Seang & Chu, is seedy. However, I spurred myself on to the effort & managed to finish the translations of the 7th & 8th chapters which is a great comfort, for now I have overcome one obstacle.[174] I am almost in despair. Chinese seems unobtainable by me & what is worse, I am awfully afraid Paine has given me his disease. It is an awful thing for me if it is true & gets abroad & the worst of it is it will all be undeserved. Tobler came up this evening and we sang & sang like nightingales. We are all seedy. It is very horrid. I am sure the Albany is unhealthy.

10. Glad to go to office this morning & this afternoon seedy. Pretty sure I have got Payne's disease & now tired I am going to bed.[175]

---

173 Flatter.
174 The seventh and eighth sections of the *Sacred Edict*.
175 The prevalence of venereal diseases and attempts to regulate prostitution had been and continued to be pressing concerns in Hong Kong for decades after Alabaster's time. On these topics see, Elizabeth Sinn, 'Chinese Patriarchy and the Protection of Women in 19th-Century Hong Kong', in *Women and Chinese Patriarchy: Submission, Servitude and Escape*, ed. Maria Jaschok and Suzanne Miers (Hong Kong: Hong Kong University Press; London: Zed Books, 1994), 141–70; Carl T. Smith, 'Protected Women in 19th-Century Hong Kong', in Jaschok and Miers, *Women and Chinese Patriarchy*, 221–37; Philip Howell, 'Race, Space and the Regulation of Prostitution in Colonial Hong Kong', *Urban History* 31, 2 (2004): 229–48, doi.org/10.1017/S0963926804002123; Elizabeth Sinn, 'Women at Work: Chinese Brothel Keepers in Nineteenth-Century Hong Kong', *Journal of Women's History* 19, 3 (Fall 2007): 87–111, doi.org/10.1353/jowh.2007.0062; Chan-Yeung, *A Medical History*, Chapter 2, 'Disease of Venus: Prostitution and Its Control'.

11. Adkins went to office. I stopped at home and worked & was seedy, the 'affair' becoming painful. I went to Chaldercot[176] who examined it & said I ought to be made a Jew[177] but did not know whether it was gonorrhoea or not. Very lazy & sleepy all day.

12. I'm a little better. Working trim today but the 'affair' very painful. I am sure I have got the gonorrhea & it is a horrid thing. However I shall go to Chaldecot again tomorrow & see what he says to it. Got a letter from King today. He is jolly but dull. An eccentric letter of course but not so entertaining as usual. Did a little work today & have to go to office tomorrow.

13. Sunday. Had to go to office & when we were there there was not much to do. After office went to Chaldecot who says I have not got the clap[178] but it is still awfully painful when I make water and even at other times. Leonard came. Saw Tatham at Chaldecot's. He was awfully confused. The *Winchester* came back. Wrote a lot of letters tho' not in the humor. The rain coming down in torrents.

14. Office and writing letters have taken up all today nearly. Just called at the bishop's. The 'affair' horribly painful & must go to Chaldecot tomorrow. Have written an awful lot of letters. Bird has applied to keep his office like a fool as the man must be and Sir J. still refuses Medhurst leave to go home. Payne is writing to Jelf. He had to stop. After hours today the teacher brought me the 'Rules of Chess' and 2 maps, one of the world – a very rum one, England a little place in the south – and another of Pekin – a very useful one indeed & probably correct.

15. Off went the mail carrying Alcock, Rymers, the bishop and a heavy load of passengers, 3 in a cabin on this side. Oh! how I would I were in it. I felt awfully home sick today and do now. I dared not go on board for I know I could not have got off again. I feel I could run away, desert, bolt & so does Adkins. Hughes exhilerated tonight, kicking up an awful row and with his

---

176 Thomas Andrews Chaldercott (1828–1883), a doctor in private practice in Hong Kong at this time, who became acting colonial surgeon on the death of Harland in 1858. He returned to England in 1862.
177 Be circumcised.
178 Gonorrhoea.

'sprig of shillela'[179] smashing open my partition or rather a hole in it. The 'affair' is awfully painful. I ought to have gone to Chaldercot's today but did not either do that or much work. The chipoo[180] is awfully hard. Been larking and humbugging all this evening. Wrote a jolly lot of letters home.

16. Still very bad. Meao at office all day. Worked at the characters & did a little work then began doing one of the chess problems. They are full of mistakes and rather ununderstandable but I hope I shall be able in time to twig the tayi.[181] Went to Chaldecot's but met him en route. He evidently does not know what the matter is at all. All I know is it is very painful. This evening had a stroll. Polly followed ½ the way & then ran home & was thrashed in consequence & then we sat down to cards for who was to get decantars. I did not mind playing for this as I rather want one & no one loses anything. Hughes took my box to send to Foochow and had not even the politeness to ask for it or thank me for it.

17. Worked away at phrases all day & did a good lot so have lots of materials when I get the teacher. Played at cards and lost the decanters. Much better today. Very little pain comparatively. Sat out in the veranda. Heard piracy going on in the distance and now, every now and then, a rocket is sent up.

18. Stopped at home. Adkins going to office. Caine goes to Amoy tomorrow. Worked away all the morning and this evening after stroll with Paine – in which we met Woodgate who told us there were 6 vacancies for student interpreters and that the Colonial Office had offered the Colonial's lodgings next door to us. I had the satisfaction of understanding a thing that nonplussed the teacher – to his admiration – it being the first thing in the book on chess which I am afraid will be a long task & then the fun began. 1st, I and Adkins dripped water down on Hughes and Payne & then we had a lot of skirmishing upstairs, I getting one ducking & giving several. At last Hughes threw some into Adkins's room & Payne ducked him, whereat he was made savage & so he & I are going to stir them up at 3 o'clock this morning tho' threatened by Hughes that he will keep it up for a week if we do.

---

179 A 'sprig of shillela' or shillelagh, was a wooden cudgel stereotypically wielded by Irishmen, referred to in popular songs and poems. Hughes was a Catholic from Newry, which is divided by the river Clanrye between County Armargh and County Down.
180 Chinese, *jiba* 雞巴, 'penis'.
181 Chinese, *dayi* 大意, 'main idea'.

19. Adkins went to office while I stayed at home. The black board is a jolly dodge. Between that, the rocking chair and a bamboo pole, I got on rather jollily today and much more to my satisfaction than usual. In the evening Tatham, with whom it is determined to break as soon as possible, came up with quoits and also Repton. Tatham brought up Lawrence & another cad in the Yankee [illegible][182] & they had a game & afterwards we had a jolly stroll with Repton who is a very nice fellow indeed. He chaffed Payne most awfully. Afterwards came home. Read the paper, which contains some attacks on Anstey. Worked with black board now to bed. Caine went to Amoy today and I wrote to Cooper. I am afraid I am getting bad again. Did not rouse up Hughes because I did not wake but Leonard came & squirted Paine.

20. Sunday. Was awakened by Leonard who likewise obliged me to jump out of bed tho' very loath so to do and after humbugging about I went down to his place and so to Church. Came home. Puddled about & then went out for a stroll. Met Woodgate who told me of Morrison's arrival. Got a letter from Chaldecot saying I need no more physic. Home & then post prandium[183] went out got a boat & heard the Ships playing jollily.

21. Went to office of course & Don Juan[184] was there. A smallish, thinnish, particularish, swellish, frizzly fellow with a treble voice and a bad reputation. I myself am seedy as is everyone else and am so sleepy that I must give up work for this night and go to bed. Nothing of note occurred today save Sir J. is going up to the north if possible. Early to bed and late to rise makes a man neither wealthy or wise but when you've muddled your brain, what's the use of working again?

22. In a rum state of mind & body. Worked and I hope to some little effect. Wretched all day. Feeling weak, sick, diarrhoeic & beastly. Had a fire. Wrote to King. A wet day & so finished.

23. Stopped at home to cram. Very bad with diarrhoea or dysentery or both. Got up at 6 but went to bed till 8 & received a letter from Sir J. about writing on soy and indigo, two very congenial subjects. Adkins is to write on building. Payne on salt & Hughes was to have – but has declined – written on stone quarrying. It is rather a nuisance but perhaps it is all for the best. After dinner played at quoits & then I, Adkins & Hughes went to call on

---

182 Possibly 'navy'.
183 After lunch.
184 I have not been able to identify this man.

Mr & Mrs Hance where we enjoyed ourselves for a short time & then after wasting an hour or so at Leonard's, home & read the paper. Find the lascars murdered a drummer boy last night[185] & now to bed.

24. In my eagerness for settling the soy question, after with great difficulty awaking Payne & getting him dressed, off I set with him to the West Point soy works. After a long walk we arrived there & there was some difficulty in shewing it to me as they said it was too high up. However, on being assured I would not mind an ascent to the moon, they stated they had no farther objection, so passing thro' the shop in which I noticed various vile compositions – potted shrimps – I go up a ladder to store rooms & after 3 more ladders all beast dirty we arrived at the roof, consecrated to soy & here the first thing that met our eyes was an immense number of wooden tubs surmounted by bamboo-mat conical covers which gave them much the effect of beehives. Not covering 1 roof only but extending to 3 or 4. In these tubs you saw the soy complete, the soy unstrained, the salt water. It quite took my taste for soy I had away to look at those tubs of beastly salt water for if made properly you would use fresh water & put salt in. However their way seems cheaper. First you boil the beans in saltwater with a little sugar, soda[186] & flower[187] & then put it to stand. Afterwards, it is put into bags and quietly allowed to strain itself & then it is put out in the sun for any time. The longer, the better. So it is a very simple process. And then the bean is taken and ground making a squashy mess much eaten by the Chinese. Having poked & peered about & finding that really there was nothing more to see & the owners declining to speak truth we came home.

---

185 *China Mail*, 24 April 1856:
   A quarrel took place on Tuesday evening between some soldiers of the 59th Regiment and the Gun Lascars, which resulted in the death of one of the former, a lad of 17 years of age, whose skull was fractured by blows of a stick. The men of the 59th were highly exasperated, and were with difficulty restrained from breaking out of barracks, to take summary vengeance, for the loss of their comrade, upon the Lascars, whom it was deemed by Colonel Graham advisable to send on board the *Hercules* for safety; but the soldiers may rest assured of receiving ample justice at the hands of the Officers and of the Civil Authorities, and that every endeavour will be made to bring the guilty to punishment. An inquest was to be held on the body yesterday, adjourned till to-morrow. Three of the Gun Lascars have since been taken in custody by the police, charged with being leaders in the affray.

China Mail, 15 May 1856, reports that 'the adjourned inquest on the body of the lad belonging to the 59th Regiment, killed in a fight with Gun Lascars, has resulted in a verdict of "Wilful murder by persons unknown"'. *Overland Register and Price Current*, 10 May 1856, reported that the drummer was called Haggarty and the root cause of the fight lay in 'a man of the regiment appropriating to himself the tauny wife of one of the lascars'.

186 Sodium bicarbonate.

187 Flour. Wheat flour was added in the bean curd making process to feed natural yeasts that provided the required fermentation.

I & Adkins went to Sir John who gave us a long oration about its being such good practice for us, &c. Home. Loitered about. Seedy. Very. Had some Lemonade & Old Meao became awfully communicative about soy which he avers every Chinaman makes. I have been very seedy all today. The Lascars had to be put aboard ship to save them from the 59 who want to attack them en masse.

25. Pouring wet day. Went to office followed by Polly whom I had some difficulty in getting home. Worked away at the Canton book & then went to Morrison. Told him of the bathtub which he says he does not want. He is rather a jolly fellow. Came home & Chinesed, Old Meao asserting that snuff is $50 a catty at Canton which I 'spect is gammon,[188] however will see & get some if it be fact. In the evening made some mess rules and regulations which will be advantageous if acted up to. It appears the drummer was killed by a kick in trying to interfere in a scuffle & the troops were almost in a state of mutiny.

26. A fine day. Birthday of the Goddess of Heaven[189] & consequently a grand day for Chinamen. Saw one procession: first a white flag, then 2 roast pigs gaily bedizened[190] surrounded by banners & musicians, then a lot of fellows dressed in red. Worked with Meao, the horrid old beast. He is awfully disgusting & now have been trying to understand this chess book but am obliged to give it up as a bad job. This evening up came Tatham & Lawrence with a rather decent fellow from the *Vandalia*. Then Leonard & finally Morrison who is not a bad fellow tho' an awful fop & he has a jolly dog. The paper contains no news.

27. A very jolly day tho' I had had a wretched night with a cold, mosquitoes, &c. Went to church in the morning & it quite reminded one of a hot summer's day at home. That quiet, warm, sunny day you often have on Sundays in England & after tiffin we went out for a sail & after having a look at the Russian prisoners on the *Hercules* we sailed along the other side of the harbor close up to Stonecutters Island passing a quarry & 2 or 3 fishing villages & at last got into a very pretty bay where we landed & had a look about hills covered with trees all round & just before you paddy fields which look very pretty now with their little bright green tufts at regular distances & the wind playing over it & just getting home by dinner

---

188 Nonsense.
189 Tianhou 天后, the sea goddess also known as Mazu 媽祖. Her birthday falls on the 23rd day of the third lunar month.
190 Dressed up.

time. We had no sooner finished it than bang went the *Fort William's* gun & off we went. We got up to the steamer & in a regular scramble got on board. No news, however, that we could find except that peace is sure & Parkes is come. Went down to Woodgate's but he was out so we did not get our letters.

28. Just out of bed whence I was roused by little Polly, for as I was comfortably snoozing I felt someone touching me in the back & looking round to confound them I saw the young gentleman with his paws upon the bed and very anxious for me to come out of it which letters being in view I did & dispatched the coolie for them & hope in 10 minutes to be reading them.

29. Last night I was so seedy & sleepy that I had to go to bed early tho' I had lots to write about. At home they are going to move to a new house. The pictures are nearly finished & they are all in tolerable health. Charly is at Oxford & Henry expects to be soon here so it is rather good news & other news there is lots of. Our new Admiral Seymour[191] is to be here tomorrow & an 84[192] viz. the *Calcutta* is to follow him. A Lord of the Treasury – an Irishman – has defaulted and cut his throat.[193] Hillier[194] is to be Consul at Siam & Bell & Forrest are to have £405 and £350 a year respectively which is very jolly for them. Wade is ill & it is rumoured that Seang was drowned in getting from the steamer this evening. After a rather jolly day's work at Chinese I, Adkins & Hughes went to the Governor's. Chapman[195] & Tait there. Chapman talking & Tait singing like steam engines. Sir John's new Secretary[196] is an awful muff[197] & has to see the billiard table ironed, &c. & so home after a very pleasant evening.

30. Another moon ended without much to look back on. Got up early. Worked Chinese till tiffin in an awful state of nervous irritability. Increased by Old Meao persisting in going to sleep. Worked till dinner. Payne going

---

191 Admiral Sir Michael Seymour (1802–1887) was appointed commander-in-chief of the East India and China Station of the Royal Navy in February 1856. The HMS *Calcutta* was his flagship. He arrived in Hong Kong on the HMS *Encounter* on 6 May 1856, see *China Mail*, 8 May 1856.
192 An 84-gun ship.
193 Alabaster is surely referring here to John Sadlier who killed himself in February 1856 by taking prussic acid, not by cutting his throat.
194 Charles Batten Hillier (1820–1856), chief magistrate in Hong Kong from 1847 to 1856. He went to Bangkok as consul in 1856 and died later that year.
195 E.L. Chapman, who worked in the Colonial Secretary's Office.
196 Abel Anthony James Gower (1836–1899) arrived in Hong Kong at this time to take up the position of private secretary to the governor. He later served in the Canton Consulate before being sent to Japan.
197 A fool, an incompetent.

to sing at the amateur choir in the Cathedral & Hughes to hear the band. I had the intense pleasure of taking about Mr Gower the new Secretary who was awfully astonished at the sight of a woman with little feet, for on my pointing one out he was rooted to the spot for 5 minutes muttering his wonderment & we went into several curio shops & bought rice paper drawings & looked at crapes,[198] &c. Some are very magnificent & not at all dear. Home. Played a game at chess. Read an *Atheneum* & saw about the most vivid flash of lightning I ever saw. It dazzled. Almost knocked me down. It was really & truly awful & then when the storm was over, we had a domestic storrum for the boy or coolie smarrashed Hughes' lamp, so he got excited & bate the coolie & was goin' to bate the boy but did not.[199] Not a farthingsworth of news in paper & so to bed. Gower is a rum fellow. Not up to English ways.[200] Eccentric & awfully polite.

May

1. A fine day. Got up early & worked Chinese well & satisfactorily this morning. The old Meao is a horrid, sleepy, old beast. He has a beautiful China snuff box, which I want to buy but he does not want to sell & just as I was settling to work after tiffin, in came Adkins who applied for the Fourth Assistantship & withdrew his application after learning it was only £216 & no quarters & then we had to go & get our pay & then Morrison & that eccentric buffer Gower who is a very rum fellow & on their departure, Leonard. I have managed to get through but little work today & am going to ponder in bed about taking the 4th Assistantship.

2. Nearly driven mad last night by mosquitoes who have bitten me all over & kept me awake till 4 this morning when after skirmishes frank[201] & rushes out of bed, &c., being dead tired I fell asleep & did not wake till 9 & prospects seem favorable for a repetition of the same tonight as there are loads of mosquitoes about today. As all 3 of us were at home I only managed to have 2 hours with the teacher but as my lamp is going out I must stop.

---

198 Crêpes, silk fabric.
199 Alabaster here is imitating Hughes's Newry accent: 'storrum' is 'storm', 'smarrashed' is 'smashed', 'bate' is 'beat'.
200 Gower was born and died in Italy, and after returning to Europe had married an Italian. Perhaps this is what Alabaster is referring to here.
201 Lusty, vigorous.

3. The lamp stopped my diary last night so I have to finish yesterday before I begin today. Well, when I had got up which I did in time, I worked away jollily tho' it was raining & as we were all 3 at home I could not have the teacher till the afternoon & I had only just begun with him & was noticing how dark it was getting when Adkins calling out, I rushed to the veranda & saw a truly wonderful sight. The wind was coming to the left. It was all dark & a cloud of spray was driven up by the wind as, accompanied by clouds & roaring grandly, it went across the harbor & rebounded from the opposite bank & then down came the rain for about ½ an hour & then, it clearing up, went down town & looked at some beautiful bracelets and ivory boxes. Home. A long dispute between Hughes and Payne about accounts in which Hughes was decidedly right but which will not add to his popularity. Today has been one of nuisance. Meao did not come in till 12 so I had none of him this morning & only 1 hour this evening which was a bother. It rained in torrents today & the water was rushing down the ravine in fine style & we had a mess dinner, inviting Leonard & Repton & were very jolly & sang & eat & drank till now & have had a merry evening.

4. Sunday. A day on which I was to have written many letters & done many things but getting up at 10 was not conducive thereunto & went to church & heard a good sermon. Home & watched a lot of little, tiny, black insects which struck me as like the world. A great bustle but little doing. The herd down below & the many struggling to rise high up. The further up, the fewer the number. Many just on the eve of success, falling headlong downwards. Nor were enemies wanting. Here, stalked horrida bella[202] in the shape of an ant destroying many. Here, was a swift and active spider emblematical of disease mowing down hundreds. Here, were fights to determine who should be first, often ending in both the tiny heroes toppling down. Here, was one unable to extricate himself from the crowd. Others disgusted with the task of mounting higher, sinking down to their former level. Here, the space being too narrow would you see a body leave & then you saw the troubles of those who were the first emigrators. Ignorance of where to go to. Storms & no shelter. In short, it seemed to remind me that I was but a mortal and that such was the world & afterwards, I & Payne went part of the way up the ravine which looks very pretty & we saw many pretty insects & flowers & came home rather the better for it & then after dinner I had another stroll home & discussion about compradores, &c.

---

202 Latin, 'horrid wars'.

5. Payne's coming of age has passed almost without remark, only known by an emblem allegorical. Sucking pig & some champagne, which rendered every one, P. especially, very aphrodisiacal. Oh! I wish I had never heard a bawdy word or done a bawdy deed. Did next to no work at all as I was seedy but had 2 or 3 delightful strolls about. Adkins too is very ill & can't work. We all had to go down to Wade who does intend to examine us it seems & has given us a new book to work up.

6. Shame. Shame. The admiral came[203] & in the evening went to reception. Only Colonel Graham there. It is very amusing to see old Hughes so eager to go, then so undetermined when there, fearing what to say & doubting what to do & so going on till he bursts out into 'a flood of contradictions to all,' Sir J. says.

7. Stopped at home. A hot day. Think I am in front. Began the novel.[204] It is very easy indeed & rather interesting. Worked. Went out with the private secretary. After a game of billiards with him, he turns out to be of an aphrodisiacal temperament. Home. Went to Leonard's with Adkins. Home, working, letters, bed. An epidemic is killing the Chinese at 50 a day.[205]

---

203 Admiral Seymour's arrival in Hong Kong on the HMS *Encounter* is noted in *China Mail*, 8 May 1856.
204 Probably the 'new book' Wade had given them to study.
205 A correspondent to the *China Mail* – 'Scrutator' – on 1 May 1856 wrote:
> Though no alarmist, I own I am rather panic-stricken at the ravages of the epidemic now extending from Tai-ping-shan to Sheong-wan … I deem this a fitting opportunity to bring to public notice, that there are upwards of 30 deaths per diem among the native population, and that their remains are strewn broadcast over the hill-side at the back of the town, in most instances without coffins, and scarcely two feet below the surface, not only tainting the air, but also the fresh-water streams which issue from the nooks and hollows in that locality. Only a few days ago, a lady and gentleman were horrified at the sight of a body in a state of decomposition, which the rain had laid bare within two or three feet of the carriage road. During last week, eight or nine men out of a gang of forty, were, to my knowledge, carried off by this epidemic in a few days – but there seems to be no registration of deaths, except in the too palpable state of the atmosphere.

The *Friend of China*, 10 May 1856, reported:
> The epidemic among the Chinese, of which we made mention the other day, is rapidly increasing, without, so far as we know, any steps being taken to check its ravages. Chinese say the mortality is after the rate of fifty a day. This, however, there can be no doubt, is an exaggeration. The Registrar General, we are told, makes the number of deaths to be 800 during the 84 days ending with the 30th ultimo. The causes of this pestilence have to be sought, doubtless, in the recently appointed graveyard immediately west of Tapingshan [sic], where corpses are interred occasionally but a few inches below the sward, and in the filth exhalations from the lanes and hills [sic]. Since the large influx of Chinese the vicinity of Taipingshan has become a huge public necessity – there being no accommodation houses for the Chinese inhabitants, as in Canton and other Chinese cities. Government must be perfectly infatuated in appointing a Chinese burial ground within the town; and unless we are to be driven out of the Colony altogether, some steps must be taken to make Sir John Bowring

8. Managed to awake old Meao by abusing the emperor & then worked away jollily. Had a row with boy and house cooly & a walk & row with Gower & was astonished to find that the examination is in June.

9. At home and at work & very satisfactory too till 5 tho' the teacher was abominably sleepy, the old brute. I managed to get on, however & after dinner up comes Gower whom we greet with a gin sling[206] and light & frivolous conversation. Waste the precious minutes till 7, when Washington Irving carries one on till 8 & letters carry one on right of 10½. There was another unsuccessful attempt made by the house coolie today, backed by the boy & teacher, to extort money.

10. The mail went, carrying with it Colonel Graham & Mrs Hillier,[207] 2 of the most popular people here. Graham was cheered off by all the troops and rowed ½ way by the sergeants & ½ by the officers, having to change the

---

exercise a little common sense. Day by day we have continued proof of the utter inability of the gentleman to fulfil the duties of his post; and for Governor we had better have Colonel Caine than him.

206 At this time, a mix of gin, sugar and water.
207 Mrs Hillier was Eliza (née Medhurst). The *China Mail*, 15 May 1856, wrote:

An independent, painstaking, and conscientious official is so great a rarity, that the departure of such a one from a limited community like that of Hongkong is severely felt. By the *Singapore*, we have lost two such men.

The one, Mr Hillier, in whose uprightness and integrity as Chief Magistrate, both natives and foreigners reposed almost unlimited confidence, and in whom Chinese especially have lost a warm and steadfast friend. Of this they seem to have been aware, by the tokens of respect they shewed him at his departure. A large procession was formed at the Temple near Taipingshan, which proceeded to Mr Hillier's residence, accompanied by music, and bearing two splendid sedan chairs, such as are used in religious processions for the gods – one chair containing a basin of water, the other a looking-glass, implying that his character was as pure as water and unstained as glass. An address was also presented to Mr Hillier by the Chinese, and a gilt tablet bearing testimony of their respect and good-will. The procession afterwards proceeded through the city, notifying to the Chinese population their irreparable loss.

But to the foreign community as well, the loss is very great, and will be more felt from the difficulty likely to be experienced in filling his place. A barrister may be procured, who will dispense to the Chinese more law, but we are not likely to have a Magistrate from whom they will receive as much justice. Mr Hillier's intimate knowledge of the Chinese language and of Chinese customs enabled him to keep down abuses and elicit truth where one ignorant of the language would fail. Alas now for the poor Chinese under the mysticisms of the law, and in the hands of unprincipled interpreters! Already is Mr Hillier's absence from the bench seriously felt.

The other departure referred to is that of Colonel Hope Graham, whose duties were less general that those of Mr Hillier, being mostly confined to the garrison, of which he was Commandant; but in the discharge of which he displayed a zeal and ability that commanded for him not only the love of the military, but the respect and hearty good-will of the civilians among whom he has resided for the last four years. The day before his departure, the 59th Regiment, with which he has been connected for nearly a quarter of a century, was mustered on parade, and addressed by him in a few kind words, that greatly affected the older soldiers;

officers, having in the first place been so late that he feared to be left behind. Mrs Hillier too was seen off by everybody. C. J. Bowring too went home.[208] I declare every mail takes home someone one knew. It is wretched. It was as usual on a mail day jollily fine but awfully hot. Had my mat taken up & the room washed. The coolie was going to do it with a basin of water & a dirty rag, sans soap, sans scrubbing brush, &c., if I had not made him get one chopchop.[209] Leonard, Morrison & Repton came up to quoits & L. & R. stopped dinner & a merry evening we have had. Tales, jokes, songs, &c. Old Payne is ½ drunk. We dosed him so with gin sling, &c. & is trying to walk it off. Did little work. Truly this is not the way to come out well.

11. Whitsunday. Got up latish & then to church to hear a tolerably good sermon. Home & tiffin to which Mr Gower drops in. After tiffin I go out for a walk with him but am driven home by rain which soaked us both & had an invitation to the governor's to dinner whither I went, Adkins going to Dent's & a sorry evening I had. Had a tolerable dinner however & some very amusing talk with Lady Bowring. Had not a single opportunity for soap[210] & felt awfully inclined to belch, so after talking to Miss B all the evening, home I came.

12. In came the Yankee corvette & saluted all day:[211] 1st the Admiral, then the Governor, then the Consul & somebody else. We had all gone down to office & had a most providential escape for while out in the Murray Battery the noise & vibration shook down a large part of the ceiling, smashing Adkin's & Payne's table. Bluff was great fun in the Battery as he took all the firing as a personal insult & threw a file of infantry into disorder by running between their legs. In the evening after a day of work the 2 Lawrences came

---

while the younger men next day greeted him with three hearty cheers, as he stepped into a boat manned by his junior officers, who paid him a parting tribute of respect by rowing him off to the steamer. The officers of the regiment had previously entertained him at their mess, presided over by Captain Romer, who, in a manly speech, expressed the grateful thanks of himself and brother officers to the Colonel for his many acts of kindness to themselves, and their full appreciation of his merits, and of the benefits conferred by him upon the regiment by his untiring solicitude for the health and welfare of his soldiers.

On Hillier, see also Christopher Munn's entry on him in Holdsworth and Munn, *Dictionary of Hong Kong Biography*, 182–83.

208 John Charles Bowring (1820–1893) was Sir John's eldest son.
209 Hong Kong pidgeon, 'immediately'.
210 Flattery.
211 This was probably the *Levant*. Strictly speaking, the *Levant* was a sloop-of-war, a corvette being the next larger class of warship.

up with Tatham & fell to quoits but it coming on to rain and they falling to cards, I came up stairs. Murrowes[212] sent a lot of coolies up the Peak to look out for the Calcutta mail armed with spears, guns, &c. I & Adkins stopped them coming down. At a sale at Captain King's, Payne & Hughes have made some wonderful bargains.

13. Called on the Gov. Went to Woodgate & borrowed a volume of the *Chinese Repository*. Home. Work. Payne and Hughes' things came home. Hughes' prints very poor. Went to the governor's. The admiral, a fine looking old fellow, there & Colonel Caine who was as friendly as possible but we soon came away & I have been sitting up reading a trashy book, *The Image of his Father*,[213] over which & *The Greatest Plagues of Life*,[214] I have wasted a good bit of time.

Plate 9. 'Sing-Song Piejon at Hong-Kong', *Illustrated London News*, 15 August 1857.

---

212 Murrow & Co., the company of Yorick Jones Murrow (1817–1884), later proprietor and editor of the *Daily Press*, a newspaper very critical of the colonial administration and, in particular, Bowring.
213 Henry and Augustus Mayhew, *The Image of His Father, or, One Boy Is More Trouble than a Dozen Girls: Being a Tale of a 'Young Monkey'*, 1851.
214 Henry and Augustus Mayhew, *The Greatest Plague of Life, or, the Adventures of a Lady in Search of a Good Servant by One Who Has Been 'Almost Worried to Death'*, 1847.

14. Between toothache and trifling wasted a valuable day. The Calcutta mail came with news of birth of a son to the emperor[215] & marriage of princess royal to prince of Prussia[216] which my toothache prevents me commenting on.

15. We hid Old Hughes' chair last night & he was in a great state this morning threatening to do all sorts of things when the boy told him. Went to office. Had lots of work. Sir J. revises the Treaty in July.[217] Woodgate gave me a book on the Amoy dialect which once belonged to Backhouse.[218] Home. Engaged the new boy for a week for trial. Played quoits & got very interested in the Yucheaoh.[219] Leonard came up. He has been laid up with fever & ague.

---

215 Zaichun, (1856–1875), the son of the Xianfeng emperor. He became the Tongzhi emperor in 1861.
216 This was, in fact, the engagement of Victoria, Princess Royal (1840–1901) – then 15 – to Frederick, Crown Prince of Prussia (1831–1888). They married in 1858. He later became Emperor Frederick III of Germany but only reigned for three months before he died of cancer. The engagement was not popular in England (or with Alabaster, it would appear) as Prussia had remained neutral during the Crimean War.
217 The treaties the British had signed with the Chinese – the Nanking Treaty (1842) and the Treaty of the Bogue (1843) – contained no provisions for revision. However, the Treaty of the Bogue granted Britain 'most-favoured nation' status. This meant that Britain automatically gained any rights granted by treaties between China and any other country. The Treaty of Wanghia (Wangxia, 1844) between the US and China included a clause stating that:
> inasmuch as the circumstances of the several ports of China open to foreign commerce are different, experience may show that inconsiderable modifications are requisite in those parts which relate to commerce and navigation; in which case, the two governments will, at the expiration of twelve years from the date of said convention, treat amicably concerning the same, by the means of suitable persons appointed to conduct such negotiation. (Article 34)

Thus, in 1856, Britain had the right to renegotiation of its treaties. See Richard E. Welch, Jr, 'Caleb Cushing's China Mission and the Treaty of Wanghia: A Review', *Oregon Historical Quarterly* 58, no. 4 (Dec. 1957): 328–57, 355.
218 John Backhouse (1818–1862) was appointed in 1843 and rose to the position of vice consul in Amoy. Retired in 1856 for health reasons, he married the following year in England but died not long after.
219 *Yu Jiao Li* 玉嬌梨, a novel by Zhang Yun 張勻, also known as *Di'an sanren* 荻岸散人 from the late Ming or early Qing, which was translated by the French sinologist Abel-Rémusat in 1826. An English version of this French translation was published in 1827 under the title *Iu-Kiao-Li: Or, the Two Fair Cousins*.

16. Dies Memorabilis.²²⁰ We have just come home i.e. I, Adkins, Payne, Hughes & Gower, from the Grand Chinese Singsong.²²¹ It was glorious. After a splendid row we landed at a place covered with stalls for selling eatables in & along we went a bamboo bridge till we came to a place where money was demanded & paid & then up some stairs into the theatre. It was an immense place. All built slightly of bamboo like this. [sketch] The stage was merely an elevation, at the back of which was the orchestra composed of bones, cymbals, gongs, drums & chins²²² – an instrument very much like cracked fiddles. Well, when we got in a young lady was talking to an old buffer [sketch] like this in a neat becoming dress. Well, after an immense lot of singing of a peculiar sort between these two, the old buffer apparently assents, when on rushes her lover to whom she is handed over, she & he throwing their legs about in a most extraordinary fashion. Well, Miss Chao takes such an awful time saying goodbye to Papa Chao that Mr Wang comes as they are kissing & helps them to a couple of backhanders which send them down as flat as herrings & the scene ends by Papa Chao cursing & Miss Chao kneeling & praying in quite a tragic manner. Scene 2. Mr Wang & Miss Chao dressed in rather handsome dresses have an awfully long confab which ends in their going away. 3. Fellows dressed in long embroidered gowns come on & walk about for some time, when in comes the emperor, a big immense fellow with an awfully red face & a most magnificent unsurpassable embroidered dress on. Flowers worked in gold & most gorgeous floss 2 or 3 inches thick. Well, down he sits & in comes Miss Chao, richly dressed & looking very pretty accompanied by two maids & begins a long harangue in verse, everything being sung to most vile and noisy music. Well, the end ont²²³ is the emperor makes her sit beside him when in comes her brother who at first wants to make a bobbery²²⁴ but soon

---

220 Latin, 'a memorable day'.
221 The illustrator responsible for Plate 9 – 'our special artist and correspondent' – described the scene (in the 11 July edition of the *Illustrated London News*), which took place in:
>a village on the other side of [Hong Kong] island: Having reached the village, a large stage of bamboo matting and talipot palm-leaves was erected in a short space of time. We passed through a crowd of Celestials and seated ourselves among them: they were very delighted. The performance was very lively … The mandarins all had flags [i.e. queues] to their backs, which is authentic; and the soldiers wore dark blue with sashes (likewise, authentic) and bamboo hats. The acting was capital, and resembled a French vaudeville. The names of the acts were posted up in neat frames on each side of the stage. The orchestra was not bad. The crowd was even better behaved than a French one.

Like Alabaster, this author travelled to the performance by boat.
222 Short for *huqin* 胡琴, the name given to the family of bowed string instruments such as the *erhu* 二胡.
223 On it.
224 Ballyhoo.

acquiesces in the arrangement, when in comes Mr Wang in a terrible rage – no longer the poor student but a great mandarin & dressed in gorgeous array – but it won't do. Out he goes swearing like blazes. 4 is a little domestic scene between Miss Chao (now empress) & dressed most beautifully in loose embroidered trousers & over that a tunic of highly embroidered silk covered with flowers. Master Chao, the comic actor, having apparently settled all to his satisfaction, goes out & in scene 5 is discovered reviewing his troops who are dressed in loose knee breeches of purple, a red sash & an open jacket, he being got up in a red gown with an embroidered girdle & a very red face. Well, he makes a speech when in comes the mighty General Wang senior, dressed magnificently – very like the emperor with a white face – followed by his troops dressed in gold silk. Well, he sits down & Master Chao coming forward & saying a lot of witty things, he gets tired & sends a soldier to slap his face & not content with that goes & tweaks his nose, whereon a scuffle ensues. Crackers are fired & Mr Chao bolts & appears in act 6 with a very much swollen nose. Explaining to his sister how he got it, she chaffs him but when the Emperor comes in, bothers him into jolliness, when in bursts Wang senior who stalks about the stage & begins to abuse Mr Chao & Miss Chao most horribly & kicks up his legs in a most indecorous manner. The Emperor stands it for some time but at last orders his degradation. He is seized, his handsome gown taken off & his hands being tied in a most scientific manner, he is lead off to prison to be tried in scene or act 7 by Mr Chao & a friend of his, who after sitting still some time (surrounded by soldiers dressed in loose knee breeches, jackets & each having 2 long & beautiful feathers in his hat), after several friends have come in & chinchinned him, giving orders for his immediate execution. So, two soldiers step forward & kneel & rising as he walks away, cut his head off & bring it to Mr Chao, but no sooner is this done when in rushes Mr Wang dressed in a very magnificent manner with a sword in each hand, accompanied by rebels, & a grand scrimmage ensues, Wang pirouetting & dancing in a most extraordinary manner & killing everybody. Even Mr Chao's friend who dodges him for a good while was at last knocked down & killed, whereon Wang struts about the stage, stands on one leg, &c., & gives you to understand that he is well satisfied & departs, whereon Mr Chao who had hidden behind a table comes out and bolts. Scene 8 is a curious one. Miss Chao seems to repent of her sins & collects an army to help Wang & is read a long lecture by Mr Wang senior who comes to life for the purpose & after many most unladylike performances (in fact most extraordinary gestures were greatly in vogue all through) returns for scene 9. Wang comes in dressed most magnificently with a most [sketch] beautiful embroidered dragon in front & little flags behind making a most becoming dress. Well, the old emperor is led in drunk with his robes off & after a spirited dialogue, Wang kicks him in the face & stomach & on his remonstrating knocks him down with Mr Wang senior's head, makes him sign his abdication & was going to make him eat the head, when a policeman came & said it was time to break up. So, with a cheer off went everybody & we had a most delicious sail home, singing as we came along & altogether I spent a most delightful evening. What astonished me most was the perfect order maintained by the crowd of coolies who though making quite a sea of heads did not make the slightest noise & were much more orderly than the wellbred frequenters of the English opera. Adkins & Payne went to office. I at home working & in the evening quoits. The new boy came today. I think he could do. He is very willing.

17. Dies Memorabilis. Soon after I was out of bed a note from Wade came telling me to go & see him which I did at 10 & was informed by him that he, having applied for at least one student interpreter to be attached to his office, Sir J. assented that having heard I had made more progress than the others, he had selected me & that henceforth I was entirely under his orders & no others. This ought to get me on in Chinese no end but will be a great bother & unless I take a deal of trouble will fix me in Hong Kong for a perpetuity. It causes great envy too. Well, after this I went & thanked Sir J. & then I, Adkins & Leonard went & had a jolly swim & enjoyed ourselves greatly, only I unfortunately cut my knee & then home to take dinner, Gower coming & afterwards Leonard & so in singing we consumed the night & are to be up at 6 tomorrow to go up the peak with Hance, &c. Wade was full of plans today. He confessed to have 50 underway.

18. Sunday. Up at 5 & off. Adkins, Payne, I & Hance set for the peak. Well, we went on jollily to the first rest, then trudged up to the gap & tho' from the mist there was no view, yet the breeze well repaid our labor & then we started for the peak, resting on the road by some beautiful water full of fish tho' so high up & had some water & biscuit. Hance was awfully amusing talking away like a good one & now darting here, now there like a good one. Well, we soon arrived at the peak and saw mist all around us but nothing more, so down we came, I & Hance turning aside here & there to get specimens & enjoying ourselves vastly. Out bursts the sun and before we arrive at the gap there is a capital view and Hance had almost made me determine to become a botanist. Down we come in time for breakfast to which Hance stayed, saying he feared not the sun, not he. Well, after breakfast, I & he took a stroll & he urged me greatly to become a collector

but was soon driven back by the sun & began giving most infidel opinions. Well, after a bath he departed & we had tiffin. Adkins going to Dent's after tiffin, I went to Wade & after a long search found out his house – a very small one & was shown in & found my lord lying on a sofa beside a table covered with papers. Well, what does he do but just go & bother about my classical education. In fact, he seems to intend to treat me much as he would a son & he told me to work up other things besides Chinese & seemed determined to make me get on though, as I thought, I am to be a feature in Hong Kong for a year if possible, unless promoted as he fears. However, I hope it will get me on well, as I think it will & as it ought. After I had left him with strict injunctions not to work more than 7 hours a day at Chinese & to go every night & see old Ying, I came home. Found Leonard there & then after dinner called on Woodgate. Found him with Capt. Parker R.N.[225] A little man with a bottle nose, funny face, potato body & short legs & Lieut. Nairs[226] of the *Coromandel* (which has smashed its rivets). A very gentlemanly fellow & after some chat I came away again. By the bye, Woodgate had his pyjamas on & now to bed very tired & sleepy.

19. Getting up at 6½ & setting to work at 7, I managed to do a little Premare[227] before breakfast & afterwards I finished the 1st chapter of the *Yucheaoli*[228] & then tried a read at Alison[229] & managed his preface but was disgusted to find on shutting the book that I had totally forgotten all of it. King sent us some bacon today. I fear tho' it is not eatable being damaged by salt water. This evening as in duty bound I went down to Wade's teacher Old Ying who received me in his room and I had a chat with the old fellow in the barely furnished apartment, old Chang coming in & they soaped me no end & lastly Wade came down & talked away. It seems I owe my being attached to the Chinese Secretary's Office to old Meao talking of me to Ying and Ying to Wade. Il faut que je prenne garde parce que ce Monsieur c'est un homme irritable a coucher.[230] It is awfully hot. All the Chinamen in trousers only & the thermometer at 95° early this morning which is a tremendous

---

225 George Charles Parker, master of the *Barracouta*.
226 Edward Nares, master of the *Coromandel*.
227 See Volume 1, footnote 141.
228 See above, footnote 218.
229 Archibald Alison, *History of Europe from the Commencement of the French Revolution in 1789 to the Restoration of the Bourbons in 1815* (1833–1843, 10 vols).
230 French, 'I have to be careful because this gentleman is irritable at bedtime'.

heat. I was escorted to Gough Street[231] most of the way by policemen with most formidable muskets as I did not know my way & Colonel Caine's name soon woke them up. I am to go to old Ying again tomorrow.

22. Sitting down to write for 3 days, for moving into Adkins' room while mine is being painted I have not had an opportunity to inscribe therein my actions, exterior relations & inward feelings. On 20, I got up early at 6. Worked at Premare till 9. Breakfast. Work with teacher till 12. Tiffin. 12½ – 3½ Chinese by myself. 3½ to 4¼ Alison's *History* & so each day has been passed up to dinner. Well, on 21, I went 1st to Hance with Adkins. Got Dr Johnston's address & in we went. Found him & wife[232] and a Mr Peasy[233] & his wife & a Chinaman who spoke English as well as I do. Well, we had a little confab about the multifarious concerns of the various dialects of China and then off I went to see old Ying leaving Adkins there & as soon as I got safely down the stairs I met Wade coming up. Well, I had an ½ hour with Ying who is a jolly old fellow and tremendously polite & thence I went to Hance who lugged out his collection of ferns and showed it me and then his library was overhauled, well repaying the trouble[234] though it is chiefly composed of those beastly philosophical German works against religion,[235] tho' he has a capital collection of classical works, all of which he has offered to lend me.

---

231 Presumably, Old Ying lived in Gough Street.
232 For Johnson, see Volume 1, footnote 134. His wife, Lumina Geertruida Maria van Medenbach Wakker (1818–1910), arrived in Hong Kong in 1851 from the Netherlands, meeting and marrying Johnson soon after.
233 Rev. George Piercy (1829–1913) was the first Wesleyan Methodist missionary in China. Based in Canton from 1851, he was engaged to his fiancée Jane, née Wannop (c. 1830–1878), around 1849, before embarking for Hong Kong. Jane arrived there in 1853.
234 This word 'trouble' appears at the head of page 137 of the second volume of the diary. The same word also appears at the head of page 139. The sentence that begins on page 136 is thus: 'I went to Hance who lugged out his collection of ferns and showed it me and then his library was overhauled, well repaying the / trouble though it is chiefly composed of those beastly philosophical German works against religion'. However, it could equally well be completed by moving straight to page 139: 'I went to Hance who lugged out his collection of ferns and showed it me and then his library was overhauled, well repaying the / trouble but when that was done I thought I should never get away'. However, the sentence made up of the last words on page 138 and the first words on page 139 makes little sense: 'Several memorable things have happened since I last wrote / trouble but when that was done I thought I should never get away'. I suspect that in his desire to catch up several days in his diary Alabaster actually completed his sentence about Hance's library twice on consecutive left-hand pages. The first attempt finishes at the bottom of page 138 with: 'Several memorable things have happened since I last wrote'. The second attempt carries on for more than four pages ending with: 'I must shut up and finish tomorrow'.
235 Possibly Ludwig Feuerbach (1804–1872) and Bruno Bauer (1809–1882). Feuerbach's *Das Wesen des Christentums* was translated by Mary Ann Evans (i.e. George Eliot) and published as *The Essence of Christianity* in 1854.

26. I have been again getting into that dreadfully bad habit of procrastination and for the last 4 days my diary has been neglected. My Chinese been progressing unfavorably. My laziness increasing. My self conceit and self contempt advancing with rapid stride, and harder and harder to fix my mind on one subject for more than 5 minutes, irritation and peevishness in the highest degree, and last but not least the fidgets, which are the bane of my existence, the thorn in my side, the cause of my humbug. Payne has cut me out in Gower's acquaintance[236] and has lost the pug which went to Sassoon,[237] tho' Payne had two tickets, Morrison 2, Gower 1, Tatham 3 & each of the Lawrences 1, making 10 out of the 25 shares but they lost it and Payne does not like having to fork out his $10.[238] Dâilleurs,[239] he & I have got on much as usual with an occasional skirmish. With Hughes the case is different. Imprimis,[240] he has been interpreting in the compradorial pidgeon in a most impertinent manner and he & I have already had a skirmish or two about that, once nearly resulting in a regular row. In secundis,[241] he has tried to chaff me & I have chaffed him till he got riled. I, then, contrary to all my Machiavellian policy which I always determine to but never do, I laugh at him; and in tertius,[242] he won't let me see his Irish papers so I don't let him see my *Atheneums* about which also we are rather sore. Adkins & I have got on well as usual. Several memorable things have happened since I last wrote.

trouble[243] but when that was done I thought I should never get away. No break was there in Hance's conversation, beginning with a robbery at the Attorney General's where tho' robbers left a dressing case on Hance's roof & the A.G. came in & said Hance's coolies would not give it up for fear they should be legally liable and going on on different subjects till I had 3 times risen to retire & Adkins had been fully instructed in all the mysteries of housekeeping by Mrs H. 21 was marked by nothing extraordinary to myself for I worked, played quoits & went to Wade's teacher as on 20, having a lonely walk there and back but Adkins in a high state of dudgeon

---

236 The meaning of this is unclear. It likely means that Payne has been socially unpleasant to Alabaster when Gower was present.
237 Probably Solomon David Sassoon (1841–1894), who worked as a clerk with his father David (1792–1864) at Sassoon's Sons & Co.
238 This appears to be some kind of raffle for a pug, a breed of dog (often confused with the Pekingese) kept by Chinese nobles.
239 French, 'Anyway'.
240 Latin, 'First'.
241 Latin, 'Secondly'.
242 Latin, 'Thirdly'.
243 See above, footnote 233.

at my having been put in Wade's Office, goes & consults Wade & the upshot of it is that Adkins writes an Official to Bowring but afterwards changes it to Woodgate & came home declaring he would leave the office for good, or else the Service, and he really thought he would but he won't. 22. Worked this day as usual and in the evening went down to Ying with Adkins, leaving Hughes in a fearful rage with me for chaffing him as I really have done considerably but more especially because I did it before Gower. It can't be helped. My tongue will lead me into difficulty & then we went in to Repton's, Payne having gone before & found a fellow named Reiry[244] & Duncanson dining there. After dessert we all started to see the singsong & came in in the middle. Got on to the stage. Found Grand Pre[245] & his wife there. Well, there was the usual row but there was a considerable lot of bawdy. A man & woman going to bed on the stage & being discovered by another lady who was wishing to be in there too. Well, I got a little information. 1 piece of cloth hanging on spears [sketch] = a camp. If the performer dies he throws a white cloth over his head & turns a somersault off the stage. A bed is curtains before 3 chairs. A performer behind a chair is invisible, &c. Back to Repton's. Duncanson goes & so do I and Adkins and Payne, leaving Reiry & Repton out on the loose. The weather is awfully hot. The time is midnight & now to bed. 23. Up as late as 7 & then unworkable lazy tho' working away all day. Rain & thunder early and the same late. Adkins got an answer to his Official, of course saying nothing at all but he seems satisfied. Smashed Payne's picture glass & he is now applying for 4th Assistantship. If he don't get it Gower will. Morrison came & sat a long while this evening chatting. He is horribly conceited. A swarm of white ants too flew up & the house is now full of them. 26. Continued to look back two pages on the night of 23. The mail came in at 8½ so next morning our letters and papers. All are well except poor Uncle who seems very ill. I wish he could get well whatever price it cost me. Henry is sure to come, he thinks, which will be jolly for me. Bowring's father and sister are

---

244 Phineas Ryrie (1829–1892). At this time a mercantile assistant with Turner & Co., he later became senior partner. During a long career as a tea merchant in Hong Kong he was co-founder of the company that began the construction of the peak tram, auditor of the Hong Kong and Shanghai Banking Corporation, first chairman of the Hong Kong Jockey Club, chairman of the Chamber of Commerce, a director of the Hong Kong, Canton and Macau Steamboat Company and a member of the Legislative Council.

245 Alexander Grandpré (1818–1864), a Portuguese man from Macau, at this time acting superintendent of police.

dead.[246] Peace is signed.[247] L'Imperatrice[248] has a very fine son.[249] The peace it seems was not well received in London for tho' the tower guns kept on blazing away, there was not a single illumination to be seen & *The Globe* newspaper[250] has gone into mourning for it, and now it being late I must shut up and finish tomorrow.

27. Now that I should work I am lazy. Now that I ought to keep my diary carefully I am careless. When I have lots to write I neglect all. News comes in everyday and I am far, far back but let one go on. On 24, after I got my letters & papers I did nothing but read them & waste my time reading all the murders which are numberless till 4 then to Leonard's. Took a boat & off & saw the review if so it can be called. Colonel Caine coming out uncommonly strong in cocked hat, &c. Well, there were lots of people there, it is true, and with the help of the drummer rather a good cheer was given & 3 salvos of small arms finished the proceedings, whereon I, Adkins & Leonard went and had a most delicious bath in the sea. It was out of one's depth directly & then home we came to a fearfully grand dinner to which Leonard came as a guest, and after drinking Her Majesty's health in champagne we felt remarkably buoyant. On Sunday too we were up early but all went to church, Adkins & Payne finding the sermon very short but then they went to sleep which accounts for it. In the evening Adkins & I off to the upper road and have a longish walk. Noticed the fearful want of water scooping up what drains thro' graveyards & this is what ½ the population of Hong Kong drink. Home to a long chat with conceited, unpopular Morrison & then to bed on a welsh rabbit,[251] to rise betimes and fall to work early on Monday morning till 10 when I get to Wade's office & find him non est,[252] however suddenly he comes & goes again like a meteor. I read an article on marriage by Medhurst[253] & another on the eagre[254] or tide at Hangchow which is a most remarkable thing. A wall of water 20 feet high

---

246 Reported in *China Mail*, 29 May 1856. As a result, *China Mail* says, Bowring did not review the troops on the Queen's Birthday, nor visit the French Legation in Macau, 'to take part in the rejoicings connected with the Birth of the Imperial Prince in Paris'.
247 The Treaty of Paris that brought the Crimean War to an end was signed on 30 March 1856.
248 Eugénie de Montijo (1826–1920), Empress consort to Napoleon III.
249 Napoléon, Prince Imperial (1856–1879), or Louis-Napoléon Bonaparte.
250 London newspaper, published from 1803 to 1921.
251 Rarebit.
252 Latin, 'he is not', but here, 'not there'.
253 W.H. Medhurst, 'Marriage, Affinity, and Inheritance in China', *Transactions of the China Branch of the Royal Asiatic Society*, part IV (1853–54): 1–32.
254 D.J. MacGowan, 'The Eagre of the Tsien-Tang River', *Transactions of the China Branch of the Royal Asiatic Society*, part IV (1853–54): 33–50.

moving down the river as far as Hangchow. Down he came. Gets Admiral Seymour in. Reintroduces me and gives His Excellency a sort of history of the Chinese language to which H.E. says, 'How wonderful!' & bolts as soon as possible & off goes Wade & about 2 comes down & tells one he will see me in 3 or 4 days or else write to me & in the evening I & Adkins went to Ying, whereon Wade called us up & gave us a lecture for about an hour & then I went to Leonard's who has got two jolly rooms & we talked till home we came & so on till today in which I worked all day. Raining in waterspouts. Everything drenched. A fearful wind. Perfectly smooth harbour. Clouds now & then, hiding everything & so on till 4 when home came the others bringing news that Mongan is to be Assistant Chinese Sec. with £300 per annum, none here being fit which riles Hughes immensely as he as usual thinks he ought to have it and Payne is to go to Shanghae which is a nuisance as Gower will be put in as 4 assistant, which will be the 2nd private secretary, then I went to Ying who is really a jolly old fellow & afterwards to Repton's where I found that consummate ass Ricketts & hence came home to bed.

28. Days pass & come. Wade has chapuhto wanle ao tati[255] examination papers which are something quite appalling to Payne who has seen them. Gower is to be 4th Assistant after passing an examination. Confound all jobbery. I have done a lot of work today but not satisfactory quite. Johnson has not answered my chit to him and I, Adkins & Payne going to Repton's. Kan si[256] found that the fellows had not come & so it was no good and accordingly singing wasted the evening.

29. Made a glorious discovery. I am only 17.[257] Hip hip hoorah. That old brute Meao told me so & for once I believe him. Borrowed Wade's Donaldson's *Grammar*[258] to help me on but have not opened it yet. I work hard but unsatisfactorily. Wade is going to live next door to us which will most jolly be. He is what one calls awfully plannish. He came up today as

---

255 Chinese, 'Chabuduo wanle. Ao! Tade 差不多完了噢他的', 'almost finished. Oh! His'. Thus, this passage might read: 'Wade has almost finished. Oh! His examination papers which are something quite appalling to Payne who has seen them'.
256 Alabaster's 'kan si' is obscure. It is probably a mistake for 'tan si' (as Alabaster would romanise it), that is *danshi* 但是, 'But'.
257 By the Western method of counting ages, Alabaster at this time *was* 17. By the Chinese method, he would have been 18. His birthday was on 14 September, see Volume 4.
258 John Williamson Donaldson (1811–1861) wrote grammars of both Latin and Greek as well as other important works of philology and Biblical criticism.

we at quoits were playing. He is a rum fellow. Moved back into my room. Went to Ying, &c., as usual. There has arrived a report that the Rose has gone down. Che puhsh tingti.[259]

30. Here goes for N° 2 of my diary. Now it must be finished & I am not in the vein to finish it. Wade commenced operations today. He came up, took possession of his house & gave directions to the carpenter. In a month the examination comes off. Wade has prepared papers for every one but as he will not look over all, it will be unfair as usual in these things. I must cram. That is certain but I feel very shaky before setting off. Especially this evening as I have been working hard all day & must do so & more for another month. It is dreadfully short time. Hughes has applied shang pay peen chu[260] so here goes for a finish to Vol. 2.

---

259 Chinese, 'Zhe bushi dingde, 這不是定的', 'This is not certain'.
260 Chinese, 'Shang bei bianzhou, 上備編著'. This reading is conjectural, first, because Alabaster's writing of 'peen' is unclear and, secondly, because it has no obvious meaning. If my interpretation of Alabaster's romanisation is correct, the whole sentence would read: 'Hughes has applied, successfully, to become provisional editor'. In August 1856, Hughes did become third assistant in the Superintendency of Trade. Given that Alabaster, when he occupied the most junior position in the office, was charged with copying out documents, it is possible that the third assistant – two grades higher – was given the job of checking them.

Alabaster Diary, Volume 3

1855

June

1. Here begins Vol. 3 of my Diary and I am sorry to have to begin it with what a fool I am. But so it is. I have this moment had an abominable row with Hughes. All about nothing and I went to great lengths and now of course regret it. Payne received news that he was to go tomorrow per *Vindex* so we gave him a dinner. Gower & Duncanson coming & Repton & Dr Hance afterwards & we had awful fun. Old Hance drunk as a fiddler & singing away like the very mischief till 12½ so we had a very enjoyable evening. Today went to church, settled accounts & lastly with Adkins called on Morrison & Wade.

2. At home. Settled the accounts which have me rather empty. Adkins at home worked away well. I happily, not at all. Somehow it is all very jolly working with one who knows considerably more than you but with an equal it is beastly & especially one who only cares for the practical part & abominates the language ∴ he won't attend to the ornamental & there is the difference between me & Adkins. He probably knows much more than I but I can enjoy it. He detests it. This evening went to Leonard's & had a most glorious sail going on at a spanking rate an immense way & then tacking in & having a jolly bathe in deeper water than usual & with a jolly bottom & thence we went to the singsong where we met Repton, Duncanson, Hudson[1] & another fellow & heard a fearful row & were nearly taken up for refusing to pay entrance. It was rather dull tho' there were some splendid

---

1   Joseph Trevitt Hudson (1826–1870), at this time merchant's clerk at Gibb, Livingstone & Co.

tumblers there who threw splendid somersaults & – a novelty in China – real women – being for the 1st time but they were nothing very peculiar tho' one was dressed beautifully. A round Polish cap, [sketch] white behind, [sketch] trimmed with fur in front & it was rather good fun. So goodnight.

3. Not out of bed till 6½. It won't do. Today has been regularly wasted. Before breakfast I did very little good & after, what with talking to Payne & not doing any Yu Cheao Li[2] because of Adkins having other pidgeon, I did not manage much. Then at 8½ down we went to see Payne off. Off we went with a spanking breeze. Off to the schooner of the seas, the schooner par excellence of all the ships that are in these parts, tho' nearly equalled by the *Wild Dayrell*. Still the *Vindex* is non pareil.

Tho' the guns are not so big,
for pirates they don't care a fig,
with long eighteen & bonny nines,
beams of oak & masts of pines.
They the tempest can outlive,
& the pirates bullets give.
Truly 'tis a jolly schooner,
& will get to Woosung sooner
than a steamer could this weather.

Here is another break in our party. Another of the ties which bind us to old England has been cut however it is not so bad as when old King went for he was both our fellow student & came out with us & was a jolly fellow besides & it was about the first change. We change about fearfully in the Service. Really. I have bought Payne's bedstead, &c. & tonight for the first time for 7 months I'm to sleep on a mattress. Only think of that for an officer of Her Majesty! God save the Queen! I may ever say so, hurrah! Gower coming up, I went down. Saw H.E. & borrowed Davis's *China*. Searched all over Sir John's library. It is jolly full of books but in the worst order possible. Everything atop & nothing at hand. I thence went to tea at Dr Johnson's, a meal I have not partaken of since I have been in China so to speak i.e. I have never had a regular English tea & after a mullimum of jabber & no information Mr & Mrs Peasy came in & Mr P. first read a chapter to the Hebrews in a horribly drawling manner & then extemporized ½ an hour's prayer during which I am ashamed to say I was in imminent peril of splitting with laughter as I fancied Adkins was snoring which it luckily turned out he was not.

---

2   See Volume 2, footnote 218.

Superficial I am. Deny it, who can?
I am a humbly aging foolish man.
Cheko tu sh cheen tsz te hwa.
Puh sh. Sh chenti. Puh sh cheati
nali hwa.[3]
Poops fal de lal
& so to bed

4. Each day as it passes exemplifies in a striking manner my shallowness of disposition, my ignorance, my former & present laziness. Each day I seem to get lazier & lazier & more stupid. Making notes, I am great in. Compilations, my delight. But when compiled I am such a fool that I never learn them. Today I have had a goodish amount of work but I am afraid I am not much the better for it, the Yu cheao li being very hard & I very sleepy. Seymour won't give Sir J. the fleet & Dr Parker is going up alone. Now is the time for he who would get on. Now is the time for intrigue from which I must keep as much as possible. Mr Johnson[4] sent me a Williams's *Middle Kingdom* today.[5] It is, as all his last batch have been, damaged by saltwater but the inside is all right & it makes ½ dollar difference in the price. Have been reading Davis's *China* this evening. It is concise and sweet but I don't remember it as I should.

6. Yesterday I am sorry to say I did not write a word of diary. Chi yin way yu niujin lae theka niujin yiting sh ko peao wo seang ta chu shuey.[6] Yesterday Wade's papers were given us to do and I have been in a confounded conflict ever since between my interest & my principle which latter will I hope gain the day & then like a fool wor kaosu hunpo ching niu jen lae[7] and consequently was most uncomfortable all night. May I never do so again &

---

3   Chinese, 'Zhege doushi Qianzide hua. Bushi. Shi zhende. Bushi jiade nalihua 這個 都是千字的話.不是.是真的.不是假的哪裡話', 'This is all from the Qianzi[wen]. No! It's true. Not false words from somewhere else'.
4   Francis Bulkeley Johnson (1828–1887), Hong Kong merchant, later in Jardine, Matheson & Co. in Hong Kong, where he was a member of the Legislative Council, and Shanghai, where he was also honorary consul for Denmark.
5   Samuel Wells Williams, *The Middle Kingdom: A Survey of the Geography, Government, Education, Social Life, Arts, Religion, Etc., of the Chinese Empire and its Inhabitants* (New York and London: Wiley and Putnam, 1848).
6   Chinese, 'Zhi yinwei you nüren lai. Zhege nüren yiding shi ge piao. Wo xiang ta chushui, 只因爲有女人來. 這個女人一定是個嫖. 我想她出水', 'This is only because a woman came. She was certainly a loose woman. I think she enjoyed herself'. Note, Alabaster's 'theka' is almost certainly a mistake for 'cheka' (as he would have Romanised it).
7   Chinese, 'Wo gaosu hunpo "qing nüren lai' 我告訴婚婆請女人來', 'I asked the Madam, "please bring me a woman"'.

may no ill effects ensue. Had a jolly bath in the ravine all among the fish, Hughes gravely contemplating the scene. Today quite seedy. I copied out the papers and then slept for about ½ the day. Sir J. lent me his *Decimal Coinage*.[8] May I get on jolly. Had a jolly bathe in the sea today. Quite a jolly ripple on the water and I managed both to dive & to float. Two great accomplishments. Also went to see Tatham who is very seedy indeed.

7. End of a most unsatisfactory week in which much bad but little good has been done. I have sinned. I have made a fool & a beast of myself. I have been deceived, bothered & humbugged. Confound it. Today I translated the *Edict*[9] so one answer is done. Hip hip hurrah! May I live for ever & chuang z les for jollipot.[10] Went partially up the ravine. Came down & read Sir John Bowring's *Decimal System*. A most interesting book. Promotion looks brisk. I must keep my eyes open.

8. Sunday. Up late & went to church, the *Fiery Cross* coming in as we went in bringing Harry Parkes & wife with it. Quarreled with Hughes. Wrote letters or rather a fearfully long one to Aunty. Went out bathing, Leonard nearly getting drowned on going in head forward into a deep hole. Afterwards we went to Leonard's & supped.

9. Went to Wade's office & was quite a jack in office.[11] Kang Sinsang is ill & all the others went to sleep. As for me I worked away like a good one at the historical writers of China.[12] Managed a good deal but have a lot more to do yet before even that semi-question is finished off but I want to answer it well as it is to be a compilation. Got through 8 vols. of *Chin. Rep.*[13] to do it besides skimming two others. Went to Gower and saw Parkes. A jolly, gentlemanly looking fellow. Lane has come down here pro tem. Everyone is going home. May I distinguish myself as I could wish.

10. Went to Wade's office. I read and collated like the very mischief. I am sure I ought to make something out of it. *Memoriae Sinicae*.[14] *Chinese Repository*. Nothing can exceed my rapacity. All are devoured. I was so engaged today

---

8   John Bowring, *The Decimal System in Numbers, Coins and Accounts: Especially with Reference to the Decimalisation of the Currency and Accountancy of the United Kingdom* (London: Nathaniel Cooke, 1854).
9   See Volume 2, footnote 24.
10 The meaning of this phrase is obscure.
11 'Jack in office', 'a person in authority who behaves in an officious manner, esp. one in a relatively minor position' (*Oxford English Dictionary*).
12 The 'historical writers of China' was evidently one of the exam questions Wade had set.
13 *China Repository*.
14 Presumably a mistake for Premare's *Notitiae Sinicae*. See Volume 1, footnote 141.

that I did not even see the mail go – being the first mail I have missed seeing – before she left 8½. An hour after getting on board Mrs Caldwell bore a son.[15] Went for a walk today. Cut Lawrence most distinctly. Leonard came up this evening. I am very seedy & ought not to have taken such a long walk with Gower & Hughes as I did. Am getting ill-tempered & very snappish which I must correct as this will never do. Saw Lane. He looks fearfully ill. I scarcely knew him. He was so altered. Pale. His whiskers growing dandified & lame. I had some difficulty in recognizing him.

11. Going to bed tired but with the consciousness of having done something towards answering the examination paper, though perhaps not much yet. It is something I have been working tremendously today & have enough to take me 6 months to do properly. Can translate the history jollily, which is more than some can. Have just proved the date in it to my satisfaction. Went out for a bath this evening. I had a swim. I can now manage swimming on my back but am far too weak to be able to swim well. Lane came up this evening. He has been fearfully ill, nearly dying from overwork. Came home with Abel Gower Esq. The more one sees of him, the rummer he appears. Am getting on at a slapping pace towards answering the history paper.

12. As is now my universal custom I went to Wade's office and made a fearful lot of notes. Tomorrow I must finish. I have got a fearful lot of materials together. Quære:[16] can I make a proper use of them? My mind is in a curious state of repletion but has scarcely been able to digest anything. It seems in a sort of fermenting state, ready to boil over at the smallest provocation and my head aching most abominably today. I made a lot of notes writing nearly ½ a notebook in French extracted from the *Memoires curieuses par les missionaires francais*[17] & this afternoon read Alison *History* about the Murder of Louis XVI.[18] What a beast égalité was. A brutal beast. Tatham came up. He has had a considerable illness & is not ill yet there is something in him which attracts me to him preciously, though I want to quietly break with him for he is sans doute[19] good natured & good nature

15   *China Mail*, 12 June 1856, noted the happy occasion: 'Births ... At Hongkong, on the 10th June, on board the P. & O. Steamer *Norna*, the Wife of H.C. Caldwell, Registrar of the Court of Judicature, Singapore, of a daughter'.
16   Latin, 'Query'.
17   This is the *Lettres édifiantes et curieuses, écrites des Missions étrangères, par quelques missionnaires de la Compagnie de Jésus*, a collection of letters from Jesuits based in China published in the early eighteenth century. An English translation appeared as early as 1707.
18   See Volume 2, footnote 228.
19   French, 'without doubt'.

has a great effect on me. I only wish I could be so. In proof of the contrary, I cuffed a small boy today. The American war steamer came in today with Townsend Harris on board, the Consul General of Japan & Plenipo.[20] to Siam and there were a fearful lot of salutes.[21] Two of 21 guns, 2 of 9 guns & 1 or 2 of 7. Whenever a Yankee comes anywhere they let everyone know it very soon indeed.

13. Got up earli-ish but as usual managed to muddle away, in looking for quotations, &c., those valuable hours and then went to the office and from 10 till 4 was writing as though for my life not stopping even for tiffin. About midday Meao came down and I translated the Canton placard[22] with his aid. It is like all the other things very easy. Home and dinner, Hughes insinuating on the road up that I had read translations of the Chinese documents which was just what I expected of him. Home. Read Alison on the separation of Fox and Burke and the State of Europe during the French revolution. How is it, I wonder, that men cannot[23] differ in politics but remain private friends. It is strange but here is a memorable instance of it: their different opinions on the French revolution separating two of the primest friends, whose friendship had lasted through life till they were both verging towards old age. This evening, finding out that it was Adkins's birthday, I went with him to Leonard whom I found at table with Calders, Pressmann[24] and Wheely. Calders is an awfully rum fellow & he & Leonard where[25] continually chaffing each other till at last C. wanting to prove something sent for his notebook of former years and read us some very curious extracts: 'I went from the railway station to the x hotel in a cab with a very pretty girl' & told us of his having kissed the King of Portugal's hand though a republican & how unfortunate he was when he went home, his father dying, and afterwards Lisbon being made a sort of hell, the Queen

---

20   Plenipotentiary.
21   Townsend Harris (1804–1878) arrived on the *San Jacinto*, putting in at Hong Kong on his way to Japan where he opened the first US Consulate there, in Shimoda. On his way to Hong Kong he had negotiated the Treaty of Amity, Commerce, and Navigation with Siam.
22   This is likely what Bowring described in a letter to Consul Harry Parkes on 3 July as 'an anonymous incendiary placard, which has been circulated in the streets of Canton, menacing the lives of foreigners who may visit the neighbouring villages'. See, Appendix A. 'Papers Respecting the Right of British Subjects to Have Free Entrance into Canton', in *Papers Related to the Proceedings of Her Majesty's Naval Forces at Canton, with Appendix* (London: Harrison & Sons, 1857), 214. A translation of what is there termed 'a hand-bill' appears on page 213. This may be Alabaster's but no name is given. At this time, a 'placard' need not have had the meaning of a 'sign' or 'poster' that it now has.
23   From the context, this should be 'can'.
24   B. Plessmann was a merchant's clerk at Dent & Co.
25   In manuscript, mistake for 'were'.

of Portugal dying[26] & minute guns being fired by all the forts & ships, so he had to stop at home till he went to England & his superstition how about 8 years ago a glass broke & the lamp was blown out on the same day that his brother died, so he is in a state today ∴ a portrait of his Aunt blew down & many other things. Pressman is a regular German. Clear enough as to intellect but unable to express himself. Wheely is a moral and edifying young man. Home through heavy rain and high wind. Tatham came up tonight. His illness has done him good. He is not so bawdy now as he used to be. He is going to stop up here pro tem. Went out for a walk with Hughes. Driven home by fear of rain.

14. Fit for nothing except sleep all day. A typhoon expected. Lane & Gower came up to dinner.

16. Last night I was not very much in the humour for writing and tonight I am still less so for I am very seedy. Yesterday evening there was a great wind & all the ships were getting into the sheltered spots and quite a swell getting up and a typhoon was & is expected. Lane and Gower came to dinner. Gower is a remarkably jolly fellow. Lane, a conceited, ambitious fellow. Today, as there was a high wind, a heavy sea & lots of rain, I could not make up my mind to go to church & stopping at home felt very seedy & put several things to rights & now am going to bed.

17. Yesterday I sat reading *The Fortunes of Nigel*[27] till past 1 & so fell asleep before I could write my diary. Went to office as usual & worked, then went out with Lane & Adkins for a sail taking Gower & Hughes with us. Well, there was a considerable wind. The boat was considerably over on one side when a little water coming over, Hughes – in a fearful fright – yelled out, 'Oh hi! Stop! I can't swim! Stop!' to everyone's great amusement tho' I confess I was nearly as much frightened as he was. Well, then we had a swim & I had two jolly plunges & so home, where no sooner had I arrived than the puer[28] told me two deliberate lies & on my preparing to lick him therefore cut for his life in a most tremendous funk & is even now non est inventus[29] & as a wind up Tatham came up as he is going to stop here protem & we fell to whist & then I fell to *Nigel* & so we did not much good

---

26   Maria II, died 15 November 1853.
27   Sir Walter Scott, *The Fortunes of Nigel* (Edinburgh: Archibald Constable & Co.; London: Hurst, Robinson & Co., 1822).
28   Latin, 'boy'.
29   Latin, 'he was not found'. In *Oliver Twist*, Charles Dickens, renders his character Mr Lively's pronunciation of this as 'Non istwentus'.

today. Got up late. Did scarcely anything before breakfast & on looking out *Fort William*, The *Erin, Canton*, a brig & Jardine's & P.& O. flagstaffs were all dressed jollily, it being the bridal day of Miss Fanny Firth & Mr Macleod of Jardine, M. & Co.[30] Jardine gave the breakfast & the plate & Walker lent the P. & O. Str[31] *Canton*. Well, tho' the weather was beastly, pouring with rain, windy, cloudy & brutal, well, they were married & all the carriages & chairs went off to East Point to the tune of 'Merrily Danced the Quaker's Wife & Merrily Danced the Quaker'[32] in a merry shower & soon after the steamer *Canton*, gallantly dressed out with flags & greens, steamed out for Macao with the bride & bridegroom under a terrific salute from Jardine's, a brig & two yachts. Wade came back today. I saw him in the office. He was in a jolly humour. Has brought 2 more teachers with him. One as good nearly as Chang or Ying. Saw but little of him however as he went to the festivities & I well employed a part of my time in translating a petition from the inhabitants of Aberdeen who it seems are miserably oppressed by pirates. Home. Adkins went out & Gower came in & soon Mr Irving made his appearance & we had a longish conversation with him. Among other topics he touched on bawdy shops & left one under the impression that it was no harm going there but that you would very likely to get robbed there[33] & on drinking which seems no harm unless you drunk bad liquor & finished by nailing us to go there on Friday at 7 o'clock precisely whereat I feel very happy. Verily he is an ass, whom any ass endued with even asinine brains might see through & then came the grand event of the day. We all went to dinner at the Governor's where I had the pleasure of sitting next to H.E. who was fearfully cross because he did not get his onions. At first we were a regular family party – H.E. & Lady B., Gower, Lane & us 3 – & after a tattling dinner in which I let fall one heedless thing we all adjourned to billiards whereat I enjoyed myself for hours. Old Hughes looking most awfully Irish in his tailcoat. Truly tails distinguish the paddy as much as caps do the German, after which sage reflection to bed.

18. The *Pekin* came in last night bringing the treaty[34] with her with which I suppose we ought to be satisfied, tho' some of the most important articles are not known publicly. Got up late. Rain & wind. The ravines transformed

---

30   The *Indian News and Chronicle of Eastern Affairs* for 1856 reported the marriage between 'Malcolm Anderson, eldest son of the late Alexander Macleod, of Helmsburgh, Dumbartonshire, to Fanny Kendall, youngest daughter of the late Samuel Firth, of Sutton-at-Hone, Kent'.
31   Steamer.
32   A Scottish fiddle tune.
33   Grammar as in manuscript.
34   See Volume 2, footnote 216.

into waterfalls, &c. Went to office. My translation was a bitchy affair. Great humbug. Wade however seemed pleased that I had done it & does not seem displeased with me. Worked most unsatisfactorily & so home leaving my pasteboard[35] at Govt. house & home & then, Lane being unable to go, I, Adkins & Leonard went for a bathe which we had after a most unsatisfactory sail, for the typhoon still hangs over us & the wind is high & gusty.

19. How the time flies. The white ants have attacked my drawers which are going to blazes. Rain, rain, rain & awfully hot. Went to office & consulted some useful Chinese books & an encyclopaedia. How strange it is that both countries should have a red book. To think that the editor of our red book had a predecessor in China.[36] Am getting on very slowly but let me hope surely as well as slowly. May I work on steadily, daily increasing my knowledge so that in time I may be of some use. All the teachers are getting sick. The houses are certainly unhealthy. Well, I hope I may get on all right but Wade is going to begin a sort of course with us on Monday. Hance has come back bringing some new specimens for which he wants me to find a name on very slender data. However, I will if I can & I think I am on the clue. Am deep in the provincial officers at present.

20. Up late. Little work ante prandium.[37] Post prandium,[38] tho' it rained magnificently, I trudged manfully down to office & by dint of excessive talking & questioning the teacher got nearly all the particulars I require respecting provincial officers so I can now set to work & clear off that question & then I had a conversation with Chang who it seems taught Medhurst, Meadows, Lay, Duus,[39] Thompson[40] & others. Thompson it seems was quite a little boy, not fit to come out here & it rained & lightened. The battery blazed away in honour of Her Majesty's accession[41] & home. I came as jolly as could be by the side of the stream which is

---

35 A visiting card.
36 The Chinese 'red book' was an official publication – with red covers – that listed all the officials in the empire. The British red book was: 'A register or directory of the British court, nobility, members of the government, and other socially important people' (*Oxford English Dictionary*).
37 Latin, 'Before lunch'.
38 Latin, 'After lunch'.
39 Nikolaj Duus (c. 1807–1861) was a Danish merchant who arrived in China in 1837 and when the colony was established moved to Hong Kong where he became a very successful businessman. He moved to Shanghai for a time during which he was Danish consul. On his return to Hong Kong he became consul for Norway and Sweden. He was also one of Hong Kong's earliest masons.
40 This is likely A.J. Thompson, a student interpreter who arrived in Hong Kong in 1852 aged only 15 but left within two years because of his health.
41 The anniversary of the accession to the throne of Queen Victoria on 20 June 1837.

full of water & all the ravines are transformed into waterfalls, the stepping stones being 6 inches or more under water. A rise of at least 12 inches in 24 hours & this evening we all went to Irving's to tea. I saw the celebrated Miss Mole[42] who is certainly very pretty, well-formed, handsome, plays well (I understand), sings well, ill-bred, ill-mannered. I had the infinite pleasure of sitting next to her at tea. Neither would she permit me to do anything for her nor would she answer civilly. Mrs Irving is rather a jolly woman tho' she has a devil of a sharp nose and is very unwell at present, as is natural. She seemed to know me & Irving asserted that she did but I do not think I ever saw her before. Then there is little Irving. A jolly little girl. Very clever, considerably sharp, by no means ugly, very agreable. She & I played at Combinations of Letters all the evening. It is a very silly, irrational, boshy, humbugging game mais il sert pour passer le temps[43] & Miss Mole, after playing two pieces – I, like a ninnyhammer,[44] standing beside her, the others being I thought very rude – sat by herself all the rest of the evening. At 9, Hughes bolted like mad fearing lest he should be hooked into prayers which we had immediately after. Long & prosy & then home. Irving is an ass. An awful ass. He seems to think he knows everything while in fact, from what I have seen, he seems to know nothing, as I shall find some day is my case. However, we spent an amusing evening, I getting quite disgusted with Miss Mole & delighted with Miss Irving, having supreme contempt for Mr Irving & a considerable liking for Mrs *do*[45] & so to bed. Read part of Fortune's *China*.[46] All botanical & rather humbuggery though goodish light reading.

21. Thunder, lightning & rain all day. Went to office & worked. The answers go on abominably slowly. Brutally slowly but nonetheless I hope they go on surely. I seem getting popular among the sinsangs & say what one will, if Wade hears from this may[47] & that I am clever, &c. he must have an impression made on him. It has made one once. It shall do so again. Wade came in tonight, bolted up into my room, found me working, blew up my teacher & entered into that I am to go to him tomorrow evening with Adkins & talk over some new plan that he has got underway. Then he bolted into Adkins & finally down below, where he talked away jollily. He, it seems,

---

42　This was likely the daughter of either George or Henry Moul, of Moul & Co.
43　French, 'but it serves to pass the time'.
44　A fool.
45　Ditto, that is, Irving.
46　This was likely either Robert Fortune's *Three Years' Wanderings in the Northern Provinces of China* (1847), or his *A Journey to the Tea Countries of China* (1852).
47　I suspect there is a missing word here.

began in '42, had an appointment in '43 & went home in '45. He came back, acted as Interpreter in the Supreme Court & was then made Acting Chinese Secretary. Lay, it seems, is first of the interpreters, after whom come Parkes, Meadows & Medhurst. Sinclair he does not think much of. Seao is to be my teacher. It will be a heavy pull but as old Meao is going away I thought it advisable, though he be an old ass, to take him. We were luckily all of us working when Wade came, whereat he was much pleased. The Yankees fired minute guns today about Washington's death[48] & I am sorry to say our ships had their flags ½ mast high, to my great disgust. The *Smyrna* was towed in today. Her mizzen mast & main topmasts being quite carried away. There are many ships in now, damaged by the late typhoon. The mail ought to be in but is not.

22. Oh! Diary or journal. When will you be to me what a former one was? When will some devouring passion, love, ambition, hate or what not fill your pages with something more than the dull & uninteresting facts which make up my life? When shall I read in your pages my plots for the gain of honour or of fame? When? I fear me never! Plot, I do! Who doubts it? But now so different from former days. I will not write them here for fear some prying knave should read them. Some inquisitive rascal with more skill than honor open locks & keys & peeping where he has no business,[49] read all my petty schemes & laugh me to scorn as well. I deserve to be laughed to scorn. Promptus et audax.[50] Have I acted up to thee today? Alas, I answer no but stop. No more humbug. Today I got up very late, obstinately refusing to get out of bed & then after a glorious bath & tolerable breakfast to which Tatham stopped, I & Adkins went to church which was crowded to an excess, I having several occasions both to show promptness & gallantry but no more. Peter Parker was in church with the Governor & there were so many strange looking people whose character my insane & boshy brain would fain analyse & so I do not remember anything at all about the sermon. Miss Mole looked ever more forbidding than ever & Buggins' brother[51] in, in church time, making a fearful row. Home to tiffin. Then we came, accompanied by Wheely & Leonard who stopped with us all the afternoon. Verily, they are rather jolly fellows & we got on remarkably well. After dinner I & A. went into Wade who had about him new plans in dozens. A new dictionary. New

---

48   It is highly unlikely that this was a commemoration of George Washington's death as that occurred on 14 December 1799; 21 June is, however, the anniversary of the ratification of the US Constitution.
49   This seems to indicate that Alabaster kept his diary locked up.
50   Latin, 'prompt and bold'.
51   On 'Buggins' see below.

vocabularies. Hundreds of dodges. Wade is a fearfully jolly & clever fellow but he can never do much good for himself while so variable. Well, at any rate, we begin a new system i.e. learning words in categories – tomorrow at 9 for 3 hours a day per Jovem.[52] Then I went out strolling & saw lots of wonderful things. Among others, a body of a beetle surrounded by myriads of ants led on by their leaders, 3 of whom were overpowering a small beetle who was there. Home & many other things. Some beautiful eggs, some just upon hatched, all the rest quite hatched & the insects surrounding them. Just before going to bed 3 minute guns[53] fired & now a bellis piu questo.[54] Puh tung.[55]

23. The mail not in. At 9 precisely I & Adkins went to Wade's & set to work till 12 & really speaking, that is nearly all the honest work I did today & feeling dreadfully seedy. As soon as it left off raining I went & took a bath in the ravine. It was splendid. The water was rushing in & the pool was so enlarged & deepened by the rain that I had quite a jolly swim in it. The ravine is splendid now, the water rushing down in fine style, bounding and burbling, &c., &c. vide[56] the Waterfall of Ladore[57] & idly bathed therein. After dinner, finished *Kenilworth*.[58] And nothing more, so bed & good night as I am not in a mood for writing.

24. A reform must be worked. I shall never get on if so be that I go on as I am going on always. Up late. Never doing any work. It will not do. Today went to Wade's. I worked away for 3 hours. Home. Demi-worked for 3½ hours. Read Alison. Evening semi-worked an hour. Old Seao is a beast. He will not give a direct answer. Bother him as I may, as I will, he will not keep to his subject, say as often as I can. Revenons à vos moutons.[59] Wan puh leang.[60] He is an old beast & I shall not keep him very long that is certain. The old

---

52 Latin, 'By Jove'.
53 Minute guns are guns fired ceremonially once every minute.
54 The phrase 'bellis piu questo' appears to be an attempt at Italian. 'Bellis' can mean 'battles' in Latin but is not an Italian word. 'Piu questo' can mean 'and also this' in Italian. What Alabaster is getting at here is obscure.
55 Chinese, *budong* 不懂, 'I don't understand'.
56 Latin, 'see …'.
57 The Lodore Falls, near Keswick in Cumbria. The falls were made famous in Victorian times through the popularity of Robert Southey's poem, 'The Cataract of Lodore' (1820). Alabaster's 'bounding and burbling, &c., &c.' is clearly a reference to the poem, much of which consists of a series of descriptive verbs in the form of, for example: 'Rising and leaping, Sinking and creeping, Swelling and sweeping, Showering and springing'.
58 Sir Walter Scott, *Kenilworth: A Romance* (1821).
59 French, a proverb, also common in English in the nineteenth century, 'Let us return to our sheep', that is, 'Let us return to the subject at hand'. Also rendered 'Revenons à nos moutons'.
60 Chinese, *wan bu liang* 完不良, 'He is really bad'.

fool knows nothing, can scarcely write a character & is such an obstinate, conceited, worthless, old fool that he will not ask any one else. The mail is not in though the weather is better. Was going to the reception but having lost or mislaid my key, I had no coat to go in so stopped at home and talked to Hance. Promptus et audax. I have not been promtus[61] et audax. May I be.

25. The mail is in – hip hip hurrah! – as I & Adkins were in with Wade. Bang went the gun! W. rushed to the window & then danced, sparred with the teacher & cut most extraordinary capers, and of course we were in a deuce of a state too till 12 when we got our F.O. letters: 1 Uncle, 1 Aunty, 2 Henry, 1 Aunt Kate, 1 Katy, containing good & bad news. Henry is coming out – hip hip hurrah! 3 cheers! Now go it! Arblaster[62] for ever! Charly, too, had got into the Union[63] & is curate elect of St Ebbes.[64] But poor little Percy has had a bad attack of croup & Aunty ill & those damned fools the Calcrafts[65] of the Royal Academy would not hang the 4 seasons[66] & all the moving is done & Aunty writes dolefully because her pictures were not sold. But that is all rectified by a letter from Uncle & 1 from Charly, for Aunty has sold two pictures. Hip! Jolly! Henry has got his appointment[67] & comes out in August & Aunty & Percy are getting all right. The letters are all jolly. Uncle makes me most thoroughly ashamed of myself as he ends so confident in me: 'Be a good boy & take care of yourself.' May I try henceforth to fulfill this. May the Lord give me strength. To think that I, who have been such a beast, such a fool, such a blaguard as I have been, should have anyone to have such confidence in me as is expressed by these 3 or 4 words. Aunty, too, writes lovingly & affectionately to me though depressed. Henry's letter is written in great excitement at his success. Poor fellow. He little knows what is before him. He & I must stick together. Never separate. He it is whom I want out here. Adkins will thus be drawn closer to me. Everything must then go well. Charly is more fraternal than ever & urges me to be confirmed & so I must be, so soon as I may be fit for it. Aunt Kate's letter makes me angry & Cousin Kate's is the silliest thing that ever coy[68] of mine did write. Uncle seems a little better in health &

---

61 Written this way in manuscript.
62 Alabaster believed that his name, historically, had been rendered 'Arblaster'.
63 The Oxford Union.
64 St Ebbe's is an Anglican church in the centre of Oxford.
65 William Calcraft (1800–1879) was a famous executioner of the time. Alabaster is making a pun on 'hangman'.
66 The *Four Seasons* was a series of watercolours (see Introduction, 'The Alabaster Family').
67 Like Chaloner, to the Consular Service.
68 Company, that is, Alabaster's friends and relatives.

though pecuniary affairs are not as flourishing as they should be. So much for home. Now for news. Woodhouse[69] goes as plenipo. to St Petersburg & the peace has been proclaimed by the heralds publicly with pomp & c.[70] The Crimean commission[71] is sitting & the gallerices[72] are after nothing more. A most uninteresting batch of news. H.E. is suffering severely from some disease. I called there today with Hughes. Dr Parker's wife has not come, to his great disappointment & so after a lazy but exciting day I meet my couch.

26. Great saluting because of the peace. The *Nankin* opened the ball which was taken up by the battery & when they had each fired off 21 guns, the *San Jacinto* took it up & fired 21 & then the *Levant* fired 21 & then the *Levant* again, *San Jacinto* again & then the *Levant* so we had 126 guns in all,[73] the Spanish steamer sulkily refusing to fire. Morrison did not get his letters yesterday thro' the stupidity of his coolie. Laid it all on me which I took most comfortably as he has 0 to do with me. Went as usual to Wade's today at 10 but found him in his shirt & pitgamas, ½ shaved & looking the rummest monster imaginable. However, in ½ an hour we went & had our lessons after which I went & made Wan sinsang's acquaintance. A very intellectual fellow for a Chinaman & then after dinner strolled out with Hughes & Gower & wandering into the Taipingshan[74] we arrived at a joss house which we entered.[75] It looked rather jolly outside & had two capital granite dogs [sketch]. On entering we found that there was 1st the outer court in which a spiral joss stick was burning & in which were several inscriptions, two rows of ornamented spears, a table with large incense bowls & up two or 3 steps was an altar but it was too dark to see anything except an incense stand on it. Hanged in two rows from it were 6 gods & goddesses, 1 a jolly nigger with a splendid beard, fierce mustachioes & a most terrific spear or mase.[76] In the middle was a mat for the buffers to kneel on and behind it were two large bronze bowls full of burnt paper, a gong, bell & drum, offerings & lanterns. I & Hughes read two sentences in Chinese which delighted

---

69   John Wodehouse, first Earl of Kimberley (1826–1902).
70   Pomp and circumstance. The Crimean War ended on 30 March 1856 with the Treaty of Paris; celebrations were held in various places in Britain and across the empire over the next few months.
71   The 'Commission of Inquiry into the Supplies of the British Army in the Crimea' submitted its report to Parliament in July 1856.
72   Galleries, that is, public opinion, journalists.
73   Alabaster seems to have left off one of the sets of 21 guns in his accounting. 126 should be 147.
74   See Volume 2, footnote 36.
75   The 'joss house' is the Man Mo temple on Hollywood Road.
76   Mace, a bludgeon.

them plagueyly[77] & they got into a great state of jollity with us. Home. Work & now I have had ½ an hour's read at Sir John's *Decimal Coinage* which leaves me in a rum state. In primus,[78] I am convinced that a decimal system is good but am in considerable doubt as to what is the best unit to take, whether shilling, florin, dollar or sovereign. However, perhaps further reading will elucidate this. 2ndly, I am convinced that a perfect decimal system of weights & measures can never be established [obscure] & that time measure, apothecary's measure & paper measure will be what will stop it. In primus, we will allow the French gramme, litre & metre to be excellent but time measure can never be decimalised while 365½ days go to a year & paper being sold by sheets will be a long time coming into a decimal system & 3rdly, I doubt much whether apothecary's measure will ever alter:

1. ∵ it would add immensely to the labour of the study of medicine, all the books being written in the old system,
2. it would give rise to endless mistakes,
3. ∵ nothing is so conservative as medicine, in witness whereof I need only adduce the general use to this day of Dog Latin,[79] and so having to my own sage mind quashed the French system by 1 good & 2 very dubious arguments I shall rest well, I hope.

27. Ill and seedy. Went to Wade. I hope the plan will go on for yitingti sh a jolly dodge tan sh Wade laoyer[80] carries it on a little too far thus he always talks about publishing it & then one can place no reliance on its continuance. However, at any rate an alteration is going to be made. Edkins is to take down the pronunciation and I the English while Wade directs & so we shall go on jollily. Worked more satisfactorily today than I usually do. Translated one of the English papers into Chinese & all the short colloquial sentences besides a little of Seu[81] to Bonham so that is rather swimming. This evening after dinner went for a walk in the hills. Went to a place where I have not been before & where there was a jolly view of waterfall, &c. & then bathed in the ravine & lastly this evening after work had a game

---

77　Plaguily, embarrassingly.
78　Latin, 'first of all'.
79　A form of vulgarised, Latinised English.
80　Chinese, 'Yidingde shi a jolly dodge danshi Wade Laoye … 一定的是 a jolly dodge 但是 Wade 老爺 …', 'It is certainly a jolly dodge but Old Man Wade …'.
81　Seu is Seu Kwang Tsin, or Xu Guangjin 徐廣縉 (c. 1785–1858). From 1848 until 1852, he concurrently held the offices of imperial commissioner for foreign affairs and viceroy of the Liangguang, succeeded by Ye Mingchen. Sir Samuel George Bonham (1803–1863) was the third governor of Hong Kong, appointed in 1848 and succeeded by Bowring in 1854.

at whist. Hughes semi-trump with Holland.[82] A piping hot day. The *San Juan*[83] went out for Manila. Sic transit gloria mundi.[84] Read some most amusing speeches made in Parliament about the naval review question which show how in peace condescend to chaff & how everything is liable to miscarriage & now though in a musing mood I will not muse but like a sensible individual retire to bed with the trite observation, 'another day is gone'.

29. Hang it man and what's to become of the diary? Yesterday, after wading in the categories I reverted to humbugging away the rest of the day. Went for a bathe after which home to dinner with Leonard & Halham[85] directly after which I slept & my nose was corked.[86] Today up desperately late & went to church & heard a good sermon. Mamma Peorce[87] and Buggins behaving in a most abominably vulgar way, talking, laughing and drawing everybody's attention to their dirty selves. This evening called on Woodgate who was out. Wade had a conversation in which Hughes accidentally made him believe that he would give up emolument in order to study Chinese. Had a longish walk home. Had a most diplomatic conversation with Hughes and to bed. Adieu.

[two full lines and two half lines crossed out thoroughly]

第一要緊的是能才其次是常心[88]

什麼呢[89]

人女男[90]

[one name crossed out]}

[one name crossed out]} – 愛的[91]

[one name crossed out]}

---

82 George Helland was a merchant's clerk at Edwards and Balley.
83 A mistake by Alabaster. The ship was the *Jorge Juan*.
84 Latin, 'Thus passes the glory of the world'.
85 J.B. Hallam worked as a tea inspector for Reiss & Co. at Canton.
86 Blocked.
87 Jane Piercy, see Volume 2, footnote 232. 'Buggins' is clearly a nickname, and from the context, likely to be a child of Mrs Piercy.
88 Chinese, 'diyi yaojinde shi nengcai. Qici shi changxin', 'The most important thing is ability. The next is constancy'.
89 Chinese, *shenme ne*, 'What?'
90 Chinese, *ren nü nan*, 'Person. Female. Male'.
91 Chinese, *aide*, 'the ones I love'.

30. & so ends another moon. June is ended. In another month I shall have left England for one year. Ignorant of when I may return, uncertain, almost hopeless, the month is ended. Waste. Waste. Waste. Time flies. How can I catch it up? Ever following, ever fleeing, wasting. Lazy, idle boy! Idle I was but now am worse. My mind is one eternal brown study.[92] I must struggle against it or if I do not I might just as well throw every other thing to the dogs. Today, went as usual next door and passed a most uncomfortable 3 hours though they help me to a command of countenance which may one day be useful to me, though not while my present absence of mind. Then home and wasted time & after dinner I, Adkins, Hughes, Tatham & Gower went up the hill & came to a jolly spot which if I were but only in the vein I might describe but shall only say we got home & afterwards I, Gower & Tatham went & caught little fish by lantern light just above the reservoir. Home now to bed.

July

1. What have I done today? The too ready answer comes. Nothing. It is a sad truth but still it is true so it must be said. In primus, I rise late. This habit seems to grow on a person. This must be stopped. In secundus, we go to Wade's. I have a little work, half of which time I, far from doing myself good, make a perfect fool of myself. Then home and waste a lot of time over tiffin & seeing the *Nankin* go out & as soon as I began to make way with the teacher, a note comes up & down we have to go & get our money. Nuisance, great & manifold & so waste the rest of the afternoon in Wade's office trying to make myself believe that I was working. Then down to Lane & Crawford's to buy Meadows's *Rebellions in China*[93] which I have not yet read but which seems to be a most eccentric but nonetheless useful book. After dinner, go for a bathe in a new place where there is a beastly bottom – muddy & disagreeable – our proper bathing place being occupied by a lot of Portuguese, male and female. Home. Work with Seao & finishing the day by cutting the leaves of Meadows' book. May tomorrow be better spent. Miss Edith Bowring has returned & I am sinking fast back down. Down, confound it!

---

92 'Brown study', 'A state of mental abstraction or musing' (*Oxford English Dictionary*).
93 Thomas Taylor Meadows, *The Chinese and Their Rebellions: Viewed in Connection with Their National Philosophy, Ethics, Legislation, and Administration. To Which Is Added, an Essay on Civilization and Its Present State in the East and West* (London: Smith, Elder & Co., 1856). T.T. Meadows (1815–1868) was the elder brother of J.A.T. Meadows, see Volume 1, footnotes 44 and 45.

2. Up & reading Meadows's book which is one of the most interesting as well as eccentric books I have read for a long time and though I cannot but think some of his views chimerical and totally disagree with others, at the same time I think that others might be carried out with great advantage to mankind generally. Though I think that he has overlooked one essential part of the English constitution i.e. the aristocracy, 'the main bulwark of English freedom,' to use his own expression. The buffer between the crown & the people. Remove it, or even its prestige, the two will clash and England's ruin will be consummated. Let then the aristocracy have a certain number of the official appointments set apart for them. Not too numerous but still in sufficient numbers to continue the prestige which at present attaches to the England's pride,[94] her aristocracy. And another body too should be represented. The monied interest. It is not enough that these should be represented in parliament, which this plan does not propose to alter, but it is necessary that there should be a certain number (small indeed in proportion to the other class but large enough to confer a degree of substantiability on the whole) of men of fortune unless indeed the salaries of <u>all</u> officials be raised far above what they are at present. In the army and navy it is not so requisite that an officer's means should be great. A man fights better for honour than for dollars, wherefore I think that a greater number of the interior appointments should be given to this department. Talent, knowledge of language & manners are more requisite for the diplomatic or provincial departments & property for the judicial. Such is my opinion. Whether good or bad I shall find out by experience. At any rate, an immense amount of information may be picked out of it. It is immensely entertaining. Today went to W. as usual. Chang sinsang has left, to our great disgust, as he was a most useful man. However, we knock on somehow notwithstanding my laziness & brown study-ness & old Seao showed himself considerably more lucid today than usual. This evening went for a bathe & had one, which of course I enjoyed, though I got several duckings while I was about it. Home to Meadows & now ad cubitum curro.[95]

3. To bed with the reflexions gained from T.T. Meadows' book that civilization is the dominance of man's moral part in the world & that to arrive at this, reverance toward God & love toward man are the only necessary agents. Humbling it is to think that the most civilized nation of the earth has not

---

94 As in manuscript.
95 Latin, 'I'm off to bed'.

yet attained the preliminary stage of the substitution of the intellectual for the physical agencies in their full degree. When the civilization of mankind is accomplished the millenium will be, for then all men will revere God & love each other. The book is a most interesting & instructive one. Full of beauties and at the same time obscured by blemishes. It is one of the most curious books I have read for a long time. Went next door at 6 but Mr W. was not at home so home we came & at 7 went & Adkins took down a list of syllables which I have since copied. Had rather a good lesson afterwards though we only got over 32 phrases & I was occupied nearly all the afternoon at it. This evening went curio hunting with Hughes & Gower. Bought 2 or 3 trifles & home. Morrison is going for a leave of absence & they talk of getting me into office, which I shall protest & attempt to engage my superior in my defence. However, at present I have heard nothing official. It will do me no harm if I manage properly. The *Bittern* went out today jollily at a great pace with all sail set.

4. Finis. The Declaration of Independence.[96] Not only did the *San Jacinto* salute but the merchant ships must needs pop away too & so there was a considerable waste of powder & a prolonged popping, every pop of which made me feel the more savage. To think that treason and rebellion should be commemorated. One of the yachts, a little yacht with only 3 guns, kept it up beautifully, blazing away in fine style but some of the large ships fired away very irregularly. Worked much as usual & read away at Meadows & still think it a most amusing & instructive book. How feeble man is when he would prove what he does not believe himself. Thus, M. on duelling wished to prove it barbarous & discivilizing but he shows that even he thinks it perfectly necessary in the present state of human cultivation & I think so too, though it ought only to be resorted to in extreme cases, as man is only justified, in my idea, in laying down his life for his God, his sovereign, his country & his family & in all other cases he is not simply erring but discivilizing in doing it. Wade today attacked the missionary system today most properly, as they preach before they can speak & translate before they can read & so make bad books, which as Ying today said of himself, the Chinese takes up a book in bad Chinese containing new doctrines, totally without explanation, which they cannot understand & so lay aside in disgust. God save the Queen is playing again. Hip hip hurrah!

---

96   Of the United States.

5. Have I acted up to my principles? No. Promptus et audax. If I be, I have not shewn it in its fullest degree as I might have done. However, I must not discourage myself but must work on, on & then perhaps I may some day be great. Would that I had Plutarch's *Lives* to read. Would that I had histories, lives, &c. & time & inclination to read them instead of invariably falling into a brown study when I read anything. Went this evening to Leonard's & read away & looked away at art journals, &c. 1. ½ folly ¼ good 1 ¼ bosh. Marry! come up there![97] Leonard came up afterwards & we carted away the evening. Waste of time, great & ruinous. Meadows' book is jolly. The more I read, the more I like it. Payne has arrived safely at Shanghae after a long passage, resting at Amoy on the way & there is considerable news from the n.[98] The remains of a Russian settlement & burnt frigate supposed to be the *Pallas*[99] have been found by the *Barracouta* & the rebels are advancing on Shanghae, so I suppose we shall have a row there anon. I wish I had some histories to refer to. I have the desire to be & only lack the requisite information & perseverance to be a diplomat, i.e. I have a waistcoat & only want the other articles of clothing to be able to dress myself. Sic transit gloria mundi.

7. Yesterday I was in a state of madness nearly all day which made me commit many things of which I am much ashamed & shall not repeat here only hoping that I may not be so mad another time. Today up late & then afterwards into Wade as usual. We worked away but did not do much today, the teachers being remarkably stupid. At 12½, down to office & when there wasted my time nicely reading extracts from the *Peking Gazette*. However as it was by Wade's order it was all right. Webb Esq., tea taster to Dent & Co.,[100] coming in. Wade unfolded many of his plans. He wants a sea voyage & does not like to go home as he would thereby lose his appointment. Mercer too came down so we did not pass an unpleasant afternoon. Wade seems up to everything & par consequence his conversation is highly entertaining though rather eccentric & odd. I must of all continue to go office. Tho' a nuisance, it is necessary I see to keeping straight with W.

---

97 'Marry come up', a phrase 'expressing indignant or amused surprise or contempt' (*Oxford English Dictionary*).
98 'The n', that is, 'the north'.
99 The *Pallas*, or more accurately the *Pallada*, was a Russian frigate launched in 1832, which, in 1854, was deployed as the flagship for Vice Admiral Yevfimy Putyatin in the Pacific theatre of the Crimean war. She was scuttled in January 1856 after being declared unseaworthy. Thus, the *Barracouta* must have found the remains of another ship.
100 A long-term and well-known businessman in Shanghai, and sometime Portuguese vice consul, Edward Webb was, at this time, working at the Shanghai branch, of Dent, Beale & Co.

This evening I have been working & then walking up & down with Adkins talking of England. I hope I shall return some day though I don't deserve it & old England will receive her unworthy son who has only yesterday found out that hindering others does not help him on & who in consequence has been doing wrong for months & only now is awakened to his error.

8. How quick is mine ruin when not upheld by religion. When once he breaks it through, how difficult it is to bind himself again thereby. So I have found it. If I had not in the first place transgressed I should not now be so base as I am. May I regain again my lost position & moral feeling. Went to office this morning & worked just long enough to find out that what I thought easy was horribly hard & this afternoon Mongan came down. He has had a long & stormy passage, meeting with a typhoon but it has been a jolly one as he called in at each of the ports on his way. He is a very nice fellow & has been very popular wherever he has been & I hope I shall get on well with him.

9. Up & into Wade as usual & afterwards at office. Mongan breakfasted at Government House this morning & was ½ starved. Told two capital stories, one of a Yankee, one of a Swede. 1. 'Well, do you see I was in the foretop looking out when I sees a whale right astern, so I sings out to Cap'en, 'Shall I lower the boats?' Says he, 'If you sees fitten to lower the boats, Mr Tomkyns, lower them & be damned.' So you see I lowered the boats & in fiftin' minits that there whale was up against the ship's side. Wal, the cap'en met me at the gangway & says, says he, 'Mr Tomkyns, you're the smartest man ever caught a whale in these here seas. Here's my knife, here's my baccy[101] pouch. Guess you'll have loan of them all this here journey. 'Cap'en,' says I, 'I don't want your knife. I don't want your baccy pouch. All I want is common civility & that of the most ordinary description.' The other was a Swedish captain who asked a captain of a man of war before a lot of ladies, 'How long is your penis?', meaning to say 'pinnace'.[102] Writing letters. Only written to Aunty, Charly & Henry. This mail not being by any means in writing trim. The *Gundreda* is in, Captain Parker has resigned and that is all.

10. The mail went with a lot of people. I have sent a most unsatisfactory budget home writing to scarcely anyone at all. Directly after the mail went out, the *Lancefield* came in, which is a capital dodge of Jardine's. The Manila

---

101 Tobacco.
102 A tender, or small boat, carried by a large vessel.

mail too is late. Wade did not get up till 12 & then did not come at 2 as he intended, so I have done scarcely anything today passing it wastefully. Leonard is going to get my box off the *Gundreda*. I went down to him & he came up with me this evening & all the rest of the day was talk & cards. Read the Critique on Grote's *Greece*[103] which is remarkably interesting. Jammed my hand in the window. It is swollen up considerably but does not hurt much.

11. At home as usual. Worked as usual. Nothing important as usual. Caine has got a leave of absence for 1 year & the Yankee *San Jacinto* has broken down. I can't go to Japan. The cunning fellows have taken a Dutchman as private secretary with them who has a cock & bull story that Forrest has had to leave Siam because he knocked down a Siamese nobleman who got in his way. There is great interest as to whether the Chinamen intend to carry out their intention of murdering every Englishman who goes out at Canton. This evening after fishing, we i.e. Adkins, Mongan & I down to Tatham's. I stopped the evening by invitation, Gower & a lawyer of the place Cooper Turner[104] coming in afterwards. This lawyer was a beast. An old, white-haired, bald man talking of women, &c. Was disgusting & not contented with anecdotes of himself, he treated us to a few family secrets, viz. that his uncle & cousin had both married whores which would be a thing most people would not desire talked about. He gave us a rather curious account too of San Francisco. The gaming seems to be carried on to an enormous extent there & cheating is quite a recognized thing & is carried on so well that though a lot of bystanders are present they can still manage it. We played too at cards & Mongan shewed us several jolly tricks with cards & afterwards we all had a walk round. Home.

13. Sunday. The fact is I waste an infernal lot of time and act in a most unmethodical, unprofitable manner, neither working well or satisfactorily, giving way to evil thoughts and becoming generally immoral & depraved. Yesterday did not write my diary because I did not get to bed till this morning. After going to Wade as usual, went to office in the afternoon & when there did not know what the deuce to do, so spent a most unsatisfactory one & then had to wait till 5 for a cap, the blessed fools having taken mine up without bringing another down & then it rained. However, at 5½

---

103 George Grote (1794–1871), *A History of Greece from the Earliest Period to the Close of the Generation Contemporary with Alexander the Great*, 12 vols (London: John Murray, 1846–56).
104 George Cooper-Turner (?1814–1860) was a solicitor, and also the Crown solicitor of Hong Kong at this time. He had also been Crown solicitor in the colony of New South Wales but had left Australia suddenly for California in 1849 accused of embezzlement.

arrived at home & found the boy could or would not get us a table or glass, so concocted one by joining mine to the other & borrowed all Morrison's things & so managed to enjoy ourselves, Connely,[105] Leonard, Repton & Gower coming so we had a nice party of 7 & sang & eat & drank like blazes. This morning, just up in time to scramble through breakfast & rush off to church where we had a good sermon from O'Dell on the necessity of our setting an example to the heathen. Mrs Peirce had to evacuate the church & I regretted not handing her out but could not quietly. Adkins has gone to Pereira's for dinner. I have been putting all my things to rights & going out with Mongan who is a jolly fellow and so the day has passed without many events but yet it has not been altogether agreeably spent inasmuch as our walks were all spoilt by the rain, &c. and I have a sort of sensation of having done nothing to get me on today.

14. A dies memorabilis[106] for me. I got my box from home. Lots of books, portraits of Aunty, Uncle, Henry, Charly, Percy & all, stationery, pictures, everything. It is wonderful how they all love me & how little I have done to deserve it. I think I am one of the worst people going. I seem to have lost every particle of heart that I ever possessed and yet tho' I have been a villain almost from my cradle, Henry, Charly, Aunty, Uncle all love me, love me deeply. Henry loves me more than a brother & I hope I love him. I wish I could learn. I wish I could work. I wish I was anything but what I am and could be properly grateful for all they have done for me. Worked very badly and yet I am going to bed tired. Brutal weather. Rain every 5 minutes & a high wind. Thermometer 80°. Poor little Bluff died. The best dog in Hong Kong. Poor little doggie.

15. Tuesday. Thermometer 80° 79°. High wind in tremendous gusts all day with very heavy rain. Supposed to be the commencement of a typhoon.

Breakfasted with Colonel Caine this morning after wasting all the time before 8 in running about the wet verandah & speculating as to whether our house would stand or not. Then down to breakfast after a great deal of bother about getting a chair. Wade, Repton & Adam Burns[107] were the only others there and we managed to eat a remarkably good breakfast somehow or other. Wade making a determination before he began to attack 3 curries & making it good. I myself managed 2 among a lot of other things.

---

105 I have not been able to identify this Connely.
106 Latin, 'A memorable day'.
107 Adam Burnes (1832–1876) was an accountant at the Oriental Bank at this time. Later, he held senior banking positions in Australia and then New Zealand.

The table was covered with flowers & looked remarkably jolly. Col. Caine is laid up with the gout but is as jolly as ever. There was one rather bawdy tale. At Macao, a gentleman paying great attention to a baby which was carried by a pretty nursemaid. She one day said her mistress was much gratified by his attention to the baby & would like to know his name. 'My name's Alcock,' says he. 'Oh!' says she, 'Oh! you naughty man. Before the blessed baby too!' After a capital breakfast, home. Wasted time till 2. Work till 4. Play cards in the evening. Old Hughes playing in such a way as to excite Adkins' ire & everyone else's laughter. Gower down with fever.

16. Wednesday. Therm. 79°. Very windy & rainy early. Frequent showers all day.

Was awoken at 3 o'clock by a tremendous wind which shook the house & made me get up & pull down all loose scrolls, &c. & make all things, in a fashion, taut & when I got up at last everything was wet in the veranda & the roof was leaking in several places. Went out & had a good blow. It was splendid. Then to Wade's. Jin[108] is given up & T'ien is to be published immediately if possible. Had a longish lecture this evening. Went down & saw Gower. He is very bad & swears they want to kill him. They are feeding him on black dose[109] & quinine which has a curious effect on him. Home & watched the showers which were very wonderful. Sometimes 2 going on at once in the harbour or one just coming in by the Lymoon[110] while another was bursting with all its fury over us.

17. Thursday. Therm. 79°. Tolerably windy & very rainy.

Another horrid day. Up late & had a showerbath in the rain. In to Wade's & worked as usual. Then back & worked. The *Antelope* came in today bringing news of the murder of Cunningham of Augustine Heard & Co.[111]

---

108 Mistake for *jen, ren* 人. See Introduction, 'Learning Chinese'.
109 A draught of senna, used as a common laxative.
110 Also spelt Lye-mun, Lei Yue Mun is the eastern entrance of the bay of Hong Kong into the China Sea.
111 Reported in *China Mail*, 24 July 1856:
   The *Antelope* brought us intelligence of a disturbance having taken place at Fuhchau on the 3d instant, in which Mr H. Cunningham was killed by a spear-thrust, which penetrated into the gallbladder. Mr Comstock's boy, it would appear, was severely beaten by thieves in trying to protect some property belonging to his master, who, coming up at the time, endeavored to rescue his servant. He also was knocked down, and, calling for assistance, brought out Mr Cunningham and Mr Vaughan, the former armed with a pistol, the latter with a sword-stick. In the struggle which ensued, Mr Cunningham was thrown down and mortally wounded.
China Mail, 16 October 1856, reports that: 'A man has been brought to confess having killed Mr Cunningham, and is to be executed forthwith'. On this incident, see also the consular correspondence in *Correspondence Respecting Insults in China* (London: Harrison & Sons, 1857), 217–20.

It seems his boy, a Canton man, caught a boy stealing potatoes & collared him &, on a crowd collecting, charged them with sword & routed them but on his attempting to capture 1 or 2, another & larger mob collected & he, like a fool, ran out with a double barreled gun and shot one or two, which so infuriated the rest that they seized him, knocked him down & tried to kill him. Comstock (a partner in the house) tried to interfere but was twice knocked down & had to run away, whereon Cunningham made an attempt to save his boy, sallying out with a revolver but was immediately stabbed & knocked down & then beaten over the abdomen & was only saved from instant death by Vaughan who brought him off by means of a walking stick sword. He died, however, directly after & the U.S. Consul has demanded full satisfaction which I doubt whether he will get. The Americans are in a great state but all English are notified not to interfere. The rebels are making great head too. Went down this even to Gowers. He is almost quiteur[112] & seemed as jolly as possible, drawing caricatures, &c. &c. & tho' in bed he had to write invitations and settle the account. Thence to Tatham's where I wasted an evening. I learnt brag[113] & so to bed.

18. Friday. Therm. 80°. Hot. Rainy. Windy. Gusty.

The week seems drawing to a close fearfully fast & I seem to have done nothing in it. Today I finished the 1st vol. of Davis on Lord Amherst's embassy.[114] I don't think the embassy could have done anything but what it did & it was very lucky that Sir G. Staunton was attached to it as the ambassador would, if it had not been for him, performed the kotow to our eternal disgrace & loss. It is a most entertaining book & contains much information. Did not go out today except to Wade & there had 3½ hours. It was tiring but I think the information obtained was such as will be useful to me for ever & a day. This evening bathed & worked with Kao. He is a jolly sort of an old fellow & makes pertinent remarks on any & everything. Has a great desire to gain information & is altogether rather a good teacher.

19. Therm. 78°. Wind, rain & fair weather in intermediate fits.

Went next door as usual. Mr Wade not very well. Got a letter from Payne who seems immensely happy. Mongan has got some Japanese books from Hakodadi & a letter from home which went there in search of him but

---

112 Possibly, *quitter*, French, 'to leave', 'to depart'.
113 A card game almost identical to poker.
114 John Francis Davis, *Sketches of China, Partly during an Inland Journey of Four Months, between Peking, Nanking and Canton, with Notices and Observations Relative to the Present War*, 2 vols (London: Charles Knight & Co., 1841).

then we have an Irish postmaster. Hughes dined at Woodgate & Mr Wade has a new plan in hand for some new affair. Adkins is to go on at 6 & I relieve guard at 7 which will not be agreeable though useful. Worked away today much as usual. Am going to make a collection of things useful against China & so am reading Davis rather attentively. The *Coromandel* is just in per Shanghae this evening. I & Adkins were out for a walk & at one place where it was dark & we were threading our way someone cries out, 'Who goes there?' Quick as thought I yell out, 'A friend!' & to our great astonishment Wade appeared & convoyed us home where I had a long talk with Adkins & afterwards with my teacher who astonished by coming out wonderfully strong on the language & literature & literati of the country whom I know nothing about.

20. Sunday. Therm. 79°. Rain. Afterwards, fine weather.

Got up much earlier than is my wont on Sunday mornings. I began making a list of my books. Read poetry & then to church in a chair. Tiger followed us in & we thought he was going to kick up a row but he did not. I & Adkins walked up with H.E. from church. I went to see Gower, H.E. asking us to tiffen. Adkins, however, rushed home with a sudden attack of diarrhea & I was left, after walking about with Gower inspecting the Siamese peacocks & fowls, &c. In to tiffen, Capt. Stuart[115] being there. Lots of news. Caine is down from Amoy. Lane is going home & the supercargo of a coolie ship has been seized & carried into the country by the Chinese. It was rather good fun. H.E. talkative, L.B.[116] chatty, S.P.[117] reserved & Capt. Stuart rough & sailorlike, like one of the old school. Afterwards went to Dent's. Saw Leonard & Wheely home. Had a fearful dinner & afterwards with Leonard & Tatham we all went out. I had a long & a sharp walk from which I have returned considerably tired, feeling however, the day to have been more satisfactorily got over than usual which is something. Read a little of Davis too.

21. Monday. Thermometer 81°.

A blazing hot day & as soon as we had been at Wade's an hour & a half, a summons came for us to go to office. I wanted to demur but Wade said I must go so I went & after I had been there ½ an hour or so, they said they did not want me, so I went & spent a most unsatisfactory afternoon ½ dead with ennui tho' there was one rather good thing. There has lately

---

115 E.A. Stuart was a captain in the 1st Royal Regiment, part of the Expeditionary Force at Canton.
116 Lady Bowring.
117 S.P. may be the Miss Pearce mentioned in Volume 1, footnote 117.

been a fearful lot of bother about some transfer of property & when they were brought to sign the deed, the owner quietly said he did not want to. Then out for a walk & lastly to sup at Leonard's. Wheely & Plessman there. A beautiful evening & a very good supper.

22. Sunday. Thermometer 83°. A piping hot day finishing with squalls & rain.

Went to Wade's as usual & worked well. He being in an excellent humour came home & worked badly at question two which is difficult & perplexing then after dinner went out for a walk. Went to the Reading Rooms. They have a good collection of books & papers but it seems rather a caddy place. Up again. Ricketts & Gibson[118] coming up in the evening & I had the only merry game at cards I have had for a long time. It was good fun & then singing & fun. The Dutch embassy calling here was saluted today. The leaders went to Bowring's grand dinner, given in honor of the bride.

23. Wednesday. Therm. 81° 79°. A fine warm morning, changing to a high wind with rain. Now great fear of typhoon.

I fear there is a typhoon just coming to catch the mail which will be an awful bother. Went into Wade as usual & stopped an extra hour & a half to help him in sorting the categories. Then home & worked inefficiently for all the afternoon & again as inefficiently all the evening. The wind is growing desperately high. I really think a typhoon is looming as already it shakes the house. Wade is sanguine that he will get to press by August & then he is going to keep two presses at work. Finished Davis's *Sketches of China* & this evening played whist.

24. Thursday. Therm. 79°. A strong N.E. Gale with occasional chops.

I scarcely slept last night & so had to make it up today & so altogether have had a most unsatisfactory day. At 1½ got out of bed & made all taut, for fear of the wind breaking in as it was shaking the house tremendously & at 5 got up for good. Had a good blow outside. Wade's bamboo work all blown down. Then bathed & read Meadows till 8¾, then dressed, eat breakfast & into Wade's where I was most abominably sleepy & for the first ½ hour could scarcely keep my head up. 12½ tiffen. Read Meadows till I fell asleep. 4½ dinner. 5½ down to the Reading Rooms & tried to read but could not though I would & so wasted an infernal long time without gaining much good. I have somehow or other managed to get my head

---

118 John Rickett and Hugh C. Gibens were both clerks at P&O S.N. Co.

nicely muddled. I used to be able to take up a book, read it & know all about it, but confound it, now I cannot for the life of me remember a single thing. I seem altogether muddled & everyone here seems to feel the same complaint, the grand desideratum being recreation. But how is this recreation to be gained? e.g. how? That is the question. What kind do you want? What? Why, society. That is the kind. But how is it to be got? By getting into society. But how are you to do that? Oh, that is quite another question. I called in at Tatham's found him & Lawrence playing cribbage. Lawrence as usual sapient on what he knows nothing about. Talking about a petition to government to allow the Colony to be governed by a republican establishment. Verily, a most sapient idea. The wind moderating, I and Mongan climbed the hill.

25. Friday. Therm. 80°. Gusty but finally cleared up.

The mail came in & excited all the various feelings which it usually does. Charly writes a beautiful letter which so affected one that I fell down on my knees & prayed to be like him. Uncle, too, writes beautiful letters to me, so full of every proof of love & confidence that when I read them I have such a sense of shame & disgust at myself as to wish myself any punishment. Aunty, too, writes so lovingly to me little dreaming what a brute I am. How I have ever deceived her & everyone else whom I have come across. Henry writes in his usual style & tells one all the news. I am an awfully selfish fellow, that there is no denying. Percy writes gaily. Poor little fellow. He has cut his hand badly & everyone is full of the illuminations which appear to have been awfully grand. What a mistake it is to make such a fuss about such a rascally peace & two parties, Henry's and Percy's, each of which passed off jollily. Aunty's pictures have gone to the Cristal Palace to which she has got a season ticket thereby & the vile *Atheneum* gives no notice of her pictures tho' it mentions those of Miss Gillies[119] confound it. The Rugely case[120] occupies all the papers. Palmer is to be hanged but those damned, confounded, beastly, canting, diabolical brutes, the puritans want to get him off as they try to do every unmitigated villain. War seems inevitable with America. They have dismissed Crampton and recognize

---

119 Margaret Gillies (1803–1887) was a well-known portraitist and water-colourist.
120 William Palmer (1824–1856), the 'Prince of Poisoners', from Rugely in Staffordshire, was executed for the murder of his friend Thomas Cook with strychnine in June 1856, and was suspected of the murder of several of his children, his brother and his mother-in-law. When Alabaster wrote, this Palmer was already dead, but that news had evidently not reached him yet.

Walker, &c. Confound them, I hope we shall thrash them into nothing.[121] An Irish paper has a most extraordinary account of a singing mouse lately found at Hughes' native place Newry.[122] Cabban writes to me a short epistle & The Honble[123] H. Stanley wants a true opinion on his *Chinese Manual*.[124] A rather ticklish business for me. Read Hall.[125] Nearly all today I was beastly seedy. Took Holloway's pills,[126] which strange to say did act as an aferunt[127] medicine. Leonard came up this evening & so finishes vol. III of my diary, journal or whatnot. May no. IV be more interesting.

121 John Crampton (1805–1886) was Britain's minister in Washington from 1852 to 1856. He was dismissed at the insistence of President Franklin Pierce after allegedly infringing the US's neutrality laws by trying to recruit soldiers for the British campaign in the Crimean War. William Walker (1824–1860) was an adventurist mercenary who led private forces into Mexico and Central America, declaring himself president of Nicaragua in July 1856 and ruling until May 1857, when he was forced out. Alabaster's juxtaposition of the two seems to imply hypocrisy on the part of the Americans, insisting forcibly on the application of the neutrality laws in Crampton's case while ignoring them in Walker's, to the extent of recognising him as ruler of Nicaragua.
122 Another account of a singing mouse from this period, this one from Suffolk, can be found in *The Zoologist* 15 (1857): 5591.
123 Honourable.
124 Henry Stanley, *Chinese Manual: Sse tse ouen tsien tchou* 四子文笺注 *Four Words Literature (with) Commentary (or) Explication* (London: Harrison & Sons, 1854). This was a translation of Artus de Lionne (1655–1713), *Phrases Chinoises, Composées de Quatre Caractères Et Dout Les Explecations Sont Rangées Dans L'ordre Alphabétique Français*.
125 Probably, Basil Hall, *Narrative to Java, China and the Great Loo-Choo Island* (London: William Tegg & Co., 1851).
126 Holloway's Pills were a patent medicine invented by Thomas Holloway (1800–1883), which were claimed to cure (to cite only the first four problems in the alphabetical list in one of his advertisements) ague, asthma, bilious complaints and blotches on the face.
127 Probably, afferent. In medicine, afferent blood vessels or nerves are those that carry blood or electrical impulses *towards* an organ or the spine.

Alabaster Diary, Volume 4

1855

July

26. Friday.[1] Therm. 80°. Rainy.

So begins vol. IV. Have spent a most unsatisfactory day. Am getting into an infernally lazy way of doing everything. Got up late. I went to Wade's where I worked tolerably I must confess. Then home. I did nothing in the evening. Gibson & Tatham came up & we were jolly. Regularly & uproariously jolly. Jolly in the widest sense of the term. It is extraordinary how soon you can get up a feeling of jollity with agreeable companions. It is extraordinary to what a pitch your jollity may go. Well, we were infernally jolly. Spouted,[2] sang & laughed & now the excitement being somewhat sobered down I seek repose having filled the 1 page of vol. IV with unmitigated bosh.

27. Sunday. Therm. 79°. Rain. Rain. Rain.

Got up about 8 & had a shower bath in a friendly cataract. It was jolly one. Just got under & then felt regularly drowned & then the exit was commendable. Then laid in bed & lounged about reading, &c. till tiffin & then read & lounged about till dinner thus wasting totally the day. After dinner went on board the *Comus*. She is a jolly little craft though small & has a nice set of officers, especially the doctor, a jolly, bald, Hindloopny,[3] ready, lively fellow & there was a nice fellow from the *Bittern* named Walsh[4] who is to dine with us tomorrow. The master Collingwood is a fine fellow

---

1 Mistake for Saturday.
2 Reciting poems, performing speeches from plays.
3 Probably a man from Hindeloopen in the north of the Netherlands.
4 I have not been able to identify this Walsh.

too. About 6'2' or more. I the smallest of 6 brethren. The ship was in beastly disorder but we managed to enjoy ourselves. Moresby[5] solicitor was on board, brutally screwed.[6] He is an awful fool. It was a change that little gunroom on board ship & so I was happy. Then we went to the Reading Rooms & I to suit my tastes must needs read *Bell's Life*[7] & had to gulp it down by the aid of *Little Dorrit*.[8] So having spent the day unprofitably we went to Leonard's, got a lantern & reverted home.

28. Monday. Therm. 79°, 81°, 79°. Fine. Glorious. Dull. Rainy. Windy.

Such variations has today displayed. Today it was a really beautiful morning. A nice breeze, a glorious sun & every thing looking green & pleasant. Received notice of my election to the Reading Rooms. Confound them, it is a bad boggled business.

1. I am proposed by Tatham & seconded by Lawrence which I do not esteem as an honor.
2. I wanted to cut it in a month & find I must prepay a quarter.
3. it is a caddy hole.[9]

Read *The Haunted Man*.[10] It is nice & pleasant tho' unnatural & mistaken. Walsh did not come. Worked well at Wade's but badly with my teacher with whom I had a regular row. My bowels are in a beastly state & so is my mind.

29. Therm. 81°, 79°. Rain.

An infernal day. No events. I have been reading Neale's *Siam*[11] till I have not an idea in my head. Went into Wade's & confound it, he kept us there 4 hours. I then came home & to work with my infernal brute who would not work & so he & I had a regular row & then in the evening played whist & read Neale. It is written in a pleasantish style but he is a great cad & humbug apparently.

---

5   William Moresby worked as a solicitor in Hong Kong until at least 1860.
6   Drunk.
7   *Bell's Life in London, and Sporting Chronicle*, published from 1822 to 1886, was Britain's most popular broadsheet that wrote about racing, as well as other sports and general matters.
8   At this time, Charles Dickens's *Little Dorrit* was being published in serial form. Instalment eight of a final 20 (Chapters 26–29) was published in July 1856. However, as it would have taken some months for publications to get to Hong Kong, Alabaster was likely reading early instalments.
9   Probably a variant on 'cuddy-hole', a small space on board ship or in the roof space of a building that is just sufficient for a person to lie down in, related clearly to 'cubby-hole'.
10 Charles Dickens, *The Haunted Man and the Ghost's Bargain, a Fancy for Christmas-Time*, first published in 1848, doi.org/10.1093/oseo/instance.00122012.
11 Fred Arthur Neale, *Narrative of a Residence at the Capital of the Kingdom of Siam: With a Description of the Manners, Customs and Laws of the Modern Siamese* (London: Office of the National Illustrated Library, 1852).

30. Therm. 79°. Fine. Fair. Rain.

Up late. Worked inefficiently. Feverish head. Achy & so to bed.

31. Therm. 79°. Rain.

So ends another month & I am sorry to have to record the fact that I don't seem to have made much progress in anything. Today as usual I was up late & then after breakfast I went into Wade & sat & worked till 12½. It is rather a nuisance sitting there 3 or 3½ hours but I think it certainly improves our construction.[12] Then home & went over some of the old category of man & then in the evening after a confab with my teacher. Played cards & then have been sitting up answering one of the questions in the examination paper which I have about 1/10th answered in 3 hours & a ½, being all included in one sheet.

August

1. Therm. 78°. Rain.

Confound it! This rain seems never going to stop. It is ruining the rice crops. What on earth are we to do? When it stops there will be no end of sickness. I already am seedy. There is news today. The Viceroy of the two Kiang[13] has promulgated a notice at Canton to the effect that the oil is all poisoned which seems probable as it is all brought from Kwangse, the rebel stronghold. 300 women & 50 men are officially stated to have been burnt at Canton & probably a much larger number have perished.[14] So much for the news. Now let me consider the deeds of today:

---

12   The explanation or interpretation of a text.
13   The viceroy of Liangjiang, or the two Jiangs (i.e. Jiangxi and Jiangnan – at this time an anachronistic designation for a province that had since been split into Anhui and Jiangsu). However, I suspect this is a mistake for the viceroy of Liangguang, or the two Guangs (Guangdong and Guangxi, or as here Kwangse), whose headquarters were in Canton. This was the famous Ye Mingchen 葉名琛. The 'rebels' were the subjects of the Taiping Heavenly Kingdom.
14   *China Mail*, 31 July 1856, reported that:
       The principal street of that part of the Canton floating suburbs called 'Sah Meen [Shamian],' has been destroyed by fire. The largest account of the loss of life, and the one which is said to have been reported to the Mandarins, estimates the number of females drowned and burnt at 300 to 400, and of males 50 or 60; while the lowest gives 100 females and 50 or 60 males. This floating street consists chiefly, if not entirely, of brothels. It stretches out from the shore in a straight line into the river, and is conspicuous at night for the brilliancy of its numerous lanterns, and the number of people in small boats thronging it. The dwellings are raised upon the floating hulls of large boats, and are constructed on the roofs, sides, and backs, principally of wood, and the bark of trees; the fronts present a very gaudy appearance, with a profusion of carving and gilding. The loss of life was occasioned chiefly by the collision of the numerous small craft, hurrying from the scene of danger. The same place was burnt about 20 years ago, and smaller fires are of frequent occurrence in the locality.

1. I was up earlier than usual which was a good beginning.
2. I went into Wade's & did not attend very much which was bad.
3. Home. I worked & blew up my teacher. Good & bad. I should not have spoken to him but have told Wade.
4. Thought of bad things. Bad.
5. Drove the thoughts away. Good.
6. Worked & loitered about. Good & bad.

4 good. 4 bad. A negative day. Henry must now have begun his travels. 2 months & he will be here I hope, I pray. God bless him. He is a brick.

2. Therm. 81°. Down town 83°. Rain. Fine.

Got up most abominably late & passed my day as usual. Read worked & played. This evening as it was fine I, Adkins, Leonard & Mongan went out for a walk & it was very jolly. Immensely jolly I may say & then we came home & played whist. Really my love of cards increases daily. Let me make a resolution never to play again. No. I see too many obstacles in its way but I make this resolution: that I will <u>never</u> play for <u>money</u> & may I keep it after cards. We had supper & now to bed full.

3. Therm. 81°, 80°. Piping hot but a beautiful day.

This morning when I woke & after a short time opened the window & getting Meadows' *Rebellions of China* made myself very jolly. Then getting out of bed I lay on my couch. I was jollier still for lying there in reach of all my books. I lay & read & thought I was jolly & when at last I was compelled to get up I still was jolly as I seemed as if nothing could make me hurry & I bathed & eat my breakfast & just as I was starting for church who should appear but Gibson who came up to go to church with us & so down we all went & heard a very bad sermon indeed, made worse by the delivery, for Irwin has a most curious manner of twisting his eyebrows in a way which seems to say, 'Now, don't think what I say is serious for it certainly is not. It's a very good joke tho',' & then he raises his voice & you think something grand is coming but it is not. Tiger was as usual walking all about the church & affording the beadle lots of work but I ought not to call him a beadle. How beadles would turn up their noses if asked to own a long-gowned, tailed Chinaman whose only weapon is as high as one of themselves. Mrs Brown[15] was there. She is an intensely jolly looking woman. A sort of motherly sort of person for whom I often

---

15 Probably the wife of W.G. Brown, lieutenant in the 1st Royal Regiment.

long to have someone to confide in & Mrs Parsons[16] is amusing. Such a clean plump little body so completely under Parsons. Then home & after tiffin lay down & read *George Dandin*[17] which established the axiom that it is bad to marry a person above you whose family are poor as rats & who are awfully proud. Then rearranged my photographs, taking down my venerable black board & then Leonard came to dinner at 5 & we drank a lot of champagne. Shame, Shame on the extravagance. & then came the grand business of the day. We got a boat & sailed & pulled across. I pulled part of the way. It was rather good fun & then we had a jolly walk o'er hill & dale. The first episode being a little dog – very small – who first set up a grand barking & then insisted on following us. A most facetious little dog & then we went up to two or three China houses round which there was an awful lot of filth & inside which there was an immense quantity of dirt. So moving out & crossing a beautiful cricket ground we came on a rustic scene. They were beating the rice from the ear & setting up the ricks to dry. This set us up too. Over the ricks went Adkins, Mongan & Leonard generally upsetting themselves & affording immense amusement to the Yokies.[18] I even attempted a haycock & cleared it but came down on ___. Old Tiger entered extensively into the fun charging every hay rick & bolting into every stream of water. Then returning by our boat we finished at Leonard's with supper & I had the intense luxury of iced water & long disputes on language & Glorious England! England! The greatest power of the world! O, England! I love you!

4. Therm. 81°. Very fine. In the evening cloudy.

A memorable event I hope has taken place today. Today, unless I am mistaken, Henry has set off from Southampton at 2 & I & Adkins drank their health. I hope they will have a pleasant voyage. Dear Henry. Worked but badly today as we did not get into Wade's till 10. I got out at 12.50, then I read at Meadows till 2, then worked till I was sent down for to get my money. Home. Out with Mongan. Quarreled with Hughes whom I must consider a mean fool & an impertinent ignoramus. Went to Tatham's who

---

16   Probably the wife of Ambrose Parsons, solicitor.
17   Molière (1688); Alabaster likely read this in the translation of Henri Van Laun, rendered as *Georges Dandin, or the Abashed Husband* (1800).
18   Probably equivalent to Yokels.

thinks himself in a decline. Home. I now like a fool have been sitting up till now reading *Little Dorritt* which I think is a most unnatural book like most of Dickens nowadays.[19]

5. Therm. 80°. Thunder & lightning. Dull. Heavy rain.

Another bad day. I got to bed about one & ½ this morning. I was roused out about 4 by thunder & lightning & managed to crawl out of bed but finally laid down on my sofa & slept soundly till I got up & into Wade's as usual. We did there a rather good day of work but nothing extraordinary happened. A middy[20] came up with a letter from Sir John requesting either Mr Wade or Mongan should go to the *Nankin* to translate to the Convoys[21] but to Mongan's disgust Wade declined.[22] Shanghae Mail too came in. Soochow is safe & the rebels have been checked by some Mongols who have been brought in. This is a dangerous experiment of the emperor, however, as they are as likely to go against him as not when the rebels are finished. After dinner it rained most awfully so Adkins & I went into Wade, he to get a *Pekin Gazette*, I to enquire what book I could read, &c. & he gave me one which is awfully hard. Then I went to the reception. I met Col. & Jun.[23] Caine coming out. However, in I went & chatted for an hour. Hart's notification[24] has called forth many letters from the missionaries, some of whom declare he asked whether Miss Aldersey[25] had whiskers or not. Now to bed. Henry I suppose has passed Ushant.

---

19 This comment echoes sentiments expressed in a widely republished review of some of Thackeray's novels originally published in 'Thackeray's Works', *Westminster and Foreign Quarterly Review* 59 (1 April 1853): 363–88, 370:

    Dickens's sentiment, which, when good, is good in the first class, is frequently far-fetched and pitched in an unnatural key … Dickens wanders frequently into the realms of the imagination and, if at times he only brings back, especially of late, fantastic and unnatural beings, we must not forget, that he has added to literature some of its most beautiful ideals.

20 Midshipman.
21 A military vessel or fleet accompanying a merchant ship, passenger vessel, etc., especially one protecting a vessel carrying supplies during a war.
22 'the assistance of both', follows, crossed out.
23 Junior. Caine's sons were George Whittingham Caine (1832, India), William Hull Caine (1836, India), Henry Monteith Caine (1838, India), Charles Henry Fearon Caine (1846, Hong Kong). If 'junior' refers to the son of the same name as the father, this would have been W.H.
24 At the time of this diary entry, Robert Hart was serving in the Ningbo Consulate. Unfortunately his journals for this period are lost.
25 Mary Ann Aldersley (1797–1868) was the first female missionary in China and is best known for opening the first school for girls in the country, in Ningbo in 1843. She had worked in Surabaya with Chinese girls since 1837. In 1861 she retired to Maclaren Vale, south of Adelaide in South Australia.

6. Therm. about 80°. Rainy.

Spent a most unsatisfactory day. Went into Wade's as usual & afterwards occupied myself all day at sorting & numbering phrases which was abominably tiring. The *Chusan* came in. Palmer is hanged[26] & the American Question[27] is nearly settled.

7. Therm. 79°. Fair with heavy showers.

Up just in time to bolt a morsel of breakfast & in next door when after several grand rows 'yün'[28] was wanliao.[29] 'Heaven' was finished,[30] so now the 2nd go over is to begin. After that nothing more transpired in the Chinese line for after humbugging about with Mongan, Dempster came in & declared everything was damned humbug, after which Caine came to dinner, after which we had a walk with him then finished the evening with Tatham & the elder Lawrence who is quite a superior sort of fellow. After this, home & letter writing. So today has passed unprofitably as far as I am concerned.

8. Began the new dodge. I & Adkins go over 天[31] by ourselves with teachers noting alterations. Mongan begins a new lay[32] with Ying and Shun & Wade goes into our corrections with Chang in the afternoon. This is a much jollier plan as we are independent & feel an interest in our work. After tiffin I translated part of Seu to Bonham.[33] Finished the rough draft this evening. After dinner I & Mongan & Gower went for a walk & after passing thro' a beautiful little wood which greatly reminded us of England we got to the Mosque & Mahometan village.[34] We wanted to go in but they would not let us, so we had a confab with a turbaned buffer who was very civil indeed & we had a lovely long talk about the religion. Oakley[35] is to resign & Hance is to go to Canton, so heigh for a change. I think I will try for a lift.[36] Just to set the stone a'rolling. Now to bed. Used up with writing letters.

---

26 See Volume 3, footnote 121.
27 See Volume 3, footnote 120.
28 *Yun* 雲, 'clouds'.
29 *Wanliao* 完了, 'completed'.
30 The first part of Wade's *Hsin Ching Lu* concerns words and phrases that fall under the category 'heaven' in traditional Chinese *leishu* 類書 or encyclopaedias. Under this category fall subsections on the sun, the stars, clouds, lightning, rain, etc.
31 *Tian* 天, 'heaven'.
32 'A line of business, job, pursuit (slang)' (*Concise Oxford Dictionary*, 1912).
33 See Volume 3, footnote 81.
34 The Jamia Masjid (also known as the Lascar Temple) was built in 1849 in Shelley Street, Mid-Levels, and later expanded.
35 See Volume 1, footnote 113.
36 A promotion.

9. Got up about 7½ & wrote till 9 when I ate my breakfast & then to work & my old man being unmanageable, I told him he was jealous & then he flew into a monstrous passion. However, I laughed at him & by laughing & reasoning together I brought him round & then we got on immensely. After tiffin attacked my Categories again & tho' I had wasted a lot of time I got on satisfactorily when I was about it & again this evening tho' interrupted by Tatham & cards, I managed to comprehend the *Sacred Edict*. I am translating a little. We went into Wade's today. Planning & it seems that I am to be thrown out again tomorrow & must go about & diplomatize a little & see what will be my best course of action under the present state of affairs.

Therm. 80°. Weather fair with occasional showers. Must be up early tomorrow so now to bed.

10. Therm. 80°. Rain. Fine. Cloudy.

The mail went. Got up early but lay down on my sofa & slept till 9. Got up & had my breakfast & then, as it was rainy & wet, wrote to Henry & at 1 went off to the steamer & got on board & saw Caine off & then we had a row after the steamer. It was very jolly going on board. It seemed to freshen one up & made one think of the day when we should be going too. Afterwards Leonard & Wheely came to dinner. Hance not coming & in the evening we had a fearfully long discussion on the currency question. On the steamer today it was worth something to see the 1 Officer, a most arrant snoot affecting the gentleman: 'I, of carse, quurte unable to say if it was fave or tan pounds they paid for a dog's passage.'[37] Hang the fellow! I felt in a grand fever with the fool. The dispute about the currency was rather a good one tho' I & Leonard quite disagreed about one thing, i.e. whether dollars were actually given in payment for goods or not. If they are not, then the Shanghae dollars being only an imaginary medium do not interfere with the trade. But if instead of being simply an imaginary medium they are an actual medium, then they certainly effect the trade inasmuch as the premium which is paid on the dollar does in the end fall upon the consumer, tho' the merchant perchance does not make any additional profit. I & Mongan called on Mrs Hance today.

11. Therm. 83. Piping hot but cloudy.

Got up by 6½ & into Wade & lucky it was that I did so for if I had not done so I should have been turned out of the new scheme altogether while now I am an integral part of it. Certainly laziness is an intolerable bane &

---

37 'I, of course, quite unable to say if it was five or ten pounds they paid for a dog's passage'.

nothing is so injurious to one. I have already lost an awful lot of influence by being so intolerably lazy as I am. When up we went & schemed at Wade's & when that & breakfast were over I went over t'ien lei[38] & then after tiffin had a satisfactory attack upon jen lei.[39] It is very satisfactory working with a will after dinner too. Fr[40] 7 to 9, I tackled the chu fen tsü lu[41] & after 2 hours made but little progress it is true but still a little & then spent the rest of the evening contending about merits & demerits. The grand concert is now going off at the club but I did not think it worth the time or the $s.[42]

---

38   *Tianlei* 天類, 'The category *heaven*'.
39   *Renlei* 人類, 'The category *man*'.
40   From.
41   From the context, this sounds like it should be the name of a text or part of a text but I have not been able to identify it.
42   *China Mail*, 14 August 1856, reported that:
>On Monday evening last the inhabitants of our Colony had the rare opportunity afforded them of hearing a professional musician of acknowledged skill. Mr Ali-Ben-Sou-Alle on that occasion introduced his two newly-invented instruments the Turkophone and the Turkophonini. We shall convey to our readers the best idea of the nature of these instruments by informing them shortly, that they are of the usual class of brass instruments, save that they have a reed instead of an ordinary mouthpiece. The former is an instrument of great compass and of excellent tone, combining the qualities of the bassoon and French horn, and would, we conceive, be a great addition to an orchestra. Of the other we cannot say much more, than that it is a silver Clarionet; and we are not so out of conceit with the old instrument (especially as Mr Ali-Ben-Sou-Alle on the same occasion gave us an opportunity of comparing the two) as to discard it for the new rival. The imitation of the Scottish bagpipes we cannot at all approve of. Why attempt imitations, when the real instrument can be easily procured, and may, we are sure, be mastered as easily as the imitation! We were greatly pleased with the execution of the artist. The class of music selected was not perhaps of the highest order; but it was calculated to please the audience, prove the resources of the instruments, and display the execution of the performer – three very important items in a musical entertainment. We were especially delighted with the fantasia on the opera of 'La Sonambula,' 'My lodging is on the cold ground,' and the Macédoine on English, Irish, and Scottish airs. Mr Ali-Ben-Sou-Alle was sadly unsupported in his performance, in consequence of the want of a pianiste – an able and well-known Amateur who had promised his assistance having been obliged by urgent business to leave the Colony on the morning of the Concert.

The *Overland Register*, 13 September 1856, concurred with many of these opinions but added: 'The imitation of the Bagpipes was very good, but we have not the slightest desire ever to hear that genuine Scottish national instrument, much less an imitation of it'. Later in the year, when Ali-Ben-Sou-Alle had returned to Hong Kong from further north in China, the *China Mail* gave its readers the benefit of a short biography:
>His father was Secretary of the Turkish Legation in Paris, and Ali, displaying at an early age a passion for music, entered as a student at the Conservatoire, and pursued his musical education until 1844, when he gained the first Clarionet prize. He was at once appointed Directeur de Musique de Marine at Senegal, where he remained three years, and on return to Paris entered the celebrated orchestra of the Opera Comique. He remained in Paris till the outbreak of the Revolution, when he crossed to England, and for two years held the responsible position of First Clarionet at Her Majesty's Theatre. He then made a professional tour through England, Scotland, and Ireland, where he learned to appreciate those beautiful national melodies which he 'discourses' so charmingly. At this time his attention was directed to the two Instruments invented by Herr Sax, the Turkophone and the Turkophonini; and making himself the master

14. Therm. 80° to 83°.

Really I ought to be ashamed of myself. Two days have gone without an entry in my precious book so here goes as a grand clearance. On Tuesday at 6.50 into Wade's after a capital bathe in the ravine & worked at the officials[43] till 8. I then worked as usual till 4 & after dinner, going for a walk with Mongan, he called at a certain Mr Stace, solicitor[44] or something of that sort with whom & his brother we tea'd.[45] He is a sensible tho' vulgar fellow enough but his brother, an engineer in the P.& O., is an awful ass.[46] However we managed to spend a jolly evening. Yesterday we worked much as usual & in the evening I & M. went for a walk on the hill & had a very pretty one till we got to the Mahometan village but then there was an awful stink of all the abominations imaginable. Near this there was an enclosure & inside that two very handsome deer & a young one. The numerous goats too on the tops of the houses, &c. was a peculiar feature of the scene. After this we all went down to Leonard's & afterwards went & had a confab with Lawrence & Tatham, winding up the evening with a long walk through the town. The *Coromandel* & Spanish steamer went out after pirates who have captured a square rigged European ship in Muir's Bay 80 miles hence & they have not returned yet.[47] This is a considerable increase in the powers of the pirates. This day I have worked & pottered about all day as usual. Leonard & Tatham coming up in the evening we played cards. Tatham is a great fool

---

of these after laborious study, he brought them forward with great success in the chief capitals of Europe. He then started for Australia, and assembling all the musical resources of that quarter, he was enabled to give the first Grand Concerts ever held in our Southern colonies.

Ali-Ben-Sou-Alle (1824–?) was born Charles-Valentin Soualle, see Stephen Cottrell, *The Saxophone* (New Haven: Yale University Press, 2013), 111–14. Paul Wehage reports that in later life he became a variety of healer establishing a practice in Paris. From the 1880s, French newspapers begin to relate that he spent time in Mysore as the director of royal music, converting to Islam and adopting the name by which he performed in Hong Kong. However, as Wehage notes: 'Since the only sources for this story are in French newspapers which quote Mr. Soualle himself, it could be that he invented the story out of thin air'. See Paul Wehage, 'Ali Ben Sou Alle: A 19th Century Frenchman in Mysore', Symphony Orchestra of India, 14 November 2016, serenademagazine.com/features/ali-ben-sou-alle-19th-century-frenchman-mysore/.

43 Elucidating on 'the officials' was evidently one of the tasks Wade had given Alabaster.
44 Described in the 1861 volume of the *Solicitor's Journal and Reporter* as practising in Hong Kong and Southampton, Edward Keate Stace was sometime secretary of the Hong Kong Law Society.
45 Had tea.
46 I have not been able to trace this maritime Stace.
47 The Spanish steamer was the *Reyna de Castilla*. Muir's Bay is a mistake, it should be Mir's Bay (see *China Mail*, 14 August 1856). As it turned out, 'there was no foundation whatever for the report of a large ship having been captured and taken in there', although five deserted pirate boats were destroyed on the expedition, the pirates 'numbering upwards of 200, being seen ascending the hills', *China Mail*, 21 August 1856.

& has lately lost all his good qualities. I wish I had never known the fellow. The weather has been very curious. Beautifully fine with occasional fierce squalls.

15. Began with a vile thing i.e. did not go into Wade at all this morning, not rising until 8 o'clock & then I did not dress & quarreled with Hughes so was quite unable to work or do anything all day. Confound it! This evening I managed 2 of the questions in sec. 1 but that is all I can fairly lay claim to having done today. The *Coromandel* has returned with a junk but how she has fared we do not yet know. Now bed. Well tired.

Therm. 83°. Very fine but a strong breeze. In the evening a severe thunder storm.

24. Here is an awful gap. The fact is however that I have either been engaged or sleepy or lazy for the last week & so have totally neglected it. On Saturday the 16, Mongan was going to Macao in the *Ann* with Gibson at 5, so I & Adkins, while we were at dinner about 4½, determined to go too & immediately packing our portmanteau, off we headed to Sir John's who gave us leave of absence. Thence we rushed down to Leonard's & he said he would go too so we got safely on board. Found there were an infernal lot of Portuguese, Mr & Mrs Rangel,[48] Scott,[49] Dixon,[50] Bevan,[51] Morrison[52] & others & just as we were starting off came Dent's boat with Leonard & directly after him Tatham. Well, as we did not particularly want to sleep we got on the forecastle & began singing & continued doing so for the greater part of the night while we threaded our way thro' the islands which presented not a single feature of interest. The *Ann* was an infernal tub but we got a fiddler[53] & had a rum sort of a supper & amused ourselves immensely. About 12 we got to Macao & a lot of boats came alongside & I & Adkins got into one & off we went. It was a rum affair, flat-bottomed with a mat-roof. Room for 2 passengers to make themselves comfortable on camp stools in the middle. The boat's furniture, &c. & a woman sculling at one end & a woman rowing at the other, viz [sketch]. Well, we got on shore

---

48 Floriano Antonio Rangel (d. 1873) was a clerk at Jardine, Matheson & Co.
49 This may have been Adam Scott who was the principle of the trading firm Adam Scott & Co.
50 Andrew Dixson (d. 1873) was the publisher of various Hong Kong newspapers, including the *Friend of China* and *China Mail*.
51 William Frazer Bevan (1819–1858) was publisher and editor of the *Hong Kong Register*.
52 Possibly George Staunton Morrison (1830–1893), at the time chief assistant and keeper of the records in the Superintendency, or perhaps W.P. Morrison, a clerk at Thomas Hunt & Co.
53 Probably here referring to a table on board ship with a low edging along each side to prevent dishes and cups falling off with the movements of the sea.

somehow & in attempting to land, head over heels I went into the water. However, that did not matter much. I got on shore & we were immediately confronted by a patrol of Portuguese soldiers. Great humbugs dressed in blue to whom Adkins declared that he was a freeborn Englishman & would knock the whole 4 over for a dollar. When this was done, we went off after the others & Leonard offering us bed accommodation at D. & Co,[54] off we went there & knocked them up. Mr Colman,[55] Dent's Canton tea taster happened to be there & of course was rather confused at being turned out of bed at that hour & not recognizing Leonard or knowing who the devil we were, came gravely up to Leonard & said 'Are you aware whose house you are in?' 'Oh yes.' said L., 'I believe we are in D. & Cos.' This of course floored him, so after making some remarks about the number of beds he retired bewildered to bed & did not find out who we were till next morning. I had a capital sleep on a sofa & was amazingly jolly. Mongan slept in the adjoining room & T. & G. down below, L. & A. paying a visit to Ahou's.[56] About 5 o'clock Gibson woke me with 'Won't you have a bathe?' So up I jumped & we all set off in boats, rowed as usual by women to the bathing place which was in a jolly adjoining bay, the praya extending along a large bay beyond which there is another called Bishop's Bay where there is a capital bottom & where we had a splendid swim. After this I dressed & rushed off to the cathedral. It is not very handsome outside but inside it is rather jolly. Altars with paintings above them covering the walls but the most curious sight was the congregation composed with only 2 or 3 exceptions of women only & the women in that infernal Portuguese dress with a chintz tablecloth thrown over their face & body which makes them look very ugly. Sitting crosslegged on the little squares of carpet there were 3 very handsome ladies dressed in the mantilla who looked very jolly. The mantilla after all is a very becoming dress. There were a lot of Chinese women there too who seemed more devout than others but I understand they are paid for it. I stopped a while & heard part of a Portuguese sermon delivered by a priest with bands of silver down his robes. It was rather jolly looking but as I did not understand the language I soon began a critical examination of all the females as they came & sprinkled themselves from pewter cuspidors & the result was that I found them unutterably ugly. The

---

54 Dent & Co., Leonard's employers.
55 I have not been able to further identify this Mr Colman.
56 I have not been able to identify this establishment.

troops passed by too. They have a good band & marched well but are an ill-regulated, ill-conditioned set of varlets. From this I returned to breakfast & here must stop for tonight.

25. Another day wasted & the mail in, of which more after, but now for Macao. After a jolly breakfast at Dent's we loitered about at home pro tem & then went off in chairs to Beale's garden[57] to see the tomb of Camoens who, by-the-by, is not Camoens but Camoes.[58] Well, we got there & it well repaid us. Such a paradise I have not seen in China. Shady, mossy, cool walks with large & handsome cotton trees & fanciful rocks on either side. Altogether an immensely jolly place. Here we wandered about & lolled on the stone seat & one of us I regret to say killed an unfortunate lizard so we wandered about till we got to Camoës' grotto. It is composed of various huge masses of rock on the top of which there is a little summer house ascended by stone steps something like this [sketch]. Inside the grotto there is a monument to Camoës with his bust, date of birth & death & several extracts from his *Lusiad*. Outside there are 2 tablets, one by a Frenchman in French, the other in Latin by I forget who & to what effect. It was a beautiful place & the green trees around were well calculated to inspire the poet while the view of the sea would set him thinking of his native land. Thence we went to the Protestant chapel & burial ground. A pretty, unpretending spot & it was good to walk among the tombs & learn that men must die whether you have rank, wealth, knowledge or power. Before the sickle of the Great Reaper you are naught. After this we lounged about a good deal & I sat down & read a lot of *The Caxtons*[59] & it did me good. That is a novel which tho' it is an imitation & a bad imitation, the characters are so virtuous that you must derive benefit from its perusal. I at last however got Adkins & Leonard to stir & take a walk so off we started & had a very pleasant one tho' the sun was hot & the glare excessive & the roads were by no means good. We got to a shady place at last & stopping there we watched the sea & the clouds & a little fort on a hill & a Parsee cemetery. The first was curious because of the shoals, the water everywhere looking quite yellow, with a few streams running thro' it. The little fort too was a curiosity. It had evidently once a church & was perched on a hill out of the way of everything [sketch].

---

57   Thomas Beale (1775–1841). His garden and aviary were famous.
58   Luís Vaz de Camões (1524–1580), author of the great Portuguese epic *Os Lusíadas*, was known in English as Camoens. He is said to have written much of the poem in a grotto in the gardens. Alabaster is mistaken that this was his tomb, as he died in Portugal in 1580 and is buried in Lisbon.
59   Edward Bulwer-Lytton, *The Caxtons: A Family Picture* (Edinburgh: William Blackwood and Sons, 1849).

All the forts here are intensely wretched, about 18 inches thick & built of mud after this fashion [sketch] & would tumble down at the first shot fired at them. The Parsees' tombs pleased me as typical of neatness. They had not a large piece of ground & this ground was sloping, so they had terraced it & two terraces already were filled with uniform stone tombs. Passing this & a curious sandstone formation, we passed over a hill which was one mass of Chinese tombs & home. Macao has not much in it. On entering you see a row of tolerable but very melancholy yellow buildings extending along the beach in front of which there is an excellent praya. To the left there is a nunnery on the hill & at the east there are forts & batteries. In the middle you see over the houses a fine & really magnificent piece of architecture i.e. the front of St Paul's Cathedral. It is all that remains of it but what there is, is beautiful & looks so old & venerable with shrubs growing out of it & clothing it with evergreens. It is a grand thing & there is nothing in China to equal it. When we got home, out we went again & after hearing some abominable bugles we heard a capital band which was really very jolly & it was curious when the Vesper bell rang to see all & everyone take off their hats & say a silent prayer. After listening to the band till we were tired we went to the hotel to dinner but the results I must defer till tomorrow. Today the mail came in with letters from Uncle, Aunty, Charly, Henry, Percy, Dada Dunlop, Katy & Captain King & not much news. All are well, however, which is good news. We have succumbed shamefully to the Yankees & are going to the dogs. Could not work. Went to Harland & spent the evening with the Staces[60] & finished by playing cards at home.

28. Rainy. Muggy. Therm. 81°.

Finished section 1 & answered question 3 in section 4. Worked badly, lazily & slovenly. Read a bit & was awfully abominable all day. In the evening played cards & drank punch. Heu me miserum.[61]

31. Therm. 83°.

Oh man! Weak are thy resolutions & ill dost thou carry them out. Here are 3 days & nothing down. On Friday I did nothing particular so in the evening I, Adkins & Tatham went & bathed most unsatisfactorily for it was nearly dark & on returning Tatham insisted on going to the singsong so we went but it was great rot & I could not be satisfied so we had to keep on changing our places & when it was over we had an infernal lot of trouble

---

60 See Volume 4, footnote 44.
61 Latin, 'Alas! How wretched I am!'.

to find our boat. Then drank tea at Tatham's & reverted. Yesterday nothing particular happened & being very idle in the evening made a lot of punch & Leonard was rather the worse. Tatham, Gibson & Rickett also there. Today went to church & could scarcely keep awake. Loafed about & broke all my resolutions. Bought a new dog. Rather a jolly one. A China.[62] Very tiny but follows capitally. Christened him Smut. Went out for a sail with Gower. Great bosh. Totally done up & can't write. Wade has gone to press.

September

1. Fine. Therm. 82° in the evening.

The first of the month has enlarged mine acquaintance by a Mr Warren,[63] Assistant Surgeon of the *Coromandel*. A very jolly fellow & a very great swell. With him we passed a merry evening & cocktails passed the time away. A true born Irish man. He sang a song which was so good we wished it had been long & though it was short 'twas monstrous good. This day I've wasted in a measure. No work has finished been, tho' much begun & now in truth I 'gin to think that I'm a humbug. Well e'en,[64] let it be. I've got a cold so now to bed. I'll go & sweat like blazes. A most appropriate simile.

2. 84° in shade. 134° in sun at 3 o'clock. Piping hot & very fine.

Here we are going to bed in a state of siege with loaded revolvers. The fact is today Grandpré,[65] the Head of the Police, finding the huts in the ravine are the haunts of ruffians who have 2 nights running attacked Duddells,[66] tonight burnt them down & we expect an attack will be made by the wretches. It is astonishing what a number of Chinamen will crowd into a little hole. Well, at any rate, the houses were pulled & burnt down & we are in momentary expectation of an attack. I have got an awful cold & can't do anything. Tatham came up & he & I had a row over whist. Silly. Silly that I am & afterwards L. came up with a brace of pistols. Got an awful cold. Got paid.

---

62 A Pekinese. See Volume 2, footnote 56.
63 Thomas Robert Warren had a long career in the medical department of the Royal Navy beginning in the early 1850s and rising to be appointed deputy inspector-general of hospitals and fleets in 1884. He died in 1906.
64 Even.
65 See Volume 2, footnote 244.
66 Duddell & Co. was a trading firm. This building was likely their warehouse.

14. Therm. 84°. Fine with occasional clouds. Splendid moon light.

My birthday. The second I have spent out of England the first in China. Now I have been nearly a year in China. What have I gained? I am afraid I must say nothing or next door to nothing. A little experience. A little knowledge. What have I lost? My temper. My energy. My virtue. My memory. Truly I must make an effort, for if I go back like this what shall I come to? Now that I begin a new year let me make some resolutions & try to keep them:

Abjuration of women.
Abjuration of wine.
Let me refrain from evil talking.
Let me work hard.

I pray to keep these resolutions for I often make them and as often break them. Let me now try to keep them. Today I was up late in the morning & did nothing. Took a walk & talked to Hughes & wasted time agreeably. In the afternoon I walked with Gibson & went to church with Gower. Dined pleasantly with Hughes & afterwards took a walk home & a stroll by moon light. Read *The Book of Ruth*[67] & one of Blair's[68] Sermons.

15. Monday. Therm. 82°. Fine & sunny with occasional showers.

Tumbled out of bed about 7 and went out with the intention of bathing in the ravine but the sun being adverse in two places & clothes washing in the other, I had to content myself with the bathroom. After breakfast again I manfully set to work and began 4 notebooks. When shall I finish them, I wonder? However they are useful & do not interfere with any other work which is a great recommendation. After tiffin I attacked the examination papers but soon gave them up. Alston[69] coming up & bringing a lieutenant of the *Calcutta* up named Windon.[70] A Baltic man.[71] One who has seen Sveabourg[72] & this totally disarranged me. After dinner went out to bathe with Leonard & Adkins & an impertinent Chinaman attempting to bargain

---

67 In the Jewish Bible.
68 Hugh Blair (1718–1800), a Scottish theologian and author. His five volumes of *Sermons* (1777–1801) were popular and influential.
69 Alfred Henry Alston (1829–1874) was a naval officer who was active in and around Canton from the mid-1850s to the early 1860s. He was author of the famous *Seamanship, and Its Associated Duties in the Royal Navy* (London: Routledge, Warne, and Routledge, 1860). He retired from the navy as commander in 1871, becoming prison governor in Usk, south Wales.
70 I have been unable to identify this Lieutenant Windon.
71 Presumably saw service in Baltic waters.
72 Now known as Suomenlinna, Sveaborg is a fortress in Helsinki Harbour dating from the mid-eighteenth century. It was bombarded in August 1855 in what is now known as the Battle of Suomenlinna during the Crimean War. Finland had been occupied by Russia in 1808.

beforehand got his head punched & had to jump into the water to cool his ire. Did not go in myself as it was an unsafe bottom & was getting dark. Home by Leonard's & Reading Rooms. No news save that the pirates have established a signal system on the peak & other side of the harbor by means of red flags which has given rise to some little excitement & now I am about to set to work on Layard's *Nineveh*[73] & sleep.

16. Therm. 84°. Fine.

Now, are the signs that generally precede rebellion rife at present or not? I decidedly fancy, 'yes.' 1. Plans of government. Are they not springing upon all sides? 2. Corruption unveiled. Is it not so day after day? Dissatisfaction & sedition everyday listened to. I really fear a revolution is at hand. 1. The plans of government. Every projector of new plans is a revolutionist in this way. His plans are either good or bad. If good, there is generally some flaw which would prevent their working & at all events they do not get adopted & the projector & all his believers become dissatisfied & welcome any change whatsoever which may seem to afford them a chance of bringing forward their plans. 2. Corruption unveiled. For corruption, though the cause is not the sign of revolutions but when they begin to unveil it then fierce war succeeds. 3. The almighty dollar, sign of decadence. Thus much for moralizing, now for facts. Got up at 6¼. Bathed & read till 8. Breakfasted & then worked with Wade till 3 when he was so ill as to be obliged to knock off. Then with teacher till 4½ after which I bathed again & read Carlyle,[74] finishing up with dinner at the Governor's. Lieutenant Dent of *Sybille* & Chaplain Beal,[75] Instructor of Youth on board the *Calcutta* & Kennedy, mid on *do*,[76] a very jolly fellow, fresh from the Black Sea & naval brigade.[77] A jolly fellow, Instructor of Youth *do do*. A humbug, Sir! I chatty but nothing worth noting, save the behaviour of Tiger who insisted in coming in & of Hughes who got excited. Harland & Chaldecot too were there.

---

73 Austen Henry Layard (1817–1894) was an archaeologist, and one of the excavators of Nineveh in modern Iraq. Layand wrote several books with 'Nineveh' in their titles that Alabaster could have read.
74 Thomas Carlyle (1795–1881), *The French Revolution: A History* (London: Chapman and Hall, 1837), doi.org/10.1093/oseo/instance.00266991.
75 Samuel Beal (1825–1889) was a naval chaplain from 1851 to 1877. He is perhaps better known as one of the earliest Western authorities on Chinese Buddhism. On retirement from the navy, he was appointed professor of Chinese at University College, London.
76 *Do* = ditto, thus, Kennedy, midshipman on the *Calcutta*. This was Sir William Robert Kennedy (1838–1916), ultimately admiral in the Royal Navy, and author of several books recounting his hunting and fishing adventures around the world while in the navy, and *Hurrah for the Life of a Sailor! Fifty Years in the Royal Navy* (Edinburgh: Blackwood, 1900).
77 The Black Sea campaign in the Crimean War.

18. My unfortunate diary. Doomed to be irregular as your master always being begun & and always getting ended indeed pitiably because there is nothing to put in you or because your master is lazy & cannot be bored. However, here goes for another attempt at resuscitation this evening. Hughes & I have had a fierce contention de cunctis rebus et quaejusdem alia.[78] 1. about 'guess' & 'deductions.' Whether they mean the same thing or things different for I hold that a guess can only be right by chance while a deduction being grounded on a mathematical basis may probably be right. So much for strife & contention. Last night we dined at Rickett's. Tate, Repton, Capt. Jamieson,[79] Hunt,[80] Hudson, Chisholm[81] being there besides ourselves & we had an intensely jolly evening singing songs, eating ice & getting drunk, to which condition several of our party sadly verged & behold the consequences today. The Albany is laid up so bad indeed that innumerable cocktails are required by some to keep themselves going. Work is nearly an impossibility & the only cry is, 'Sleep!' I have been reading Carlyle & boshing most of the day. 4 hours next door & 2½ at least at home but 'twas much cry & little wool.[82] A fact worthy of contemplation. Have got a cold. Not a loose cold but a light cold which is a nuisance. *Lady Mary Wood* is in with no particular news & in a week I hope Henry will too. Hughes & Gower are going to Macao on Saturday but I don't think I shall. Mrs Loraine is dead.[83]

19. 84°. Fine & Hot.

So pass day after day. Thermometer so & so. Weather hot, but what are the effects? Alas, none. What have I done here? Simply nothing. Nothing at all. For effects I had better been in England. Today I learnt nothing, did nothing. A melancholy fact to think of. Melancholy indeed. Waste. Blank. Waste. Blank. So wags my world. Went to the band. Saw Repton, Hudson, Leonard, Gower, Wade, Gibson, Ricket, &c. I homed after a walk, Gibson coming up. I quashed Chinese. I played whist. Finis.

---

78 Latin, 'About everything and then some other things'. This is a misquotation of a Latin phrase that appears in Canto 16 of Byron's *Don Juan*: 'De rebus cunctis et quibusdam aliis'.
79 Captain Charles Jamieson, who was master of P&O steamers on the Pearl River, in which capacity he assisted the Royal Navy in their actions against pirates. Later, he became inspector of opium and owner of an opium hulk.
80 W.H. Hunt was a clerk at Gibb, Livingstone & Co.
81 I have not been able to identify Chisholm.
82 An expression meaning a lot of activity but little outcome.
83 Jessie Lorrain, née Grieve (1816–1856), was the wife of Dr William Buchan Lorrain (1804–1857).

21. Therm. today 86°.

Facts. Saturday. Did not work. A summons served upon one in the suit of Afow for $17.06. Wade very ill taking 2 blue pills[84] every 3 hours. Bathed. Had a capital swim. Hughes, Mongan & Gower went to Macao per *Willamette*. Hudson, Leonard & Wheely came to dinner. An unjolly affair. Repton & Rickett drop in afterwards but there was no singing or jollity. Sunday. Got up as usual. Saw Wade. Still seedy. Church. Bad sermon. Almost fell in love with Miss Forth,[85] a lady old enough to be my mother. Home. Tiffin. Laziness. Dinner. Go out. Church. Sermon on Mrs Loraine. Bad. Home. Kennedy called. Lawrence ill. Monday. Wade still ill. Answered the summons. Saw Stace.[86] Mitchell presided.[87] Very like Uncle Greeves.[88] Made a fool of myself. Compromised the affair. Home. Laziness. Attempt at work. Went out to see funeral of French officer. Died in 2 hours of apoplexy. Got there. Saw procession. 1 sailor boy with crucifix, coffin, French, English & American Sailors 750 odd marines, English, French & American naval officers, W. Woodgate, jacks, governor's carriage, rag, tag & bobtail. No band. Burial service scamped over by 3 priests. 3 vollies.[89] All is over at 3 o'clock. Yesterday he was in perfect health. Home. Into Lawrence's. Drink tea. Capt. or Skipper Webb of *Remi* there. An old rake. Home. So finis. Sensations: laziness with occasional anxiety. Great confusion. Great lassitude.

23. Therm. 85° at night. Fine. Thunder.

Up at 6. Bath. Little Chinese. Breakfast. Work. Lei[90] & tsa hua.[91] Old Hsiao regularly mad. Tiffin. Finished section II after fearful quarrelling. Dinner. Long walk with Hughes, Plessman & Mongan. Met soldier's funeral. Home. Stomach ache. Carlyle. Gibson comes up. Cards. Carlyle. Bed. Henry will very likely be here tomorrow. Gower seedy. Adkins *do do*.

---

84   Blue Pills, or Blue Mass, were a medicine common in the nineteenth century and earlier, which was taken to cure a wide range of ailments. Its main active constituent was mercury. A typical dosage was two to three tablets per day, thus Wade's dosage was very high, and represented many hundred times the now recommended safe level of mercury ingestion.
85   Probably a daughter of F.H.A. Forth, colonial treasurer (1808–1876).
86   Edward Keate Stace was a long-time solicitor in Hong Kong, and would have appeared for Alabaster.
87   William Henry Mitchell was assistant magistrate at this time.
88   John Greeves was married to Katherine Alabaster (1814–1892) who was the sister of James Chaloner (Chaloner's father) and Mary Ann (Aunty).
89   Volleys, salutes of gunfire.
90   *Lei* 類, categories.
91   *Zahua*, probably 雜話, 'miscellaneous stories', colloquially 'chat'. From the context, this may refer to a part of a text Alabaster was studying.

24. This night a year ago I arrived at Hong Kong so that now I am no longer a griffin.[92] Experience I have certainly gained but am much the same as to foolery as I was last year. This year I must reform. Today worked tolerably & this evening, after hearing the 59th band and taking a walk, I & Mongan went to the Asiatic. Beal, Chaplain of the *Sibylle*, reading a paper on Japan, &c. Rather good tho' he had to leave out ½ of it.[93] Miss Irwin[94] being there & I must say I saw more of her than I heard of the paper. She is rather a jolly girl but too forward. However, I intend to fall in love with her. Tasted some sake which seems to be a composition distilled from cockroaches & ketchup. Lot of Japanese books there. Nice neat little things in curious paper covers. Sake jar [sketch]. Drinking cup [sketch]. Foxes tail. Capercailyie,[95] &c., &c. A thunderstorm at 5 this morning. The peals of thunder resembling a smart fusillade. The *Sybille* went out having lost its steward by sudden death. It was towed by the *Coromandel*. The *Barracouta* came in. Saw Lawrence of course & tea'd with him. He is nearly well & has got a new lamp whereat he is jolly. Henry, I hope, will arrive tonight.

25. 26. No mail yesterday did but little work in the evening. Saw Leonard who has fallen ill today. Did nothing. The *Winchester* coming in & saluting. The rain coming down in torrents all day. Went to reading rooms & saw Gibson also laid up.

October

9. Fine Cloudy. 77° & 78°.

Here we are again. Henry is come all right, &c. Today up at 6½. Bath. Read Machiavelli. Took my tonic & colloquialized as usual. Walsh[96] of *Bittern* & Mairs[97] or some such name, staff surgeon of 59th, came to tiffin. Two jolly

---

92 A griffin was an Anglo-Indian term for a newcomer or greenhorn.
93 *China Mail*, 2 October 1856, reports:
    At a Meeting of the China Branch of the Royal Asiatic Society, on Wednesday evening the 24th September ... The Rev. J Beal ... read his paper, giving an account of places visited during a late cruize to the Gulf of Tartary, and the Coasts of Japan. The paper was one of very great interest, and was illustrated by a collection of arms and utensils of various kinds, and especially by some excellent photographs by J. Austen, Esq ... There was also a supply of Japanese Saki, of which several members partook.
94 The daughter of J.J. Irwin, see Volume 2, footnote 169.
95 Scottish spelling of capercaillie.
96 William Walsh was acting lieutenant on the *Bittern* at this time.
97 John Henry Gouldsbury Devenish Meares (1836–1877) served in the Army Medical Department from 1855, on qualifying in the Royal College of Surgeons of Ireland. After seeing service in China in 1856–57, he was in Malta as well as England and Scotland, reaching the rank of surgeon-major.

fellows. After tiffin classicalized & then took Jacko and Smut out for a walk & swim. Jacko swims & dives jollily. Home. Machiavelli. Dinner & whist. Sic transit gloria mundi.

11. Fine Day.

Took my tonic. Colloquial & classic as usual & after that a mess dinner. Tronson[98] came. A jolly fellow who sung many songs in very good style. Jackson,[99] too, a middie came in the room of Kennedy. A most extraordinary *rencontre*.[100] I knew his brother very well. He was in the same class with me. I was rather astonished by his asking, 'Did not you go to King's College?' to which I answered, 'Yes' & we were friends at once. He is an intelligent, nice little fellow. I shall like him very well. Had a long talk with Gower about Hughes whom we agree in considering a beast & had two tiffs with Henry. One on scientific grounds, he denying that I could perceive light & darkness & the other was he wanted to come the elder brother on my damning the boys' eyes, whereon I told him that I did not come here to be lectured by him or anyone else.

12. Sunday. Fine & hot.

After a bad night in which I was disturbed by the dog & rats I got up at 5. Had a bath and started with Adkins to the *Baracouta* whereon he had a bath & we breakfasted in the gunroom. Home & breakfasted again but did not go to church. After church, Ray[101] came. He is a jolly old fellow tho' he has not so much talk in him as I should have expected. He stopped tiffin & dinner & we rather enjoyed ourselves & afterwards had a talk with Howlett.[102] He is a rum fellow. The *Comus*, *Encounter*, *Fiery Cross*, and *Shanghae* all came in

---

98 Dr John Mortlock Tronson was a naval surgeon who became a member of the Royal College of Surgeons in London in 1852, and an MD from the University of St Andrews in 1861. He died in Sydney on 30 January 1863, where he had been serving on the *Orpheus*, the flagship of the Australian squadron. He did not sail with the *Orpheus* on its next voyage as he was suffering from the illness that would kill him but, as luck would have it, the *Orpheus* sank on 7 February off Auckland with 189 of its 259 crew lost. Tronson is known for his *Personal Narrative of a Voyage to Japan, Kamtschatka, Siberia, Tartary, and Various Parts of the Coast of China in* H.M.S. Barracouta (London: Bradbury and Evans, 1859).
99 Jackson was serving on the *Barracouta*.
100 French, 'meeting'.
101 I have not been able to identify Ray.
102 Herbert George Howlett was a student interpreter who was appointed in May 1856. He later served in the consulate at Dengzhou (i.e. Yantai). He was an alcoholic and was forced to resign from the Consular Service in 1872.

today. Russia has given up Kars and the Serpent Isles[103] & is making grand preparations for the coronation.[104] The Prince of Prussia is wounded in a fight with the Riff[105] pirates. The King of Naples[106] has sent back a defiant answer. The Eastern King[107] is torn to pieces by 5 buffaloes and that is all.

15. Damn Hughes and his impertinence. Today the mail went. Did no work. Up at 6½. Wrote letters then idled and bathed and, as Jenkins[108] would call it, basnached[109] about till 12 when I, Henry, Mongan & Howlet went on board the mail steamer.[110] Saw old Ray off. There is a curious assortment of passengers this time. The Duke of Valambrossa,[111] next heir to the Sardinian throne, and poor Nixon[112] who is totally mad from sunstroke. Afterwards went on board the *Comus*. Saw the gun carriages of the guns which they had to throw over board. It seems they have had a fearful passage. A hurricane lasting 48 hours. The guns not visible for the water and the ship quivering and quaking. Everything battened down and every strip of canvas blown away & everyone expecting to go down. Jenkins must be a bold and good man for in the height of the tempest he read the prayers for the shipwrecked to the crew and then had 8 guns thrown overboard. Markham[113] came to dinner. He is a fine, tall, gentlemanly, clever, handsomish, fast fellow. Talks nicely. Kept it up late and now to bed.

---

103 Kars is a city in north-eastern Turkey that had been occupied by Russia since 1828. Serpent Island, or Snake Island as it was also known, is a small, barely populated outcrop in the Black Sea also occupied by Russia, in this case since 1829. Both places were ceded to Ottoman Turkey at the Treaty of Paris that concluded the Crimean War in March 1856. Snake Island is now controlled by Ukraine (*Ostriv Zmiinyi*), though it has also long been claimed by Romania (*Insula șerpilor*).
104 The coronation of Tsar Alexander II took place on 26 August 1856 by the Julian calendar or 7 September by the Gregorian.
105 The Berber Rifians live in the Rif region of northern Morocco.
106 Ferdinand II, King of the Two Sicilies (1810–1859, r. 1830–1859) was in dispute in 1856 with Britain over their influence in Sicily.
107 Yang Xiuqing (d. 1856), the so-called Taiping Eastern King, was killed by senior commanders of the Taiping administration on 2 September for plotting to usurp the Taiping Heavenly King, Hong Xiuquan.
108 Robert Jenkins (1825–1894), at the time Captain of the *Comus*, which was involved in the suppression of pirates. He also served in Syria, the Arctic, New Zealand and Fiji, ultimately rising to the rank of admiral.
109 Obscure. Possibly related to banjaxed.
110 The P&O Steamer *Shanghai*.
111 This was Riccardo Giovanni Maria Stefano Manca-Amat, second Duke of Vallombrosa and fourth Duke of Asinara (1834–1903). I do not know why he was in Hong Kong at this time.
112 I have not been able to identify Nixon.
113 John Markham (1835–1871) was appointed as a student interpreter in 1852. At the time of this entry he had just been made second assistant in the Superintendency. At the time of his death he was acting consul in Shanghai. Coates notes that Markham was appointed through the patronage of the then foreign secretary, Lord Malmesbury, and had 'a total disinclination to learn Chinese'. He was the grandson of the private secretary of Warren Hastings, famous in the history of British colonialism in India. See Coates, *The China Consuls*, 74, 499.

P.S. The Duke of Valambrossa is a tall, fine, coarse, snobby, sensual-looking buffer.

17. Yesterday nothing notable happened. Jackson come up & he, I, Howlett & Gower went curio hunting & I found an old buffer who talked Mandarin so after much talk home. Of public news, there was a grand meeting to advise Sir J.B. what to do, &c., &c., which carried all its motions. Today the usual amount of work being got through, we tea'd at Irwins, Miss Mole being remarkably amiable. A German missionary too was there & after wishy-washy discourse, singing, &c. to Lawrence's whence home.

18. I & Hughes had a damned row at dinner. I got rather muzzy like a fool and told him my mind regarding his behavior respecting the room, &c., and he was riled & being rather drunk…

19. Adkins, Hughes, Gower & Leonard went to Macao to stop a week. A wretched bad day. Rainy & seedy.

20. Hot. Showers.

The Canton affair is not settled yet.[114] The *Coromandel* went today & the *Calcutta* & *Winchester* are going in a day or two. Worked in at Wade's all day. Now very tired so to bed.

24. Here have 4 days gone by & I have put nothing down tho' there have been all descriptions of jollity going on. 1. The *Calcutta*, *Samson*, *Encounter*, *Barracouta*, *Comus*, *Sybille* & *Coromandel* have all gone to Canton. 2. Yeh ming shan[115] has refused all satisfaction. 3. The *Barracouta* has taken the Bogue Forts. 4. Wade has gone to Canton. 5. The *Encounter* is lying off Canton. 6. I have been working hard.

27. I have been in better temper than usual.

---

114 Alabaster's 'Canton affair' referred to actions surrounding the seizure of the ship *Arrow* that effectively began what is now known as the Second Opium War. On the events alluded to in this part of the diary (and their aftermath), see the Introduction.
115 Ye Mingchen.

November

13. Weather tolerable. Very beautiful sky & moonlight night.

Temper, bad. Health, diarhoeic. Events. Capture of the Bogue Forts after a short resistance by the *Calcutta, Baracouta, Hornet* & *Coromandel*.[116] Achun came but was told to come tomorrow. Wrote letters & had a despatch to Yeh to copy. Bathed in ravine. Chinese studies most unsatisfactory.

20. Particulars arrived concerning the Yankee difficulty. It seems the Yankees had determined to leave us to fight it out when the boat bearing this message from Parker to the Commodore was fired on which riled the Yankees. So next day tho', *Levant* & *Portsmouth* went to smash the forts to all tarnation & after 20 minutes firing a lull ensued. On this the Yankee officers began to brag of the efficient manner on which their 8 inch shells had brought the matter to a speedy conclusion when 'bang!', they went at it again till night fall, the Yankees getting considerably knocked about & not being able to take the forts. Well, next day they were going at it again & sent a boat ahead to take soundings, so the Chinamen took the Chinaman's head off with a round shot & then just as everyone was going to work, Peter Parker steps up and stops all fighting & sends a letter to Yeh demanding an apology in 24 hours, to which Yeh retorts that he has given them a licking & is going to annihilate them. The *Annandale* too has had a fight with a junk today. The remaining two receiving ships arrived from Cumsingmoon. Caldwell is down at Canton on 700 a year. Today as usual I went to office at 12. Lady B. sent for me so I went & saw H.L.[117] & I am to go every day for the present to tell her all the news of the place. Saw Lawrence, Gibson, &c. Worked with Hsiao in the evening reading some of the *Trimetrical Classic*[118] which is very easy. Ordered new trousers & waist coat.

23. As is sure to be the case with me, something new having occurred I leave off my diary till it is all over. On the 21 in the morning I went down town & at the stationer's was told that the Chinese intended to shut up shop on the 22nd being discontented with the working of the Nuisance Act.[119]

---

116 I have not been able to identify Achun.
117 Her Ladyship.
118 The *Sanzi jing* 三字經, a beginner's primer where all phrases are three characters long.
119 This would refer to either Ordinance No. 8 (16 April 1856), 'An Ordinance for Buildings and Nuisances' or No. 12 (12 June 1856), 'An Ordinance to Regulate Chinese Burials, and to prevent certain Nuisances, within the Colony of Hong Kong'.

26. I, Henry and Mongan breakfasted at Colonel Caine's and as a matter of course had a capital breakfast. The Colonel as jolly as usual. I made a fearful bull saying we expected quarters out next mail which excited a roar. Col. Caine too told us a good story. He had 2 pointers out, so when the ship arrived he went down & was met by the captain who told him that 2 very savage bull dogs had come. This of course disgusted Caine who however told him to get them off which the captain after some bother did & the ferocious bulldogs turned out two docile pointers. After breakfast we went shopping. Bought a dinner service, &c. then home & out again to call on Irwin with H & M. Saw Irwin but no one else & were invited to tea & toast on Friday. After this we went off to the Russian frigate *Aurora* which arrived today. Went on board. None of us able to speak French. In fact I made a most infernal hash of Chinese & French however we went over it, the officer on watch being remarkably civil & the men drawing up in line. They are fine men but dirty & grovelling looking. The ship is a nice old tub but is kept clean. She has no guns on her lower deck. After our inspection we chowed.[120] Home, taking a pull ourselves & then Gibson & cards.

---

120 Ate.

Appendix

The following vocabulary list is found in the first volume of the diaries, starting from the back, upside-down.

Pronouns

I

我	wo	I			
你	ni	You	sometimes	您	lin
他	ta	He			

but except in very intimate conversation it is considered rude to use one of these, and such words as the following are used instead

門生 or	學生 or	晚生	}
munsang	hiohsang	wunsang	} I your disciple
小弟	siauti	I your younger brother	
小的	siaou-teh	I your humble servant	
罪人	tsuijin	I a sinner	
老爺	laou ye	You sir	
老大[1]	laou ta jin	Thou great man	
大老先生	ta laou sing sang	noble master	
相公	seang-kung	Sir	
老人家	laou jin kia	Old sir	

---

1   Alabaster left out the final character here.

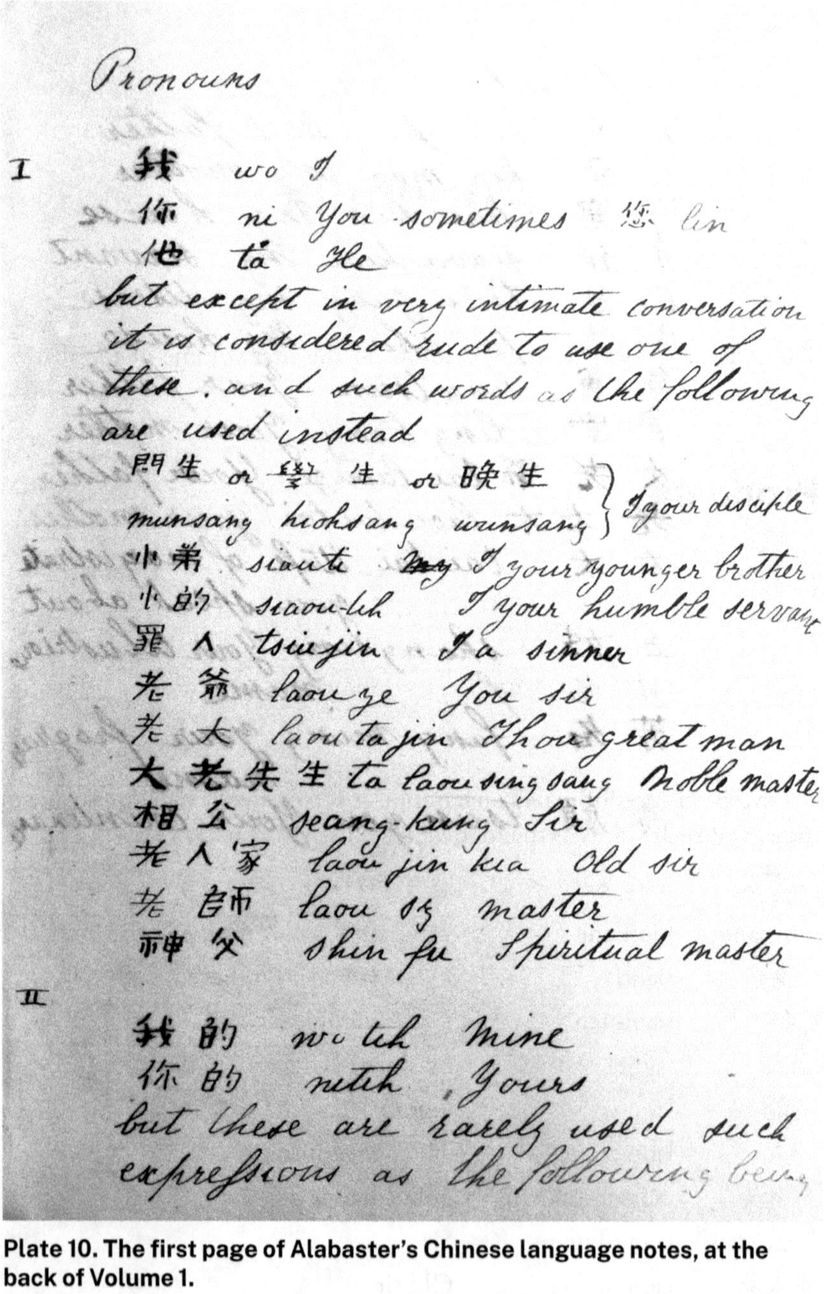

Pronouns

I
- 我 wo I
- 你 ni You sometimes 您 nin
- 他 ta He

but except in very intimate conversation it is considered rude to use one of these, and such words as the following are used instead

- 門生 or 學生 or 晚生 munsang hiohsang wunsang } I your disciple
- 小弟 siaute I your younger brother
- 小的 siaou-teh I your humble servant
- 罪人 tsuijin I a sinner
- 老爺 laou ye You sir
- 老大人 laou ta jin Thou great man
- 大老先生 ta laou sing sang Noble master
- 相公 seang-kung Sir
- 老人家 laou jin kia Old sir
- 老師 laou sz master
- 神父 shin fu Spiritual master

II
- 我的 wo teh Mine
- 你的 neteh Yours

but these are rarely used such expressions as the following being

Plate 10. The first page of Alabaster's Chinese language notes, at the back of Volume 1.

APPENDIX

老師	laou shy	master
神父	shin fu	Spiritual master

II

我的	wo teh	Mine
你的	niteh	Yours

but these are rarely used such expressions as the following being employed

家父	kia fu	My father
家母	kia moo	My mother
家寒	han kia	My house
小价	siaou kiai	My servant
賤恙	tsien yang	My disease
敝處	pi chu	My house
令尊	ling tsun	Your father
令堂	ling tang	Your mother
太老爺	tai laou ye	Your father
老太太	laou tai tai	Your mother
太太	tai tai	Wife of magistrate you speak about
上姓	shang sing	Your illustrious name
芳名	fang ming	Your fragrant name
尊顏	tsun yen	Your countenance

Select Bibliography

Manuscript Sources

Diaries of Sir Chaloner Alabaster. Library of the School of Oriental and African Studies, University of London, Archive and Special Collections, MS 380451.

Adkins Family of Milcote, Weston-on-Avon – 1855–1879. Warwickshire County Record Office, CR 3554.

Bowring Papers. John Rylands Library, University of Manchester, GB 133 Eng MSS 1228–1234.

Foreign Office: Consulates and Legation, China: General Correspondence, Series I. National Archives, FO 228.

Alfred Woodhead. 'Life in Hong Kong, 1856–1859'. Hong Kong Public Records Office.

Newspapers and Journals

Allen's Indian Mail
Bell's Life in London, and Sporting Chronicle
China Mail
Friend of China
Illustrated London News
Indian News and Chronicle of Eastern Affairs
North China Herald
Overland Register and Price Current
Solicitor's Journal and Reporter

Internet Sources

'Gwulo: Old Hong Kong'. gwulo.com.

'London Street Views'. londonstreetviews.wordpress.com.

Printed Sources

Abe, Kaori. *Chinese Middlemen in Hong Kong's Colonial Economy, 1830–1890*. Abingdon: Routledge, 2018. doi.org/10.4324/9781315543949.

Alabaster, Adrian. *A Quintet of Alabasters*. Knebworth: Able Publishing, 1997.

Alabaster, John S. *An Alabaster Quest: A Claim to North American Indian Land, 1837*. Occasional Monograph No. 4, The Alabaster Society, 2011.

Alabaster, John S. *Sir Chaloner Alabaster Correspondence (1840–1880)*. Occasional Monograph No. 2, The Alabaster Society, 2005.

Alison, Archibald. *History of Europe from the Commencement of the French Revolution in M.DCC.LXXXIX to the Restoration of the Bourbons in M.DCCC.XV*. 10 vols. Edinburgh: W. Blackwood and Sons, 1833–1843.

Alston, Alfred Henry. *Seamanship, and its Associated Duties in the Royal Navy*. London: Routledge, 1860.

Altenburger, Roland. 'Two Cousins: Jean-Pierre Abel-Rémusat's and Stanislas Julien's Translations of Yu Jiao Li'. In *Crossing Borders: Sinology in Translation Studies*, edited by T. H. Barrett and Lawrence Wang-Chi Wong, 145–80. Hong Kong: The Chinese University of Hong Kong Press, 2022. doi.org/10.2307/j.ctv2pfq2rn.10.

Anon. *Correspondence Respecting Insults in China*. London: Harrison & Sons, 1857.

Anon. *Further Papers Related to the Rebellion in China*. London: Harrison & Sons, 1862.

Anon. *Historical and Statistical Abstract of the Colony of Hong Kong, 1841–1920*. Hong Kong: Noronha & Company, Government Printers, 1922.

Anon. *Papers Related to the Proceedings of Her Majesty's Naval Forces at Canton, with Appendix*. London: Harrison & Sons, 1857.

Anon. 'Thackeray's Works'. *The Westminster and Foreign Quarterly Review* 59 (1 April 1853): 363–88.

Anon. *The China Directory for 1862*. A Shortrede & Co., 1862.

Anon. *The China Directory for 1863*. A Shortrede & Co., 1863.

Anon. *The Chronicle and Directory for China, Japan and the Philippines for 1864*. Hongkong: Daily Press, 1864.

Anon. *The Chronicle and Directory for China, Japan and the Philippines for 1865*. Hongkong: Daily Press, 1865.

Anon. *The Chronicle and Directory for China, Japan and the Philippines for 1869*. Hongkong: Daily Press, 1869.

Anon. *The Chronicle and Directory for China, Japan and the Philippines for 1870*. Hongkong: Daily Press, 1870.

Anon. *The Hongkong Directory, with List of Foreign Residents in China*. Hongkong: Armenian Press, 1859.

Barrett, T.H. *Singular Listlessness: A Short History of Chinese Books and British Scholars*. London: Wellsweep Press, 1989.

Beaven, Alfred B. *The Aldermen of the City of London, Henry III – 1908, with Notes on the Parliamentary Representation of the City, the Aldermen and the Livery Companies, the Aldermanic Veto, Aldermanic Baronets and Knights, etc*. London: Eden Fisher & Co, Ltd, 1913.

Bickers, Robert and Jonathan J. Howlett, eds. *Britain and China, 1840–1970: Empire, Finance and War*. Abingdon: Routledge, 2016. doi.org/10.4324/9781315687735.

Bickley, Gillian, ed. *A Magistrate's Court in Nineteenth-Century Hong Kong: Court in Time*. Hong Kong: Proverse Press, 2005.

Blair, Hugh. *Sermons*. 5 vols. Edinburgh: William Creech, 1777–1801.

Bodell, James, *A Soldier's View of Empire: The Reminiscences of James Bodell, 1831–92*, edited by Keith Sinclair. London: Bodley Head, 1982.

Bowring, Sir John. *Autobiographical Recollections of Sir John Bowring, with a Brief Memoir by Lewin B. Bowring*. London: Henry S. King, 1877.

Bowring, Sir John. *The Decimal System in Numbers, Coins and Accounts: Especially with Reference to the Decimalisation of the Currency and Accountancy of the United Kingdom*. London: Nathaniel Cooke, 1854.

Bowring, Sir John. *The Kingdom and People of Siam*. London: John W. Parker & Son, 1857.

Bowring, Philip. *Free Trade's First Missionary: Sir John Bowring in Europe and Asia.* Hong Kong: Hong Kong University Press, 2014. doi.org/10.5790/hongkong/9789888208722.001.0001.

Braga, Stuart. *Making Impressions: A Portuguese Family in Macau and Hong Kong, 1700–1945.* Macau: Instituto Internacional de Macau, 2015.

Bruner, Katherine F., John K. Fairbank and Richard J. Smith, ed. and narratives. *Entering China's Service: Robert Hart's Journals, 1854–1863.* Cambridge, MA: Council on East Asian Studies, Harvard University, 1986. doi.org/10.1163/9781684172627.

Bulwer-Lytton, Edward. *The Caxtons: A Family Picture.* Edinburgh: William Blackwood and Sons, 1849.

Carlyle, Thomas. *The French Revolution: A History.* London: Chapman and Hall, 1837. doi.org/10.1093/oseo/instance.00266991.

Carroll, John M. *Edge of Empires: Chinese Elites and British Colonials in Hong Kong.* Cambridge, MA: Harvard University Press, 2005. doi.org/10.4159/9780674029231.

Carter, Kathryn. 'The Cultural Work of Diaries in Mid-Century Victorian Britain'. *Victorian Review* 23, no. 2 (Winter 1997): 251–67. doi.org/10.1353/vcr.1997.0013.

Cavendish, Francis W.H. and Edward Hertslet, comps. *The Foreign Office List of 1857.* London: Harrison, 1857.

Cavendish, Francis W.H. and Edward Hertslet, comps. *The Foreign Office List of 1863.* London: Harrison, 1863.

Chan-Yeung, Moira M.W. *A Medical History of Hong Kong, 1842–1941.* Hong Kong: The Chinese University of Hong Kong Press, 2018. doi.org/10.2307/j.ctvbtzp1t.

Choi, Henry Sze Hang. *The Remarkable Hybrid Maritime World of Hong Kong and the West River Region in the Late Qing Period.* Leiden: Brill, 2017. doi.org/10.1163/9789004341166.

Chu, Cindy Yik-yi, ed. *Foreign Communities in Hong Kong, 1840s–1950s.* Basingstoke, Hampshire: Palgrave MacMillan, 2005. doi.org/10.1057/9781403980557.

Coates, P.D. *The China Consuls: British Consular Officers, 1843–1943.* Oxford: Oxford University Press, 1988.

Cohen, Paul A. *Between Tradition and Modernity: Wang T'ao and Reform in Late Ch'ing China*. Cambridge, MA: Harvard University Press, 1974. doi.org/10.1163/9781684172719.

Cooke, George Wingrove. *China: Being 'The Times' Special Correspondence from China in the Years 1857–58*. London: G. Routledge & Co., 1858.

Cooley, James C. *T.F. Wade in China: Pioneer in Global Diplomacy, 1842–1882*. Leiden: Brill, 1981.

da Silva, António M. Pacheco Jorge. *The Portuguese Community in Hong Kong: A Pictorial History*. 2 vols. Macau: Conselho das Comunidades Macaenses, Instituto Internacional de Macau, vol. 1, 2007, vol. 2, 2010.

Davis, John Francis. *Sketches of China, Partly during an Inland Journey of Four Months, between Peking, Nanking and Canton, with Notices and Observations Relative to the Present War*. 2 vols. London: Charles Knight & Co., 1841.

Davis, John Francis. *The Chinese: A General Description of the Empire of China and its Inhabitants*. London: Charles Knight, 1836.

de Prémare, Joseph Henri Marie. *The Notitia Linguae Sinicae of Prémare*, translated by J.G. Bridgman. Canton: Office of the 'Chinese Repository', 1847.

Dennys, Nicholas. *The Treaty Ports of China and Japan*. London: Trubner & Co., 1867.

Disraeli, Isaac. *Curiosities of Literature*, edited by Benjamin Disraeli. 3 vols. London: Routledge, 1863.

Drémeaux, François, ed. *Hong Kong, French Connections: From the 19th Century to the Present Day*. Hong Kong: Bonham Media, 2012.

Eitel, E.J. *Europe in China: The History of Hongkong from the Beginning to the Year 1882*. London: Luzac & Company, 1895.

Ellis, Henry T. *Hong Kong to Manilla, and the Lakes of Luzon, in the Philippine Isles in the Year 1856*. London: Smith, Elder & Co., 1859.

Endacott, G.B. *A Biographical Sketch-Book of Early Hong Kong*. Hong Kong: Hong Kong University Press, 2005.

Endacott, G.B. *A History of Hong Kong*. London: Oxford University Press, 1958.

Endacott, G.B. *An Eastern Entrepôt: A Collection of Documents Illustrating the History of Hong Kong*. London: Her Majesty's Stationery Office, 1964.

Fairbank, John King. *Trade and Diplomacy on the China Coast: The Opening of the Treaty Ports, 1842–1854*. Cambridge, MA: Harvard University Press, 1953.

Faure, David. *Colonialism and the Hong Kong Mentality*. Hong Kong: Centre of Asian Studies, University of Hong Kong, 2003.

Feng, Bangyan and Nyaw Mee Kau. *Enriching Lives: A History of Insurance in Hong Kong, 1841–2010*, translated by Violet Law. Hong Kong: Hong Kong University Press, 2009.

Feuerbach, Ludwig Andreas. *The Essence of Christianity*, translated by Mary Ann Evans (i.e. George Eliot). London: John Chapman, 1854.

Fortune, Robert. *A Journey to the Tea Countries of China*. London: John Murray, 1852.

Fortune, Robert. *Three Years' Wanderings in the Northern Provinces of China*. London: John Murray, 1847.

Gay, Peter. *The Bourgeois Experience: Victoria to Freud. Vol. 1, Education of the Senses*. New York: Oxford University Press, 1984; *Vol. 4, The Naked Heart*. New York: Oxford University Press, 1996.

Grainger, John D. *The First Pacific War, Britain and Russia 1854–1856*. Woodbridge: The Boydell Press, 2008.

Grote, George. *A History of Greece from the Earliest Period to the Close of the Generation Contemporary with Alexander the Great*. 12 vols. London: John Murray, 1846–56.

Gutzlaff, Charles. *Journal of Three Voyages along the Coast of China, in 1831, 1832, & 1833, with Notices of Siam, Corea, and the Loo-Choo Islands*. London: Frederick Westley and A.H. Davis, 1834.

Gutzlaff, Charles. *Journal of Two Voyages along the Coast of China, 1831, & 1832, the First in a Chinese Junk, the Second in the British Ship Lord Amherst, with Notices of Siam, Corea, and the Loochoo Islands, and Remarks on the Policy, Religion, etc., of China*. New York: J.P. Haven, 1833.

Hall, Basil. *Narrative to Java, China and the Great Loo-Choo Island*. London: William Tegg & Co., 1851.

Hamilton, Sheilah E. *Watching over Hong Kong: Private Policing 1841–1941*. Hong Kong: Hong Kong University Press, 2008.

Hertslet, Edward, comp. *The Foreign Office List of 1865*. London: Harrison, 1865.

Hertslet, Edward, comp. *The Foreign Office List of 1866*. London: Harrison, 1866.

Hertslet, Edward, comp. *The Foreign Office List of 1877*. London: Harrison, 1877.

Hertslet, Edward, comp. *The Foreign Office List of 1881*. London: Harrison, 1881.

Ho, Pui-yin. *The Administrative History of Hong Kong Government Agencies, 1841–2002*. Hong Kong: Hong Kong University Press, 2004.

Ho, Vincent Wai-kit. 'Duties and Limitations: The Role of United States Consuls in Macao, 1849–1869'. In *Americans and Macao: Trade, Smuggling and Diplomacy on the South China Coast*, edited by Paul A. Van Dyke, 143–52. Hong Kong: Hong Kong University Press, 2012.

Holdsworth, May and Christopher Munn. *Crime, Justice and Punishment in Hong Kong: Central Police Station, Central Magistracy and Victoria Gaol*. Hong Kong: Hong Kong University Press, 2020.

Holdsworth, May and Christopher Munn, eds. *Dictionary of Hong Kong Biography*. Hong Kong: Hong Kong University Press, 2012.

Howe, Octavius Thorndike and Frederick C. Matthews. *American Clipper Ships, 1833–1858*. Vol 1. New York: Dover Publications, 2012.

Howell, Philip. 'Race, Space and the Regulation of Prostitution in Colonial Hong Kong'. *Urban History* 31, no. 2 (2004): 229–48. doi.org/10.1017/S0963926804002123.

Kennedy, Sir William Robert. *Hurrah for the Life of a Sailor! Fifty Years in the Royal Navy*. Edinburgh: Blackwood, 1900.

Kim, Jaeyoon. 'The Heaven and Earth Society and the Red Turban Rebellion in Late Qing China'. *Journal of Humanities and Social Sciences* 3, no. 1 (2009): 1–35.

King, Amelia Kay. 'James Keenan: United States Consul to Hong Kong'. MA thesis, North Texas State University, 1978.

Kinnis, John. 'Contributions to Medical Military Statistics of China'. *The Transactions of the Medical and Physical Society of Bombay* (1847–48): 3–34.

Kwan, Uganda Sze Pui. 'Transferring Sinosphere Knowledge to the Public: James Summers (1828–91) as Printer, Editor and Cataloguer'. *East Asian Publishing and Society* 8 (2018): 56–84. doi.org/10.1163/22106286-12341317.

Kwong, Chi Man and Tsoi Yiu Lun. *Eastern Fortress: A Military History of Hong Kong 1840–1970*. Hong Kong: Hong Kong University Press, 2014. doi.org/10.5790/hongkong/9789888208708.001.0001.

Layard, Austen Henry. *A Popular Account of Discoveries at Nineveh*. London: John Murray, 1852.

Layard, Austen Henry. *Nineveh and Its Remains, with an Account of a Visit to the Chaldean Christians of Kurdistan, and the Yezidis, or Devil Worshippers; and an Inquiry into the Manners and Arts of the Ancient Assyrians*. 2 vols. London: John Murray, 1849.

Layard, Austen Henry. *The Monuments of Nineveh*. London: John Murray, first series 1849, second series 1853.

Lejeune, Phillipe. *On Diary*, edited by Jeremy D. Popkin and Julie Rak, translated by Katherine Durnin. Honolulu: Hawai'i University Press, 2009. doi.org/10.1515/9780824863784.

Le Sage, Alain-René. *The Adventures of Gil Blas of Santillane*, translated by T. Smollett. London: J. Osborn, 1749.

Lobscheid, William. *Grammar of the Chinese Language*. Hong Kong: Office of the 'Daily Press', 1864.

Mayhew, Henry and Augustus. *The Greatest Plague of Life, or, the Adventures of a Lady in Search of a Good Servant by One Who Has Been 'Almost Worried to Death'*. London: David Bogue, 1847.

Mayhew, Henry and Augustus. *The Image of His Father, or, One Boy Is More Trouble than a Dozen Girls: Being a Tale of A 'Young Monkey'*. London: H. Hurst, 1848.

Meadows, Thomas Taylor. *The Chinese and Their Rebellions, Viewed in Connexion with the National Philosophy, Ethics, Legislation, and Administration, to Which Is Added an Essay of Civilisation and Its Present State in the East and West*. London: Smith, Elder & Co., 1856.

Medhurst, W.H. *English and Chinese Dictionary*. Shanghai: The Mission Press, 1848.

Medhurst, W.H. 'Marriage, Affinity, and Inheritance in China'. *Transactions of the China Branch of the Royal Asiatic Society*, Part IV (1853–54): 1–32.

Millim, Anne-Marie. *The Victorian Diary: Authorship and Emotional Labour*. Abingdon: Routledge, 2013.

Mills, John. *The British Jews*. London: Houlston and Stoneman, 1853.

Milne, William, trans. *The Sacred Edict Containing Sixteen Maxims of the Emperor Kang-Hi, Amplified by His Son, the Emperor Yoong-Ching; Together with a Paraphrase of the Whole by A Mandarin*. London: Black, Kingsbury, Parbury and Allen, 1817.

Munn, Christopher. *Anglo-China: Chinese People and British Rule in Hong Kong 1841–1880*. Richmond: Curzon Press, 2001.

Munn, Christopher. 'Colonialism "in a Chinese Atmosphere": The Caldwell Affair and the Perils of Collaboration in Early Colonial Hong Kong'. In *New Frontiers: Imperialism's New Communities in East Asia, 1842–1953*, edited by Robert Bickers and Christian Henriot, 12–37. Manchester: Manchester University Press, 2000.

Munn, Christopher. 'Hong Kong, 1841–1870: All the Servants in Prison and Nobody to Take Care of the House'. In *Masters, Servants, and Magistrates in Britain and the Empire, 1562–1955*, edited by Douglas Hay and Paul Craven, 365–401. Chapel Hill: University of North Carolina Press, 2004.

Neale, Fred Arthur. *Narrative of a Residence at the Capital of the Kingdom of Siam, with a Description of the Manners, Customs and Laws of the Modern Siamese*. London: Office of the National Illustrated Library, 1852.

Ngo, Tak-Wing, ed. *Hong Kong's History: State and Society under Colonial Rule*. London: Routledge, 1999.

O'Sullivan, Patricia. *Policing Hong Kong: An Irish History*. Hong Kong: Blacksmith Books, 2017.

Purdy, John. *Sailing Directions for the Strait of Gibraltar and the Mediterranean Sea*. London: R.H. Laurie, 1841.

Rosado, Pepe. *The Convent: An Illustrated Guidebook*. Gibraltar: FotoGrafiks Design, 2012.

Russell, Gillian. *The Theatres of War: Performance, Politics, and Society 1793–1815*. Oxford: Oxford University Press, 1995. doi.org/10.1093/acprof:oso/9780198122630.001.0001.

Sayer, G.R. *Hong Kong 1841–1862: Birth, Adolescence and Coming of Age*. Oxford: Oxford University Press, 1937.

Scarth, John. *British Policy in China: Is Our War with the Tartars or the Chinese?* Edinburgh: Smith, Elder & Co., 1860.

Scarth, John. *British Policy in China: Italy for the Italians and China for the Chinese*. Edinburgh: Smith, Elder & Co., 1860.

Scarth, John. *British Policy in China: Neutral War and Warlike Peace!* Edinburgh: Edmonston and Douglas, 1861.

Scarth, John. *Twelve Years in China: The People, the Rebels, and the Mandarins*. Edinburgh: Constable, 1860.

Scott, Sir Walter. *Kenilworth: A Romance*. Edinburgh: Constable and Ballantyne, 1821.

Scott, Sir Walter. *The Fortunes of Nigel*. Edinburgh: Archibald Constable, 1822.

Sinn, Elizabeth. 'Chinese Patriarchy and the Protection of Women in 19th-Century Hong Kong'. In *Women and Chinese Patriarchy: Submission, Servitude and Escape*, edited by Maria Jaschok and Suzanne Miers, 141–70. Hong Kong: Hong Kong University Press, 1994.

Sinn, Elizabeth. 'Women at Work: Chinese Brothel Keepers in Nineteenth-Century Hong Kong'. *Journal of Women's History* 19, no. 3 (Fall 2007): 87–111. doi.org/10.1353/jowh.2007.0062.

Sinn, Elizabeth and Christopher Munn. *Meeting Place: Encounters across Cultures in Hong Kong, 1841–1984*. Hong Kong: Hong Kong University Press, 2015.

Sinn, Elizabeth, Wong Siu-lun and Chan Wing-hoi, eds. *Rethinking Hong Kong: New Paradigms, New Perspectives*. Hong Kong: Centre of Asian Studies, University of Hong Kong, 2009.

Smith, Carl T. *Chinese Christians: Elites, Middlemen, and the Church in Hong Kong*, new edition with introduction by Christopher Munn. Hong Kong: Hong Kong University Press, 2005.

Smith, Carl T. 'Protected Women in 19th-Century Hong Kong'. In *Women and Chinese Patriarchy: Submission, Servitude and Escape*, edited by Maria Jaschok and Suzanne Miers, 221–37. Hong Kong: Hong Kong University Press, 1994.

Smith, George. *A Narrative of an Exploratory Visit to Each of the Consular Cities of China and to the Islands of Hong Kong and Chusan, on behalf of the Church Missionary Society in the years 1844, 1845, 1846*. London: Seeley, Burnside & Seeley, 1847.

Smith, Henry Stooks. *The Annual Military Obituary for 1856*. London: Longman, Brown, Green, Longmans, and Roberts, 1857.

Stanley, Henry, trans. and ed. *Chinese Manual: Recueil de phrases chinoises, composées de quatre caractères, et dont les explications sont rangées dans l'ordre alphabétique français*. London: Harrison and Sons, 1854.

Staunton, Sir George. *An Abridged Account of the Embassy to the Emperor of China, Undertaken by Order of the King of Great Britain from the Papers of Earl Macartney*. London: John Stockdale, 1797.

Steinitz, Rebecca. *Time, Space and Gender in the Nineteenth-Century British Diary*. Basingstoke: Palgrave MacMillan, 2011. doi.org/10.1057/9780230339606.

Talbott, James. *The Christian School-Master*. London: J.F. and C. Rivinton, 1782 (originally published 1707).

Taveirne, Patrick. 'The Religious Case of the Fengzhen District: Reclamation and Missionary Activities in Caqar during the Late Qing Dynasty'. In *The History of the Relations between the Low Countries and China in the Qing Era*, edited by W.F. Vande Walle and Noël Golvers, 369–418. Leuven: Leuven University Press, 2003.

Thackeray, William. *The History of Samuel Titmarsh, and The Great Hoggarty Diamond*. London: Bradbury & Evans, 1849.

Tronson, John M. *Personal Narrative of a Voyage to Japan, Kamtschatka, Siberia, Tartary, and Various Parts of the Coast of China in H.M.S. Barracouta*. London: Bradbury & Evans, 1859.

Tsang, Steve. *A Modern History of Hong Kong, 1841–1997*. London: I.B. Taurus, 1997.

Wade, Thomas Francis. *The Hsin Ching Lu 尋津錄, or Book of Experiments; Being the First of a Series of Contributions to the Study of Chinese*. Hong Kong: Office of the 'China Mail', 1859.

Wade, Thomas Francis and Walter Caine Hillier. *Yu Yen Tzu Erh Chi 語言自邇集: A Progressive Course Designed to Assist the Student of Colloquial Chinese as Spoken in the Capital and the Metropolitan Department*. 2nd ed. Shanghai: Statistical Department of the Inspectorate General of Customs, 1886.

Wakeman, Frederick. *Strangers at the Gate: Social Disorder in South China, 1839–61*. Berkeley: University of California Press, 1966.

Ward, Barbara. 'Kau Sai: An Unfinished Manuscript'. *Journal of the Hong Kong Branch of the Royal Asiatic Society* 25 (1985): 27–118.

Wehage, Paul. 'Ali Ben Sou Alle: A 19th Century Frenchman in Mysore'. *Serenade*, 14 November 2016.

Welch, Richard E. Jr. 'Caleb Cushing's China Mission and the Treaty of Wanghia: A Review'. *Oregon Historical Quarterly* 58, no. 4 (December 1957): 328–57.

Wells Williams, Samuel. *The Middle Kingdom: A Survey of the Geography, Government, Education, Social Life, Arts, Religion, etc., of the Chinese Empire and its Inhabitants*. New York: Wiley and Putnam, 1848.

Werner, E.T.C. *Autumn Leaves: An Autobiography with a Sheaf of Papers, Sociological & Sinological, Philosophical & Metaphysical*. Shanghai: Kelley & Walsh, 1928.

Wong, J.Y. *Deadly Dreams: Opium and the Arrow War (1856–1860) in China*. Cambridge: Cambridge University Press, 1998. doi.org/10.1017/CBO97805 11572807.

Wong, J.Y. *Yeh Ming-ch'en: Viceroy of Liang-Kuang (1852–58)*. Cambridge: Cambridge University Press, 1976.

Wong, Kam C. *Policing in Hong Kong: History and Reform*. Boca Raton: CRC Press, 2015. doi.org/10.1201/b18199.

Yip, Ka-che, Yuen-sang Leung and Man-kong Wong. *Health Policy and Disease in Colonial and Post-Colonial Hong Kong, 1841–2003*. Abingdon: Routledge, 2016. doi.org/10.4324/9781315672373.

[Zhang Yun 張勻]. *Iu-Kiao-Li: or, the Two Fair Cousins*, translated by anon. from French. London: Hunt and Clarke, 1827. Originally published in Chinese as *Yu Jiao Li* 玉嬌梨 and translated into French by Jean-Pierre Abel-Rémusat.

Zhou, Xun. '"Cosmopolitanism from Above": A Jewish Experience in Hong Kong'. *European Review of History – Revue européenne d'histoire* 23 (2016): 897–911. doi.org/10.1080/13507486.2016.1203879.

www.ingramcontent.com/pod-product-compliance
Lightning Source LLC
Chambersburg PA
CBHW071739150426
43191CB00010B/1635